D0477906

Caution! Music & Video Downloading: Your Guide to Legal, Safe, and Trouble-Free Downloads

Russell Shaw and Dave Mercer

Wiley Publishing, Inc.

Caution! Music & Video Downloading: Your Guide to Legal, Safe, and Trouble-Free Downloads

Published by
Wiley Publishing, Inc.
111 River Street
Hoboken, NJ 07030-5774
www.wiley.com

Copyright © 2005 by Wiley Publishing, Inc., Indianapolis, Indiana

Library of Congress Control Number is available from the publisher.

ISBN: 0-7645-7564-3

Manufactured in the United States of America

10 9 8 7 6 5 4 3 2 1

1B/RY/RR/QU/IN

Published by Wiley Publishing, Inc., Indianapolis, Indiana

Published simultaneously in Canada

No part of this publication may be reproduced, stored in a retrieval system or transmitted in any form or by any means, electronic, mechanical, photocopying, recording, scanning or otherwise, except as permitted under Sections 107 or 108 of the 1976 United States Copyright Act, without either the prior written permission of the Publisher, or authorization through payment of the appropriate per-copy fee to the Copyright Clearance Center, 222 Rosewood Drive, Danvers, MA 01923, (978) 750-8400, fax (978) 646-8600. Requests to the Publisher for permission should be addressed to the Legal Department, Wiley Publishing, Inc., 10475 Crosspoint Blvd., Indianapolis, IN 46256, (317) 572-3447, fax (317) 572-4355, e-mail: brandreview@wiley.com.

LIMIT OF LIABILITY/DISCLAIMER OF WARRANTY: THE PUBLISHER AND THE AUTHOR MAKE NO REPRESENTATIONS OR WARRANTIES WITH RESPECT TO THE ACCURACY OR COMPLETENESS OF THE CONTENTS OF THIS WORK AND SPECIFICALLY DISCLAIM ALL WARRANTIES, INCLUDING WITHOUT LIMITATION WARRANTIES OF FITNESS FOR A PARTICULAR PURPOSE. NO WARRANTY MAY BE CREATED OR EXTENDED BY SALES OR PROMOTIONAL MATERIALS. THE ADVICE AND STRATEGIES CONTAINED HEREIN MAY NOT BE SUITABLE FOR EVERY SITUATION. THIS WORK IS SOLD WITH THE UNDERSTANDING THAT THE PUBLISHER IS NOT ENGAGED IN RENDERING LEGAL, ACCOUNTING, OR OTHER PROFESSIONAL SERVICES. IF PROFESSIONAL ASSISTANCE IS REQUIRED, THE SERVICES OF A COMPETENT PROFESSIONAL PERSON SHOULD BE SOUGHT. NEITHER THE PUBLISHER NOR THE AUTHOR SHALL BE LIABLE FOR DAMAGES ARISING HEREFROM. THE FACT THAT AN ORGANIZATION OR WEB SITE IS REFERRED TO IN THIS WORK AS A CITATION AND/OR A POTENTIAL SOURCE OF FURTHER INFORMATION DOES NOT MEAN THAT THE AUTHOR OR THE PUBLISHER ENDORSES THE INFORMATION THE ORGANIZATION OF WEB SITE MAY PROVIDE OR RECOMMENDATIONS IT MAY MAKE. FURTHER, READERS SHOULD BE AWARE THAT INTERNET WEB SITES LISTED IN THIS WORK MAY HAVE CHANGED OR DISAPPEARED BETWEEN WHEN THIS WORK WAS WRITTEN AND WHEN IT IS READ.

For general information on our other products and services or to obtain technical support, please contact our Customer Care Department within the U.S. at (800) 762-2974, outside the U.S. at (317) 572-3993 or fax (317) 572-4002.

Wiley also publishes its books in a variety of electronic formats. Some content that appears in print may not be available in electronic books.

Trademarks: Wiley and the Wiley Publishing logo are trademarks or registered trademarks of John Wiley & Sons, Inc. and/or its affiliates. All other trademarks are the property of their respective owners. Wiley Publishing, Inc. is not associated with any product or vendor mentioned in this book.

WILEY

About the Authors

Russell Shaw is an author, journalist, technology analyst, and online educator based in Portland, Oregon. He has written numerous books and articles about multimedia content creation and enjoyment, wireless networking, digital photography and video, Web site content and design, and online investing. A train fanatic and a lover of the outdoors, he is proficient at carrying a camera bag and a backpack simultaneously.

Dave Mercer is the founder of Servata Online Applications. He is a computer consultant who has advised corporations, government, and non-profit organizations on information processing.

Credits

Acquisitions Editor
Michael Roney

Project Editor
Cricket Krengel

Copy Editor
Gwenette Gaddis Goshert

Editorial Manager
Robyn Siesky

Vice President & Group Executive Publisher
Richard Swadley

Vice President & Publisher
Barry Pruett

Project Coordinators
Maridee Ennis
Emily Wichlinski

Graphics and Production Specialists
Beth Brooks
Lauren Goddard
Heather Ryan

Quality Control Technicians
Joe Niesen
Brian H. Walls

Proofreading
TECHBOOKS Production Services

Indexer
Johnna VanHoose

Cover Design
Anthony Bunyan

To Nancy, who by her
serenity, grace, and love,
has earned a place
in my heart.
And, thanks to the universe,
for sending me omens.

Introduction to Music and Video Downloading

*C*aution! Music & Video Downloading: Your Guide to Legal, Safe, and Trouble-Free Downloads is aimed at helping you protect yourself from the many dangers you'll encounter in your quest to find and enjoy the best music and video the Internet has to offer. The dangers come in many forms: risks to your pocketbook, your privacy, your data, your job, and so on. Because understanding your computer and the dangers facing you is the first step in protecting yourself, this book covers a bit about the technical side of computers. But don't worry. You won't be bored by jargon that only computer experts understand. Everything is written in everyday terms or well defined in numerous sidebars, with plenty of screenshots to show you exactly what's happening.

Why Music and Video Downloads

Everyone downloads files, but music and video are particularly interesting because they allow you to do something besides work or play games on your computer. The Internet has literally thousands of radio stations playing all day long, and for those of you with broadband connections, quality video is available. Computers are becoming easier to use and more of an appliance, so you can have fun and work too. And if you want to build a large collection of your favorite hits, the Internet is the best place to go.

You can apply the things you'll learn in this book to any type of files you download, even Web pages and e-mail. In fact, you'll find information helpful for stopping spam, pop-ups, and other annoying (and possibly dangerous) forms of advertising in Chapter 6, many ways to protect your network in Chapter 7, and the ins and outs of protecting your privacy in Chapter 8.

Get Rich Quick on the Internet

So you've decided to enrich your life with music, video, and other forms of art. And you want to do it at Internet speed. You *can* get *art*-rich quickly on the Internet, but don't believe that Nigerian general when he offers you 25 percent of 20 million dollars, if only you'll send your bank account numbers to him.

The Internet is a compelling place, full of great things, interesting information, and at the same time, files that are potentially disastrous to your computer and your personal information. When it comes to copyrighted files that you may download without permission, the Internet can cause you legal problems you would not wish on anyone.

The purpose of this book is to give you the knowledge and tools you need to get the most out of the Internet's vast storehouse of music and video, while informing you about and helping you protect yourself from the scams, rip-off artists, and malicious virus spreaders.

This book assumes that you have a computer connected to the Internet or have access to one. It doesn't really matter whether you are running a Windows-based PC, a Mac, or a Linux machine; all the browsers operate in much the same way, and downloading files, storing them, and playing them back isn't very different on these computer types either.

Viruses, worms, spyware and Trojan horses affect each of these computers, but since Windows-based PCs are so much more common, there are more dangers facing Windows computers. Privacy concerns and legal issues are present no matter which type of computer you use.

What Is Digitized Music and Video?

Before you can protect yourself while downloading music, video, and other rich media file types, you need to know what you're dealing with. Here's a quick introduction to the subject of digital media files; I have tried to make it as interesting and painless as possible.

When you listen to a live musical production, you're hearing the actual notes played as sound waves hitting your ears. The sound waves rattle your eardrums, activating nerves cells that signal your brain. The music you hear is really "composed" in your brain by sophisticated auditory algorithms genetically hard-wired into you. Your brain acts as a computer processing raw data into sounds.

The sound waves bouncing off your eardrums are waves of compression and dispersion in the air. When you hear a live production, you are listening to an analog version of the sound, meaning the sound is continuous. When you listen to a digital version of the same sound, what you're hearing is a reproduction of the original sound that was made from tiny digital segments of data sampled from the original analog sound waves.

Under the right conditions, digital reproductions are indistinguishable from analog productions, because the digital samples are so small and the reproduction capacity of the computer or player so fast and accurate that your ear can't tell the difference (but critics say they can tell the difference, and some prefer vinyl recordings, claiming a richer sound).

Anything real can (theoretically) be digitized and reproduced; audio, video, tactile sensations, even smells, and many other forms of input. The two big advantages of digitization are perfect long-term storage (so long as the storage media is intact, the bits are safe and can be used to faithfully reproduce the original) and the ability to manipulate the digital bits with a computer.

Lucent Technologies (formerly Bell Labs) claims to have first demonstrated digital music in 1957, and since then a variety of digital recording technologies have been introduced, as well as many digital music formats. Any digital music recording technology uses a microphone to capture sound and turn it into an electrical signal, and then samples the electrical signal in very small intervals. The sampling process generates a set of numerical values corresponding to the actual audio input at that exact time. This set of numbers in encoded into a particular audio format, so that you end up with a file containing digital data. Reproducing the original sound is then a matter of reversing the process, reading out the numerical values and turning them into an electrical signal (that drives a speaker) in the precise sequence and speed at which they were recorded.

Sampling and compression

So what is important about this sampling process? Recording audio, video, or other forms of input accurately requires a high sampling rate. If you sample once every minute, you'll never be able to turn that into a good reproduction of the original, but if you sample once every second, you'll be much closer, and if you sample once every 1/1000 of a second, you'll begin to fool the ear into thinking it's hearing "real" sounds instead of reproductions. But sampling at a high rate means collecting lots of data. Sample at too high a rate, and no CPU could process the data fast enough to reproduce it (and the file would be so big it couldn't be stored on a normal computer anyway).

So you have to find a sampling rate that is fast enough to fool the ear (or eye) and yet not so fast that you overwhelm the computer or player reproducing the sound. A typical sampling rate for CD quality sound is 44,100 samples per second.

Even audio files sampled at this rate are a bit too big to be transmitted efficiently over most Internet connections, so there are compression schemes that shrink down the file size. Some compression schemes shrink files while preserving all data (loss-less compression), and some shrink files even more by deleting some of the data (lossy compression). There's nothing wrong with lossy compression schemes for audio and video media file types, so long as the sound or video that is reproduced still sounds or appears good enough for the purpose. For example, you don't really care if you get CD quality sound out of a long distance telephone call, so long as you can still understand what the other person is saying.

The format in which the audio or video data is stored is also important, as no files can be played back without the appropriate software. Some software player applications play many file types while other are limited to a few or only a single one. And some are proprietary to a particular manufacturer, limiting your choice of playback options.

Digital dangers

Almost anyone with the right equipment and software can make a digital recording of music or video, and the equipment and software is easy and cheap to obtain. But then again, so are guns in some communities. The name on the file or other external information associated with it gives no assurance of the actual digital content of a file, nor its status as a file you are legally entitled to download and use. As I explain in several chapters, however you could be downloading an illegal copy or, even worse, downloading music or video with malicious software hidden inside.

How to Use This Book

In each chapter, you'll see numerous screenshots that show you step by step what's being done: going to a particular site, installing the player or editing software, using the software, as well as using your own browser or system. And you see examples, written step by step in plain English, so you can perform the same steps on your own computer as you follow the screenshots. The screenshots are mainly Windows-based, but some the text includes some information for Mac and Linux users as well.

For the technically inclined, you'll find some sidebars that discuss the detailed, behind the scenes workings of computers and file systems, system requirements for player and editing software, and defining computer jargon relating to music and video files.

Who should read this book

This book is for you if you use a computer, specifically if you want to use a computer to download and share music and video files safely. You may have lots of experience with computers or just a little, you may be young or old, or you may be technically inclined or just smart enough to turn the thing on. Regardless of where you are coming to this book from, know that following every step in this book won't guarantee that you'll never get a virus, but it will help prepare you, inform you, and protect you from known threats.

This book is partly a guide to music, video, and other interesting resources on the Internet, and partly a safety manual to help you learn to protect yourself and your computer while having fun on the Internet.

Chapter-by-chapter synopsis

Each chapter of this book is aimed at a specific topic concerning music and video downloads. Some are more technical than others, but all of them are written in language you can understand. You'll start off learning the differences between file-sharing and direct downloading, and proceed to the major file sharing and direct download sites on the Internet. Then it's on to detailed information about files and file systems, no matter what type of computer you are using. Next, you'll get a look at malicious software and how to protect yourself and your network, and finally you'll learn about how to make your own music and video and how to transfer these files to take with you.

Part I: Safely Choosing and Using Music Services

Part I gives you the basics that you need to know to get started downloading and file sharing.

Chapter 1: In this chapter, the differences between file sharing and direct downloading are discussed, as well as typical features of file sharing and direct download sites, the risks involved in file sharing or direct downloading, and how to identify problem sites or files. At the end of the chapter is a checklist to help you decide when to swap files and when to download directly.

Chapter 2: This chapter covers the major direct download sites. It includes system requirements and download instructions for various applications, as well as a discussion of terms, conditions, and privacy policies. Sites reviewed include Apple iTunes, the new Napster, MusicMatch, and more.

Chapter 3: Chapter 3 reviews the major file-sharing services. It also goes through installation of their file-sharing software applications, discusses system requirements, and examines their terms, conditions, and privacy policies. Services reviewed include Gnutella, Kazaa, Morpheus, and others. A short introduction to using file-sharing software is included, as well as detailed information about how file sharing works.

Part II: Protecting Yourself Technologically and Legally

Part II tells you how to keep your computer safe from some of the hazards on the Internet, from potentially nasty spyware to very nasty copyright-related lawsuits.

Chapter 4: In this chapter, the basics of computer hardware, files, file systems, and operating systems are discussed. Included in the discussion are Windows (such as Windows XP as well as some earlier operating systems, on), Mac OSX, and Red Hat Linux, various file system types, setting user and group permissions, how files are stored, and filenames and file extensions.

Chapter 5: In this chapter, downloading and file-sharing dangers are discussed, including the major forms of malicious software and other dangers. Viruses, worms, Trojan horses, and spyware are examined, as well as identity theft, privacy issues, legal issues, and other significant problems.

Chapter 6: This chapter discusses all the ways you can protect yourself from malicious software and files. Anti-virus, anti-pop-up, and spam-filtering software are reviewed, the costs and benefits examined, and how to find and install them are followed step by step.

Chapter 7: In this chapter, I explain the concepts of computer networks, and how to protect your network-enabled PC. The Internet is explained as the largest computer network, with safety concerns you need to be aware of. The rest of this chapter covers safeguards you can implement to keep your Internet-connected PC safe from the risks inherent in Internet networking and network connections.

Chapter 8: This chapter covers protecting your privacy. The personal information you should protect (and why), where this information can be found publicly (and on the Internet), your privacy rights at the various levels of government, and how you often trade your privacy for the right to buy products are examined. What you can legally do to protect your privacy as a consumer is also covered.

Chapter 9: In this chapter, protecting yourself from illegal files is discussed. The nature of legal and illegal files is examined, and how to identify and protect yourself and your children from illegal or obnoxious material is covered as well. Finally, I discuss what can happen to you if you download illegal music and video files, and what you should do if you are caught.

Part III: Legal and Safe Fun with Downloaded Media

Part III tells you how to take your legal downloaded media with you as you make your rounds, and how to use that media to create fun music and video projects such as video with music, or even a slide show of the photos you have taken with your digital camera.

Chapter 10: This chapter discusses the process of downloading music and video files to your PC, and then to your Portable devices. Several popular portable music and video players are introduced and explained. Then, I go on to show you how to work with proprietary portable player software — as well as PC-based media player software — to transfer these files. I also explore the fascinating world of ring tones, which can play music on your cell phone.

Chapter 11: In this chapter, an entirely new production is created. You'll learn how to record your own music and video files, obtain legal music and video files from multimedia editing software sites, or work with your own digital photographs stored on your PC. Then, you will work with this content to make your own movie, or slide show. Numerous software tools, from inexpensive to high-end, are reviewed and their capabilities discussed.

Part IV: Appendixes

This book includes three appendixes, all of which are great resources. This section also includes a glossary of useful terms.

Appendix A: The first appendix covers music and video services from where you can order legal music files, and download them to your PC.

Appendix B: This appendix describes utilities you can use to protect your PC from viruses and other maladies that sometimes are part and parcel of the download process. I also discuss other peer-to-peer networks and technologies that some digital music and video file traders use enthusiastically.

Appendix C: In this appendix, you are offered a real-life, case history that describes the process of finding, purchasing, downloading, and playing a legally downloaded music track.

Glossary: The glossary offers a resource of relevant terms used in this book.

Acknowledgments

Thanks to my agent, Carole McClendon of Waterside Productions, for all she has done for me.

Contents at a Glance

Introduction to Music and Video Downloading vii
Acknowledgments xv

Part I: Safely Choosing and Using Music Services 1
Chapter 1: Direct Downloading or File Sharing:
Making the Right Choices for Efficiency and Safety 3
Chapter 2: Managing Your Risk by Choosing
the Best Direct-Download Service 15
Chapter 3: Managing Your Risk by Choosing the Best File-Sharing Service 43

Part II: Protecting Yourself Technologically and Legally 75
Chapter 4: Behind the Scenes: What Really Happens When File Sharing 77
Chapter 5: Dangers of Downloading or Sharing Files:
The Nature of the Threat 101
Chapter 6: Protecting Yourself and Your Computer 119
Chapter 7: Protecting Your Network 133
Chapter 8: Protecting Your Privacy 147
Chapter 9: Protecting Yourself from Illegal Downloads 165

Part III: Legal and Safe Fun with Downloaded Media 187
Chapter 10: Safely Downloading Media to Portable Devices 189
Chapter 11: Creative and Legal Music and Video Projects 213

Part IV: Appendixes 227
Appendix A: Music and Video Services 229
Appendix B: Useful Information 233
Appendix C: Chronicle of a Typical Digital Download 237
Glossary 247

Index 257

Contents

Introduction to Music and Video Downloading vii

Part I: Safely Choosing and Using Music Services   1

Chapter 1: Direct Downloading or File Sharing: Making the Right Choices for Efficiency and Safety. 3

Downloading Music and Video Files 3
File Sharing versus Direct Downloading. 4
Typical File-Sharing and Direct-Download Sites 5
    File sharing on Kazaa 5
    What Kazaa does for you 6
    Direct downloading on Musicmatch 6
Other Ways to Download Music and Video 7
    Getting files by disk or e-mail 8
    Finding files and FTP sites with a search engine. 8
Risks of File Sharing and Direct Downloading. 10
    Security risks 10
    Legal risks. 11
    Quality concerns 12
    System concerns 12
Top Points for Consideration when Choosing Between
    File Sharing and Direct Downloading 13
Summary. 13

Chapter 2: Managing Your Risk by Choosing the Best Direct-Download Service 15

Using Direct Music and Video Download Sites 15
    Downloading files 16
    Finding direct-download sites 17
    Understanding the major direct-download sites 23
    Understanding filenames and extensions 24
    Using Napster. 27
    Tuning in to Apple iTunes. 29
    Musicmatch 32
    Getting Real with Real Network's RealRhapsody 33

Downloading and installing RealRhapsody 33
Connecting with Sony Connect 34
Introducing MSN Music 36
Top Ten Things to Consider when Installing and
Using Downloaded Software 39
Summary 41

**Chapter 3: Managing Your Risk by Choosing
the Best File-Sharing Service** **43**

Understanding How File Sharing Works 43
Using File-Sharing Networks 45
The Gnutella file-sharing network 46
The Freenet file-sharing network 46
Other file-sharing networks 46
Using File-Sharing Services 47
Shareaza 48
BearShare 56
eDonkey and Overnet 60
LimeWire 62
Morpheus 4.1 64
Kazaa 67
Deciding Which File-Sharing Application to Use 71
Network connections 71
Open-source software 71
Freedom from popup ads and spyware 71
User interface 71
Features 72
Documentation 72
Top Five Things to Consider for Safe and Satisfying File Sharing 72
Summary 73

**Part II: Protecting Yourself
Technologically and Legally**   **75**

**Chapter 4: Behind the Scenes: What Really Happens
When File Sharing** **77**

Computer System Basics 78
Computer hardware 78
Operating systems 82
Drives and Files Systems 84
Boot disk 85
Hard disk drives and partitions 85
Understanding File Basics 88
Bits and bytes 88
Files 89

Understanding File Systems 93
Managing Your Files 93
    Files and folders 95
    File properties 95
Permissions, Users, and Groups 96
    What are permissions? 97
    Users and groups 98
Top Ten Techniques for Mastering Your System 98
Summary 100

Chapter 5: Dangers of Downloading or Sharing Files: The Nature of the Threat 101

Understanding the Threats to Your PC 101
Remote Access Threats 102
    Evil software 103
    How the Bad Stuff Gets to Your PC 113
Meet the Bad Folks 113
    Hackers and crackers 113
    Scam artists 114
    Identity thieves 115
Eight Essential Techniques for Staying on Top of Computer Threats . . . 116
Summary 117

Chapter 6: Protecting Yourself and Your Computer 119

Ways to Protect Yourself 119
    Securing your e-mail 120
    Spam 120
    Anti-spam software 121
    Web-browsing security 127
Ten Ways to Protect Your Computer from Suspicious
    E-mail and Spyware 130
Summary 131

Chapter 7: Protecting Your Network 133

Understanding How the Internet Functions 134
    Physical connections 134
    The Internet as a network 135
Understanding Internet Network Threats 136
    Recognizing file-sharing security risks 136
    Server exploits and attacks 138
Securing Your Network: Keeping the Bad Guys Out 140
    Be safe by visiting encrypted Web sites 141
    Physical security and firewalls 141
Ten Useful Ways to Protect Your Network 144
Summary 145

Chapter 8: Protecting Your Privacy 147

Living in a Fishbowl: Modern Life and Privacy. 147
    Getting to know you: The good and the bad. 148
    Privacy services that look out for you 150
Encryption and Pretty Good Privacy (PGP) 154
Staying Clear of Spyware 155
    How to stay clear of spyware 156
    Cleaning out spyware. 157
What to Do If Your Online Identity Has Been Stolen. 160
Ten Indispensable Techniques for Protecting Your Privacy 161
Summary 163

Chapter 9: Protecting Yourself from Illegal Downloads 165

Understanding Copyright Law 166
    Copyright law and digital downloading 169
    Changes to copyright law 171
Understanding Trademark Law 174
Trademark Law and the Internet 176
Distributing Music Legally 176
    Clarifying the licenses you will need 176
    Obtaining a sound recording license 181
What Can Happen to You 181
    Hunting for copyright violators 182
    Real-life violations 182
Ten Vital Ways to Protect Yourself Legally when You
    Download or Distribute Music and Video. 185
Summary 186

Part III: Legal and Safe Fun with Downloaded Media   187

Chapter 10: Safely Downloading Media to Portable Devices. 189

Using iPod and iTunes 190
    Downloading and installing iTunes on your computer. 190
    Setting up an Apple iTunes account 192
    Transferring music from iTunes to your iPod 196
Introducing Other Portable Media Players. 197
    RCA/Thomson Lyra. 198
    Rio Cali 199
    Creative Rhomba 199
    Samsung YP55V 200
    ARCHOS Gimini 220. 200
    Transferring files to portable music players 201

Enjoying Downloaded Digital Media on Other Portable Devices 207

    Downloading a movie to your laptop. 207

    Downloading ring tones 209

Six Great Ways to Have Fun with Digital Media on Portable Devices 210

Summary 211

Chapter 11: Creative and Legal Music and Video Projects 213

Working with Digital Video Editing Software. 213

    Transferring video files from camera to PC 214

    Finding free and legal music for your Web site 216

    Finding legal music files included in video editing programs 216

Creating and Sharing Multimedia Scrapbooks. 220

    Producing a music slideshow with PHOTOJAM 4. 220

Legal Restrictions 223

    What will get you into trouble. 223

    What might get you into trouble 223

    What won't get you into trouble 224

Six Clever Ways to Have Fun with Downloaded and Legal

    Digital Media 224

Summary 225

Part IV: Appendixes   **227**

Appendix A: Music and Video Services. 229

Appendix B: Useful Information. 233

Appendix C: Chronicle of a Typical Digital Download 237

Glossary 247

Index 257

Safely Choosing and Using Music Services

In This Part

Chapter 1
Direct Downloading
or File Sharing:
Making the Right
Choices for Efficiency
and Safety

Chapter 2
Managing Your Risk
by Choosing the Best
Direct-Download
Service

Chapter 3
Managing Your Risk
by Choosing the Best
File-Sharing Service

Direct Downloading or File Sharing: Making the Right Choices for Efficiency and Safety

◆ ◆ ◆ ◆

In This Chapter

Downloading 101: Where to start getting music and videos

Using typical file-sharing and direct downloading sites

Understanding the risks of file sharing and direct downloading

Using FTP sites and major search engines

Choosing between file sharing and direct downloads

◆ ◆ ◆ ◆

Downloading music and video, in its popular form, has been around only a few years and is still evolving. It has little in common with other forms of trading files because you never know what you're going to get. Downloading music and video from the Internet can be great fun and very exciting, but you've got to be savvy to protect yourself. This chapter looks at the various ways you can download files, the sites that offer files for download or sharing, and the risks and rewards of file sharing and downloading.

Downloading Music and Video Files

You've downloaded files already, whether you know it or not. When you view Web pages, you're downloading files. When you put a floppy disk or CD-ROM in your computer and copy files to your hard drive, you're downloading files. When you upgrade your software, you're downloading files. When you check your e-mail, you're downloading files.

There are few activities as ubiquitous and yet as mysterious as downloading or sharing files. It's ubiquitous because everyone who uses a computer does it, and it's mysterious because few people *really* understand the risks they're taking or how to protect themselves.

But you don't have to be a geek or a computer whiz to have fun. Computers are finally becoming as easy to use as refrigerators, washing machines, or microwave ovens; just switch them on, and use your favorite settings to perform your tasks. With the right information, you can be safe and have fun too. I'll start by defining the top two methods for downloading music and video files from the Internet.

File Sharing versus Direct Downloading

First, a few definitions. *Downloading* is the act of getting a file; *uploading* is the act of sending a file. *Direct downloading* means getting a file whole (often by paying for it), while *file sharing* is the act of trading files in small bits and pieces with other folks (often at no cost to you). When you listen to tracks from an Internet radio station, the file is *streamed* to you (as in *streaming audio* or *streaming video,* meaning it plays back on your player software without the entire file being completely downloaded and you don't get to save it). Listening to streaming music is not the same as downloading or file sharing.

Whatever way you get a music or video file, you are copying bits to your computer: in RAM memory, to your hard drive, or burned onto a CD or DVD. How you copied those bits is not as important as where you got those bits, because there are risks associated with each file-sharing or direct-download site.

These are the primary risks:

- ✦ **Security issues.** Does the file contain viruses, worms, or spyware? Will the file crash your system, destroy your data, or talk about you behind your back (communicate with its maker without you knowing)?

- ✦ **Legal issues.** Is the file an illegal copy (stolen goods), or do you have the right to possess and play back the file? If the file is legal, what limitations does your contract impose?

- ✦ **System issues.** Is your system prepared to handle the file with enough hard drive space, processing power, RAM, and the appropriate player software to run the file? Depending on compression or lack thereof, 1 MB a minute is an average time/memory ratio for a downloaded file, but this ratio can be much larger. So, if you have 500 downloaded songs of four minutes apiece, that's 2 GB right there.

- ✦ **Quality issues.** Is the file corrupted or of poor quality? On some digital music files, poor quality reveals itself in hissing and skipping. Did you get what you paid for (if you did pay for it)?

Note Some free (and mostly illegal) download sites list the file size of all tracks available for download. You will notice some differences in available files for identical tracks. Substandard music files can be smaller in size than their superior counterparts. That can be because the person making the file available for download set up a tape recorder next to their PC, played the track "over the air" and into a PC microphone, transferred it to their PC's music directory, from where it was made available for download.

You can mitigate your risks by learning all you can about the two main ways to get music and video files (file sharing or direct downloading) and by finding and using sites that you can depend on. A more detailed discussion of risks is provided later in this chapter.

Typical File-Sharing and Direct-Download Sites

Finding file-sharing and direct-download sites is fairly easy, and you've probably heard of a few from your friends. I'll take a look at a couple of the most popular of these sites and see what they have in common.

File sharing on Kazaa

Kazaa can be found at www.kazaa.com. At this Web site, you'll find the current versions of Kazaa. As of this writing, versions 2.7 (free, supported by ads and pop-ups) and 2.6. (for $29.95, without ads or pop-ups) are available. Running on both a PC and a Mac, the Kazaa software is a desktop application that allows you to connect to other computer users and search for and trade files. It comes with the Kazaa Media Desktop Interface that helps you search the Web for files.

The Kazaa software uses peer-to-peer (P2P) technology to allow you to communicate with other Kazaa users and share files.

 Cross-Reference For a detailed discussion of P2P, please see Chapter 7.

The term P2P primarily indicates that you are connecting to other computers directly instead of connecting through a central server. The files you search for and download come from other users of the system and are not stored in some server at Kazaa headquarters. Besides making the system more practical, this strategy has some positive legal implications for Kazaa.

Interestingly, the Kazaa Web site mentions that some users are automatically designated as Supernodes, meaning that they serve an important function for other users by storing local lists of files offered for sharing by all users "near" them, based on the fact that the Kazaa software detected that they have a "modern computer and a broadband connection."

According to the Kazaa site, being automatically designated a Supernode is harmless to your computer, and that's true under some circumstances. Still, as you will learn in Chapter 9, you may be vulnerable to detection by connection-sniffing software used by music industry organizations looking for copyright violators.

There can also be fundamental issues of system performance and fairness. Having a utility such as Kazaa on your desktop and trading files with it uses up some of your connection bandwidth and computer memory, slowing your system down. Also, when someone else is using your computer and bandwidth without paying for it, it seems a little unfair. And if it's happening to your work computer and connection, your boss may not appreciate it.

What Kazaa does for you

Kazaa provides software that allows you to make P2P connections to other users of the same software across the Internet, and the software has search features to help you find the files you crave. When you find a file you want, you can download it and play it using Kazaa's software.

That's about it. It doesn't sound like much when it's put this way, but there's really nothing magical about being able to search for a file, find it, download it, and play it. What the file-sharing sites really try to offer is ease of use, security, anonymity, safety, quality, low (or no) cost, and so on, all lumped under the heading of "user experience."

Cross-Reference   In Chapter 3, you'll find a more detailed look at the similarities and differences between the major file-sharing sites and how they stack up in key attributes.

Direct downloading on Musicmatch

Direct-download sites such as Musicmatch differ from file-sharing sites primarily in that they store files on a central server from which you can search and download. You can find Musicmatch at `www.musicmatch.com`. Like Kazaa, Musicmatch is a desktop software application for downloading and playing files (currently Musicmatch Jukebox 9.0, with new versions released every 3 to 6 months), but the software connects directly to the Musicmatch server, searches for files on it, and downloads from that server. The basic player software and jukebox are free (currently you can get a Plus version with more features for $19.99), but individual tracks are 99 cents, and whole albums are $9.99.

The Musicmatch software helps you search for and find tracks, but also comes with a special matching feature that helps you find new music you might like. It plays whole files for you, but it also functions as an Internet radio appliance, allowing you to listen to streaming audio. It also allows you to store your own CDs in a library file. With this function, you can create playlists and classify the songs you want to listen to by style of music, or even by individual artist.

Desktop Software Applications

Software performs work for you. When your computer starts up, there is a small piece of software that checks the machinery to see whether it is ready for the operating system to take over. After the operating system takes over, your desktop application software has the ability to run. Desktop software applications are what most of us use all day long to perform our jobs and have fun. Some desktop software applications, such as browsers and e-mail software, are designed to connect to the Internet and communicate with other computers. Sometimes, part of the work performed by a desktop software application is actually done on another computer to which the software connects. Just a few years ago, the term *desktop software application* meant a standalone application that didn't talk to any other computer or communicate across the Internet. Today, those boundaries are rapidly blurring.

Like many direct-download sites, the Musicmatch software is free but the tracks cost money. You might think that is a disadvantage, but sometimes, if the price is right, paying for something has serious benefits. The music tracks available for purchase are likely to have been professionally prepared by the artist's record company. However, in the rare event that you have downloaded a clunky file of poor sound quality, you can ask for your money back.

 Cross-Reference In Chapter 2, the major direct-download sites are reviewed and issues like this discussed in more detail.

Other Ways to Download Music and Video

The terms upload and download are synonymous with sending and receiving, respectively. So when you upload a file, you send it or copy it from your computer to another computer or to a disk. And when you download a file, you retrieve it from another computer or disk and place it on your own computer. With that in mind, file sharing and direct downloads are not the only ways to find and download music and video. If you have a friend who happens to have a track you want, your friend could do any of the following:

✦ Copy it to a CD, DVD, or even a floppy disk, and give it to you

✦ E-mail it to you

✦ Post it to a Web site and give you the URL

✦ Upload it to an FTP site for you to download

Music and video files are just like any other file type; they can be copied and passed around quite easily. But there are still the same concerns about legality, quality, security, playability, and size. Just because your friend has a track doesn't mean that it is legal, free of viruses, or playable on your player.

Inconvenience Dead Ahead

A number of these MP3 sites force you to go through inconvenient registration procedures before you can download. There are also multiple reports of these download sites passing the e-mail and other contact information they gather about you to third parties, some of which may send you unwanted e-mail pitches. I discuss this topic in more detail in Chapter 8.

And since music and video files are often large, especially if they are high quality, fitting the track on a floppy disk or sending it by e-mail may be difficult. If you are attempting to redistribute a 5 minute long, 5 MB music file, that could be bigger than your e-mail service provider allows. The file will also be several times the size of the 1.44 MB capacity of most 2-side, double-density floppy disks.

Getting files by disk or e-mail

You probably already understand how to copy a file to a floppy or burn it to a CD. And e-mailing files as attachments is deceptively simple as well; in addition to the fact these files may be too large to send, you should be sure that you don't send so many files or such large files that you overload your recipient's mailbox. Plus, if your recipient has a slow dial-up connection, it may take him or her a long time to download the files you send.

Note   Web-based e-mail services such as Yahoo! and Hotmail offer much more mailbox space than they once did; however, personal mailboxes on other services often still have a 5 to 10 MB limit per message.

Cross-Reference   If you want more details about copying files and creating CDs, there is more information in Chapter 10.

Finding files and FTP sites with a search engine

You can also use the major search engines to find music files and anonymous FTP sites that offer music for download. Follow these steps to use Google to find sites that offer music and video files.

1. **Go to the Google main page at** `www.google.com`. If you've not used the Google search engine before, you will find it a very good resource for searching the Web.

2. **Type** Finding MP3 files **in the Google search field, and click Google Search.** You'll get a list of sites that help you find MP3 files. The ones you're looking for are search engines specializing in MP3s. For example, consider MP3search at `www.mp3search.com`. Figure 1-1 shows this site.

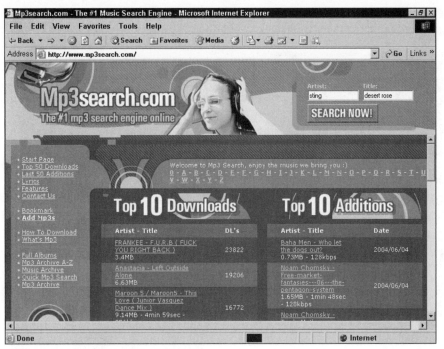

Figure 1-1: The MP3search Web site

In addition to these steps, you can use Google's search box to directly look for files by extension. If you type in, for example, **"Tom Petty"** and **"MP3"** (in quotes), Google will dish up a search results page likely to include several MP3 files available for direct download.

The difference between this site and file-sharing or direct-download sites is that you are not required to buy anything or install any software to use it (although it does offer a program called GetRight for $20 that helps you download tracks more efficiently, but it's not required). Your browser does all the work.

You can also use search engines to help you find anonymous FTP sites. Logging in to an FTP site is done with an FTP client, such as CuteFTP or WS_FTP, but usually you can make your browser work as an FTP client. All you have to know is the FTP host-name (such as `ftp.bigtip.com`) and a username and password for the site. If the FTP site allows anonymous access, you can usually use "anonymous" as the username and your e-mail address as the password. Even a fake e-mail address will often work.

Figure 1-2 shows the Wicked Downloads site (`www.wickeddownloads.com`), which has a variety of links to FTP sites. Note the disclaimer about the files not being veri-fied and also about anonymous FTP sites commonly requiring uploads for the privi-lege of downloading. You have no guarantee that the files you're downloading are legal or free of viruses, so caveat emptor.

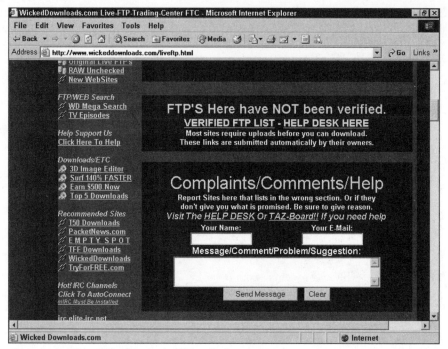

Figure 1-2: The Wicked Downloads Web site

Risks of File Sharing and Direct Downloading

As was discussed earlier in this chapter, you encounter five categories of risks anytime you share files or download them directly: security, legal, system, quality, and sites that sell your registration information to third parties who may spam you.

These legal and quality risks are present no matter how you acquire files, because in most cases you can't tell what's in the file by name, and after you open a file (double-click or play it back), it's usually too late then. In fact, some files, on some operating systems, can do their damage even without being opened. The following sections look at the risks in order of immediacy and try to quantify the risks in terms of the damage that's possible.

Security risks

The first risk you face, whenever copying a file to your computer, is that the file may contain a virus that could cripple your system or destroy your data. This is not necessarily the biggest risk you face, just the most immediate one. Running anti-virus software can mitigate this risk by examining the newly copied file for virus "signatures." However, if a virus is brand new, your anti-virus software won't have the appropriate signature in its database yet.

So, to prevent your system data from being lost, always back up your files, especially critical data files. You can reload your operating system and software applications, but data that hasn't been backed up can be very time-consuming and expensive to recover (if it can be recovered at all).

Prevention

On your hard drive, the files that make your computer work are the operating system (OS) and software applications. You should have the original disks that came with your system and any software you bought, so you can reload your OS and applications if they get destroyed. But you need to back up data files. You can do this in several common ways: copy data files to floppy disks, burn files to CD, copy files to a tape backup, or copy files to an online backup site. How frequently should you do this? If you use your computer only a little or place a low value on your files, perhaps you should back up your files once or twice a month. If you use your computer every day and place a high value on your files, perhaps you should do a backup twice a day. And make sure that you become familiar with procedures for restoring lost files; some automated backup software is very easy to use for backups, but difficult or confusing for restoring files.

Viruses from your system can also infect someone else's computer or might have a low-level infection. Viruses often hold off damaging your system until they've had a chance to reproduce. Some viruses copy themselves onto disks or CDs; some send themselves via e-mail to everyone in your address book; some even transmit themselves to your Instant Messaging buddy list.

And sometimes viruses aren't out to damage your system; they simply want to spy on you. An unscrupulous person can gain much by capturing your personal information and transmitting it back to headquarters. By the way, this is exactly the same mechanism used legitimately by some software makers, and with your permission no less! Read the fine print in that privacy policy or software license agreement before you install it, please!

Cross-Reference

You'll find much more about viruses and how they operate in Chapters 5 and 6, and about privacy policies and software license agreements in Chapters 2 and 3.

Legal risks

Some files (such as underage pornography) are patently illegal to own. Simply possessing such files exposes you to enormous legal risks, not to mention the associated damage to your standing in the community. But if you're not a pedophile, you're at no risk, right? Wrong!

Because you have no way of knowing, definitively, the contents of a file without opening it (and even that may not be enough), a perfectly innocent download on your part could result in an illegal file being present on your hard drive, without you knowing anything about it.

This is an extreme example; a more common legal risk is simply copying files that you don't have a right to copy. For example, did you buy all the software you're running? Or did you copy it from a friend's disks? Or did you get it when you bought your computer used? Many, many people have bought used computers with an operating system and software applications already present, but if you read the fine print in software licenses, you'll see that there is no provision for transferring the software license when the computer is sold. And you're certainly not legally entitled to make copies of other people's software.

And then there is the practice of *burning* or *ripping* (terms for copying media files to disk) tracks from CDs. Controversy abounds about how much right an individual has to make copies of music they have purchased for personal use, but clearly copying and selling them or even copying and giving them away is illegal. The Recording Industry Association of America (RIAA) has been filing lawsuits against individuals for violating copyright laws by illegally copying music for several years now.

Cross-Reference   Chapter 9 has a great deal more information about intellectual property, the RIAA, and protecting yourself from illegal downloads.

Quality concerns

When you download a file, if it is free of viruses and is legal, you still have to consider quality. For music and video files, if the original material is of low quality, the file will be low quality, no matter how clean and perfect the recording. Even if the digital music file you have downloaded may seem large enough to be of good technical quality, it can be afflicted by poor musical quality. In such cases, you are likely to open the file to find the digital file actually sounds like it was transferred from a tape recorder from the back row of a stadium. Just as in the pre-download world, crap is still crap even if the cover of the CD looks great.

Many other factors can lead to poor quality, such as using an incorrect sampling rate, the wrong format for a particular use, or too much lossy compression (see the Introduction for more details about digitizing music and video, sampling rates, and compression).

System concerns

If all else is well, the final concern is your own computer system. If you've downloaded a fine collection of music files, you're not going to get much out of it if your system doesn't have enough space to store them, enough RAM and CPU power to play them back properly, or a good enough sound card and speaker set to output the music. You should know enough about your system to determine its capabilities. Consider spending some money for upgrades if necessary. Upgrading your computer is relatively inexpensive these days, and you can get great sound capability for just a little money. It's more important to make sure that all parts of your system are equally capable, because there's no point in having a great set of speakers and wimpy sound card.

 Chapter 4 has more information about what kinds of hardware to buy and how to match it up.

Top Points for Consideration when Choosing Between File Sharing and Direct Downloading

1. **Cost:** Sharing files doesn't cost anything, but you have to be careful not to accept illegal files or get viruses. Direct downloading copyrighted music files isn't always free, but it is usually legal.

2. **Legality:** If you've paid for a file, it is more likely to be legal, meaning that your fee legally entitles you to certain storage and playback privileges.

3. **Ease of use:** You can find music and video files by searching the Internet, calling around to your friends, and so on. But using file-sharing or direct-download software is easier, because the major companies put lots of effort into their desktop applications.

4. **Privacy:** File-sharing services afford more privacy in most cases, because you don't necessarily have to provide your personal information in order to use them. Direct downloading, especially for a fee, means that you're giving billing information to the company, which in many cases entitles them to market to you via e-mail or other means.

5. **Security:** Direct-download sites generally offer more security, because it's in their interest to double-check each file they offer to make sure that it is virus-free. Because direct-download sites get their music files from the manufacturer, it's much more likely that they are free of viruses (but not guaranteed). File-sharing services such as Kazaa do incorporate anti-virus protection, but of course there is no perfect anti-virus software so a malicious person could share files that are infected.

Summary

Many Web sites and software programs make the process of obtaining music and video files easy. These Web sites and programs generally fall into two categories: file sharing and direct downloading.

File-sharing sites provide software that uses P2P technology to let you search for and download files from any other user's computer. Direct-download sites provide software that lets you search for and buy files directly from their server.

In this chapter, as well as in chapters to follow, I describe these sites, software programs, and how to use them effectively, safely, and legally.

✦   ✦   ✦

Managing Your Risk by Choosing the Best Direct-Download Service

◆ ◆ ◆ ◆

CHAPTER 2

In This Chapter

Using direct music and video download services

Understanding Napster

Using Apple's iTunes

Getting "real" music with RealRhapsody

Making merry with Musicmatch

Acquiring safe and satisfying music files

◆ ◆ ◆ ◆

Y ou're ready to load up your player with thousands of hits, but where do you go for the best deals, the best service, and the safest downloads? New music sites are popping up all over, and not all of them are friendly, reliable, or even real. This chapter guides you to the top sites, compares music deals, and shows you how to avoid the marketing scams and worse.

Using Direct Music and Video Download Sites

You've probably heard of Napster and other music sites from their legal battles, so you may be wondering whether you should try them, how they work, and if you're going to be sued if you use them. While Napster did have legal problems back in 2001 the new Napster does business another way, and it's likely that you'll find music happiness there.

Napster is now different because it has joined the ranks of direct-download sites. The original Napster was a file-sharing service. File-sharing services provide access to files via the computers of members of these services who are logged on to those utilities, while direct-download sites provide files from their own hard drives or Web servers specifically intended for distributing these files.

In 2003, Steve Jobs premiered the Apple iTunes online music store, the first major, high-profile, direct-download music site to really connect with users. Before iTunes, digital file purchase options were limited. Some services, such as Liquid Audio, were around for years, but only offered a limited menu of songs and in a proprietary format not readily compatible with music player software included on most PCs. Of course, some music sites did not make actual files available for download, but only offered 30-second sound samples from CDs with the CD itself made available for shipping the old fashioned way — by delivery to your door, not to your hard drive.

Faced with these restrictive choices, large numbers of users did not pay for their downloaded music. Instead, seeking substantial song and musical artist choices, they preferred to download music for free from file-sharing services, many with the impression that if a file could be found, it must be legal to download it. After Apple's iTunes was established, it changed the way music was sold. A big part of the change is the compatibility of the iTunes software offered as part of the package with the iPod portable music player also made by Apple. Plus, the $0.99 -per-song pricing helped a great deal.

Downloading files

Direct-download sites allow you to copy files from their computers to your own computer. Although you could use their sites to download any type of file, they commonly specialize in certain well-known file types, such as music or video.

Direct musical file download sites have several things in common. For example, direct-download sites require that you install their proprietary software in order to use their service. Major browsers such as Internet Explorer, America Online's built-in browser, and Opera are capable of performing file downloads, but may not allow the download site to maintain as much control and security as they'd like.

Caution   Downloading and installing software, even professionally developed software from major companies, involves risks. Although it's unlikely that you'll have problems with software from the companies mentioned in this chapter, you should understand the risks. The major risks are that your system might not have the resources to handle the software or might be incompatible with the software, or that your system may be infected with a virus or even communicate information about you to the company without your knowledge. Make sure your system is compatible and has enough resources by reading the System Requirements, and then read the license agreement to find out what the software does after it's installed.

Direct-download sites also commonly maintain a library of files for download; the broader the selection the better. To make it easy for you to use their library, they supply search capabilities in their software you download, or even on the main Web site for these services. Again, major browsers are capable of supporting search capability, but direct-download software has specialized search functions optimized for the sites' particular file libraries.

So how do you choose the best one? Although they all have some things in common, they differentiate themselves by their selections, terms and conditions, fees, and extra services. But you'll also find differences in other areas that are not touted by the download sites. For example, the software offered by some download sites may be less invasive of your privacy than others.

Tip   Apple's iTunes site offers audio books as well as music.

Finding direct-download sites

In this chapter, the major direct-download sites are examined in detail, so the facts in this book are a good starting point for finding reliable direct-download sites. But anyone can set one up, if he has the resources. All it takes is a server, some player software, a collection of music or video files, and a good Internet connection. But which ones are legal, authorized, reliable, reasonably priced, fair in their terms and conditions, secure, and easy to use? Good questions. This chapter covers all these aspects of the sites' offerings; in the end, you should be able to answer these questions for yourself based on the inside facts provided.

Just because the Web site looks real and sounds authoritative doesn't mean it has any legal authority to offer music or video files for sale. You might get bogus or defective files, or even end up with a serious virus or spyware.Illegitimate music files have afflicted digital downloaders for several years. One of the most high-profile cases occurred back in 2002. In that year, a BBC online report (currently found at `http://news.bbc.co.uk/1/hi/entertainment/music/2486023.stm`) noted that some fake copies of tracks from *Escapology* (by Robbie Williams) appeared on the Internet a few days before the album actually was released. The speculation is that the fake copies were placed online by the record label to make it harder for people to find "real" illegal copies. Regardless of how the files got on the Web, the point is that these fakes could just as easily have been viruses, Trojan horses, or *adware*. Placed on your PC during file or utility downloads, adware tracks what Web pages you visit, and then serves you spam ads or e-mails based on your preference.

Prevention   Double-check the background of download sites, and check up on other user's complaints before installing and using the software.

So how do you tell bogus sites from real sites, and how do you know whether a real site is authorized to sell you music? Although you may not be inclined to go the lengths outlined here for every music service you use, at least you'll know how to begin checking out the legitimacy of a site. This section contains a few effective ways to check up on sites.

Note   These tips work for any Web site, not just direct-download services.

Check the domain name registration. You can do this by going to a Web site such as Network Solutions (www.networksolutions.com) or any other domain-name registration company and performing a whois (pronounced "who is") search. The whois command is actually a Unix command that has found its way into the modern world as the Internet method for checking the registration of domain names. Figure 2-1 shows the Network Solutions site.

To use the whois command at Network Solutions, click the whois link and then enter the domain name and the domain extension (for example, enter **napster.com**, not **www.napster.com**) as shown in Figure 2-2.

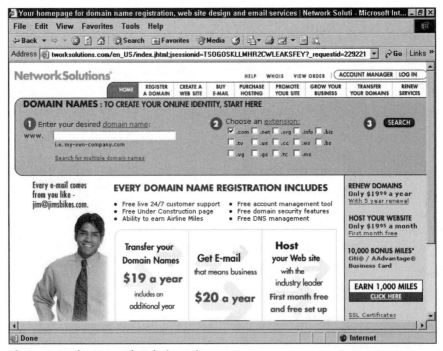

Figure 2-1: The Network Solutions site

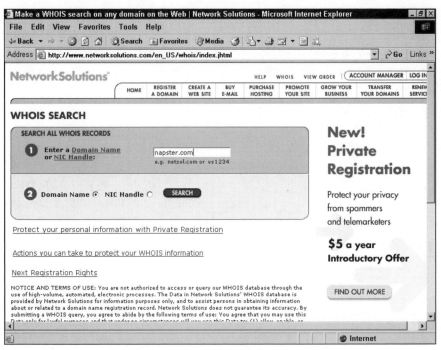

Figure 2-2: Using whois at the Network Solutions site

The Network Solutions site employs a system that displays a short set of characters that you have to recognize and enter before the system will complete your request. (This helps them block robot software from electronically using their whois without permission.)

Enter the characters shown, and you'll see the registration information for the domain name, even if the domain is not registered through them. The screen should be similar to Figure 2-3.

You can tell lots from a domain-name registration: who owns the name (and often, as in this case, the parent company), where the owner is physically located, some contact phone numbers and e-mail addresses, the domain-name server, and so on. However, note that it is possible for domain-name registrants to fake this information as well, and the domain-name registrar gives no guarantee of the validity of any information in a domain-name registration.

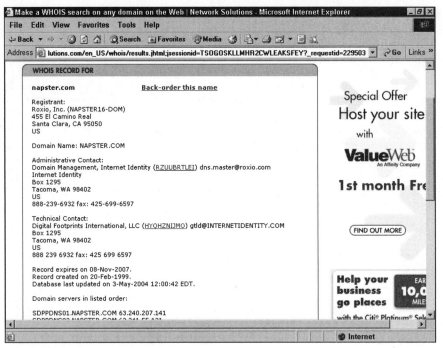

Figure 2-3: Domain Registration information

Also, registrants sometimes register DBAs, or names of holding companies. Because of these inconsistencies, this information will tell you little if anything about the site's legitimacy. Finally, Network Solutions and most other registrars seem to have recently implemented an inquiry limit for their whois pages, sometimes half a dozen per day. Abuse the privilege, and you may get a bounce-back message

What Is Spyware?

Spyware is software that, once installed, communicates to the outside world via your Internet connection and without your knowledge. Legitimate software often does this as well, but usually tells you in the license that it is going to do so. Some software items may have perfectly benign reasons for talking to their makers, such as looking for recent updates or patches. But it's an uncomfortable feeling when the communications take place behind the scenes with no warning. Installed software generally has access to your entire system, and you never really know what might be sent out.

To go one step further, go to the D&B (formerly Dun and Bradstreet) Web site (www.dnb.com), shown in Figure 2-4. Notice that I entered the name of the parent company (Roxio Inc.), not the domain name, in the D&B Web site's search form. The result of the search is shown in Figure 2-5.

You can also get a fairly detailed outline of the owner at the comprehensive business information Web site, Hoover's Online (www.hoovers.com) The information about Roxio Inc. at the Hoover's Online site includes the main product lines of the company, some background on the company, a list of officers, the company's recent financial performance, and more (see Figure 2-6).

Seeing this kind of information in well-known sites such as Hoover's and D&B goes a long way toward proving the site is legitimate. Fake sites would have a very hard time generating this much corroboration.

So the Napster.com site looks and sounds real and authoritative. This still leaves many open questions about the software, reliability, security, terms and conditions, and so forth. Take a closer look at these issues by examining the major direct-download sites.

Figure 2-4: The D&B Web site

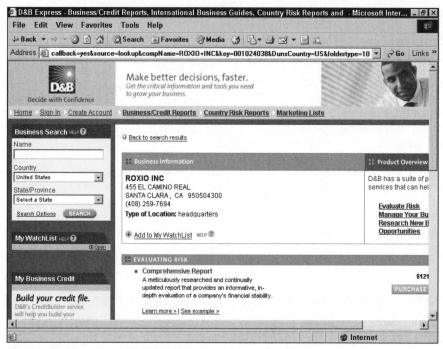

Figure 2-5: Search results for Roxio Inc. at the D&B Web site

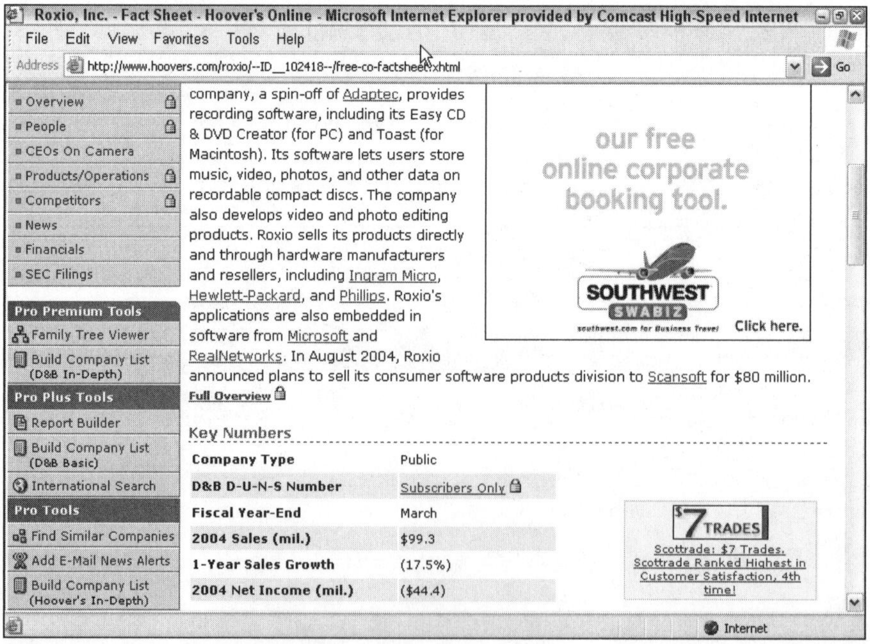

Figure 2-6: Search results at Forbes for Roxio Inc.

Understanding the major direct-download sites

By definition, direct-download sites are commercial, meaning they sell files to you. You are nearly always required to install their software, and sometimes can only play the files you download with their software.

So what do they have in common, and how can you make a choice as to which one to use? The following list discusses some criteria for judging them. The three most important things to look for when considering a site to be your preferred music store of choice are:

✦ **Price.** Like any products for sale, you can find a number of pricing schemes on the direct-download sites: by the file, by the album, subscription rates, free trials, discounts, and so on. To compare prices, you first need to understand what you're buying. After all, a song for $0.99 might seem like a great deal, unless you can only play it once. To figure out what you get when you make a purchase, take a look at some of the sales terms on the site before you buy. Some download sites allow CD burning, some do not. Some allow CD burning but only a certain number of times, or for a certain period after the track is downloaded.

✦ **Library.** The term library is synonymous with selection, meaning that a site with a large library of files for sale has a large selection to choose from. There are hundreds of categories of music, not to mention other kinds of files, and no site carries them all. Some sites are specific to the music of their own recording labels, while others carry a wide variety of music (but perhaps not specific labels' music). Some sites specialize in certain file types such as mp3.

✦ **Ease of use.** Is proprietary software required? That is certainly not a negative feature, but if you tend to run a number of other programs and have an older computer, the software may slow your PC's performance. In that case, you may be better off purchasing digital music from a Web page-based service (such as mp3.com), rather than one that forces you to install special software to buy and play the music.

Caution

Like insurance and other less-well-understood products, the songs sold by each company differ in what you can do with them. You can know what you're getting only by either reading the terms and conditions very carefully, or by going to a consumer site that lists the differences in a table so you can make an informed decision. Don't assume that just because you can download a song and copy it that you have the right to do whatever you want with it. You can easily stray into illegal territory by doing the wrong things, which is exactly what you're hoping to avoid by paying for the song in the first place.

Understanding filenames and extensions

To play a digital music file, you will want to ensure that your music player software can handle files with specific extensions. For example, most music software utilities can handle mp3 files, but few, aside from iTunes, can play files encoded in Apple's proprietary iTunes format (which has an hkdb file extension).

Here's some basic information that will help you understand how file extensions work.

Web page files are composed of plain text, written as HTML tags, Javascript, and ordinary text characters. Web page files may be named anything, but they usually end with .htm, .html, .php, .asp, .cfm, .jsp, or something like that. The filename extension (the last three or four characters after the final dot in the filename) is meaningful, because your browser knows to display the file as a Web page when it ends with one of these file extensions.

But if the file ends with .mp3, your browser may prompt you with a little notice asking whether you want to save the file or open it (and telling you that opening files can be dangerous because they may contain viruses).

Still, if you happen to have an MP3 player software application installed, and your browser knows to use it, you can opt to open the file and play it directly. So again, you can use your browser to download MP3s or any other file type. If you use your browser to download a file type that your browser doesn't recognize or for which you don't have a player installed, you can just save it. Then later you can install the appropriate player software and play back the file.

Common file types

Table 2-1 lists some of the common audio and video media file types by their file extension. Media files are often compressed because audio and video files contain massive amounts of data in order to offer superior picture and sound quality at playback, and therefore do not travel well on the Internet. *Lossless* compression means the file can be restored with all its data, while *lossy* compression means that some data is lost. Many of the file types listed here use lossy compression but still produce good quality when played. Some of the file types can be streamed (played across the Internet even before the entire file has been received).

Keep in mind that just because a file has a particular extension does NOT guarantee that the file is actually that type; a common trick is to change a file extension so that the file can masquerade as another type while hiding its true type and thereby sneaking into your system.

Table 2-1
Common Audio and Video File Types

Extension	Sponsor/Name	File Type
.mp3	MPEG	Audio, compressed
.wav	Microsoft, waveform	Audio, uncompressed
.ra, .ram	Real Networks, real audio	Audio, compressed
.avi	Microsoft, audio video interleave	Video/audio, uncompressed
.mg2, .mp2, .mp4	Motion Picture Experts Group, MPEG-4 Yes, but .mg2 is not the same thing as .mp4.	Video/audio, compressed
.mov	Apple, Quicktime	Video/audio, compressed
.rm, .rv	RealMedia	Video/audio, compressed
.swf	Macromedia, Flash	Video/audio/animation, compressed

Software license

As sure as I am that you always read (and understand) the complete terms of software license agreements before installing the software, I want to take a close look at some of the terms common to software licenses for direct-download services.

Most download music site licenses include the following provisions and restrictions:

✦ Generally, you are not allowed to use, download, upload, copy, print, display, perform, reproduce, publish, license, post, transmit, or distribute any songs or other information you download from these services.

✦ You are responsible for getting any necessary permission and paying any necessary licensing fees for the music or other material you choose to record. If you violate the copyright laws, there may be fines or criminal charges brought against you, even if you don't get any commercial benefit from the illegal copies you distribute. If you violate an artist's copyright, you cannot hold the music store where you bought the track or tracks liable.

✦ Some services have restrictions regarding the number of PCs on which you can play CDs you have burned from legally purchased music. For example, Musicmatch restricts each burned CD to a maximum of seven PCs.

Agreeing to a software license is in many cases the same as physically signing a contract. READ THE LICENSE before agreeing. In most cases, a little common sense will tip you off to disagreeable terms, so don't be put off by lots of legal mumbo jumbo.

Terms and conditions

Terms and Conditions found on many direct-download sites are quite similar to Terms of Use (sometimes called TOS, or Terms of Service) found in direct-download software license agreements. For example, the Musicmatch terms and conditions specify how you may use the Musicmatch software and its services.

Note

These services include Musicmatch On Demand, which is a service that allows you to purchase tunes from Musicmatch Jukebox and Musicmatch Radio. For either $4.50 or $2.95 a month (as of this writing), you can subscribe and listen to any of more than 200 Musicmatch radio stations.

✦ **Use of Web site information.** Basically, this term restricts using the Web site except for personal, informational, non-commercial uses.

✦ **Use of software.** In addition to the specific license terms in the software license, this term restates your obligation to read and abide by Musicmatch's software license, and also makes it clear that you have the responsibility to ensure that you do not use the software to violate anyone's copyrights.

✦ **Use of Musicmatch On Demand or Musicmatch Radio.** You will be able to use Musicmatch to search for songs by your favorite artists. If you decide to access either of these services to purchase or listen to music you have found by doing your search, the terms spell out how you will be charged, such as "no pro-rated refunds" and "renewal charges will be billed automatically."

The remaining terms are mostly regarding how and when you will be billed, and what you get.

Caution

You must read the sections on definition of service, billing, and opting out of service carefully, because you may find that you're going to be billed whether or not you ever use the service. The amounts may be small, but a no-refund policy can be pretty annoying if you have to pay for something you don't use.

Privacy policies

Privacy policies abound on Web sites, and they are typically long and filled with legalese, although some sites do attempt to put their policies into plain English. The policies you see on Web sites are sometimes mandated by the states in which the sites operate, but in each case they generally follow the same guidelines. Most sites prominently state that they respect your privacy, while at the same time making it clear that if you let them they'll sell your name to anyone, they'll make statistical summaries (without personally identifiable information) available to third parties without your permission, and they abide by laws restricting them from collecting information about users under the age of 13.

The most effective Web site privacy policies have clear, "opt-out" language that make it clear to you how you can contact the site and request that your name and contact information not be sold to third parties. In terms of contact information you will need to notify the company you want to opt out of these practices, Web site privacy policies should either link to a form where you can submit your opt-out request, or give e-mail, physical address, and a phone number for a department or individual able to take care of this for you.

A simple "webmaster@..." e-mail link is not enough. If you send your opt out request to the site's Webmaster, he or she may be in a different department, or not even with the company. Plus, Webmasters are more concerned with technical issues than customer service matters. So, the more specific the opt-out contact information on the site, the better the privacy policy.

However, you'll find that the privacy policy specific to the installed software is a little different than the one regarding use of the Web site. For example, many direct-download software applications check your installation to see whether you need upgrades, and it may install those upgrades without your knowledge. They also identify your installed software so they can check to see whether it is being used in accordance with the Terms of Use.

Web site privacy policies that clearly state if or how personally identifiable information will be used often bear the seal of approval of either or both major Web privacy policy certification agencies, such as the BBBOnline (the Better Business Bureau's online division), or TrustE, a voluntary, not-for-profit organization especially devoted to online privacy.

 More information about each of these services is included in Chapter 8.

Using Napster

In 1999, a college student named Shawn Fanning had a brilliant idea: Make files from any computer available to any other computer, as though they were all connected inside one giant hard drive. The technical name for this type of file sharing is peer-to-peer (P2P) networking, but Shawn wanted to optimize the system he created for swapping music files, so he added a music search capability, plus instant messaging and other features. The result was the original Napster.

Napster was eventually forced out of business by large organizations representing the mainstream music industry, but it has resurfaced with a business model resembling the successful Apple iTunes music service. Now that Napster is legal, it sells music for $0.99 per track, or you can get the whole album for just $9.95. It also boasts a library of more than 700,000 songs from all genres of music. The service also offers 15 songs for $14.95.

You can find Napster at `www.napster.com`.

Terms and conditions

As of this writing, Napster offers seven days of free downloads when you join its premium service. But, Napster wants a credit card number in order to sign up, even to get the seven-day free trial. Following the trial, you are billed $9.95 per month.

The Napster Terms and Conditions document can be found on the Web site, of course, and it has the usual restrictions and notices. One interesting caveat is contained in it stipulating that you are responsible for how you handle the track after it is purchased. The tracks they provide have some kind of digital watermark or other identifying code inserted, and if you remove it, you're on your own.

System requirements

Napster's player application requires a PC running Windows XP/ME, Internet Explorer 5.1 or higher, and Windows Media Player 7.1 or higher. As with other download sites, a fast Internet connection is a major time saver. Note that if you happen to be running an incompatible operating system (such as Windows 98), the site doesn't allow you to download the software for installation on a compatible machine. Currently, there is no Mac-compatible version.

Privacy policies

Napster's privacy policies indicate that when you sign up for the service, you have the option of consenting to having your personally identifiable information as well as your purchasing patterns shared with music companies that have partnered with Napster. However, Napster's privacy policy also says "any personal registration data that we share is not authorized by us to be transferred by the recipients of that data to third parties or used for mass distribution of emails or other activities that might be considered 'spamming.' We do not share your credit card account information with Partners or any other third parties. "

In other words, if Napster notifies one of their music company partners that you have purchased a track by a given artist, that music company partner is not allowed to release that information to one of their business partners. Like most other legal digital downloading services, Napster does not share your credit card account information with Partners or any other third parties.

Software installation

Software installation of the Napster 2.5 software is fairly straightforward. You first see the screen in Figure 2-7.

Figure 2-7: The Napster installation process begins.

This screen simply tells you to follow instructions and set up Napster on your desktop. After the InstallShield software takes over, you have the opportunity to set the location of the software, the speed of the connection, and your settings, and then do the final install, respectively.

Tuning in to Apple iTunes

Apple iTunes is Apple's entry into the online direct-download music-store business. Apple already had a very successful music player called the iPod, and Apple brought great credibility to the marketplace, but a site like this was a gamble nonetheless. Fortunately, Apple got it right, and the iTunes store sold a million songs the first week. The iTunes service and the software it uses are available in Windows as well as Mac-compatible versions.

You can find Apple's iTunes at `www.apple.com/itunes`.

The Apple iTunes music store currently claims to offer more than one million songs, including those of the major music labels such as BMG, EMI, Sony Music Entertainment, and more. The store gives the impression that more attention is given to songs that are currently popular; although from the size of the library, the average user probably would find what she's looking for regardless of popularity.

Going to the iTunes download page offers instructions and system requirements for getting the Windows or Mac version of iTunes. It also offers a chance to subscribe to Apple's newsletters (fortunately, signing up for the newsletters is not required) as shown in Figure 2-8.

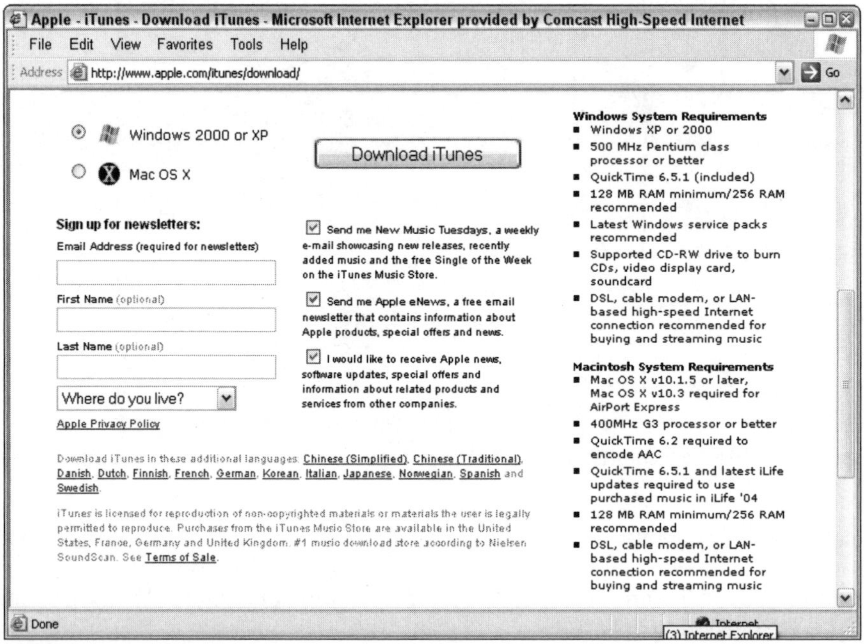

Figure 2-8: The Apple iTunes download screen

Terms and conditions

Like other direct-download software, Apple limits your right to download and copy material for personal use. Specifically, iTunes' terms and conditions require you to use the music you purchase in the following ways only:

✦ **For personal, noncommercial use.** That means you cannot distribute the music you purchase on iTunes to your friends, either for a fee or just as a free attachment to an e-mail.

✦ **On a maximum of three computers at one time.** This prevents excess copying and distribution.

✦ **Burning your own CDs or DVDs.** If you burn a CD of songs you have purchased on iTunes, and then either give the CD away or sell it, you are violating your agreement with iTunes. If you are caught, your account with iTunes will be subject to suspension.

Privacy policy

Apple's privacy policy sounds very friendly, but like so many others it basically says they collect personally identifiable information about you for business purposes, and other information (not personally identifiable) all the time. And they intend to share this information with other Apple businesses worldwide.

System requirements

The Apple Web site says that iTunes 4.5 (for Windows) requires Windows 2000 or Windows XP with a QuickTime-compatible audio card. The site also recommends that you have the latest Service Pack for your computer using Windows Update. For additional capabilities, such as creating CDs or DVDs, you may need an iTunes-compatible CD or DVD burner or a QuickTime-compatible video card. And obviously if you're going to download large files, a DSL, cable modem, or local area network (LAN) Internet connection is recommended.

Software installation

Software installation for Apple's iTunes is fairly straightforward, offering the typical choices of program location, assignment of file type by file extension (meaning if you double-click the file, the iTunes player will open it), and so on.

The system requirements for using iTunes with a Windows PCs are Windows XP or 2000 on a computer with a 500 MHz Pentium class processor or better. iTunes comes with QuickTime 6.5.1 and requires 128 MB RAM minimum/256 RAM; a supported CD-RW drive to burn CDs, video display card, and soundcard; and DSL, cable modem, or LAN-based high-speed Internet connection.

For Macs, Apple requires Mac OS X v10.1.5 or later, Mac OS X v10.3 required for AirPort Express, and a 400 MHz G3 processor or better. You will also need QuickTime 6.2 because it is required to encode AAC; QuickTime 6.5.1 and the latest iLife updates are required to use purchased music in iLife '04. You must have a minimum of 128 MB RAM, but 256 MB RAM is recommended. Apple also suggests you have a DSL, cable modem, or LAN-based high-speed Internet connection for buying and streaming music.

Musicmatch

Musicmatch began in 1997 as a service for matching a person's musical interests with the appropriate tracks. In late 2004, Musicmatch was purchased by Yahoo!, which may ultimately integrate its new acquisition into its impressive collection of existing digital content services.

The Musicmatch Web site can be found at www.musicmatch.com and offers sophisticated software allowing the user to enter his tastes and then receive a (hopefully) matching playlist.

The software has matured over the years, now offering a Jukebox feature, an Internet radio station (or network, as it's billed), and most recently a direct-download service. The current software version is Musicmatch 9.0. The Musicmatch site claims that more than 500,000 tracks are available in their library, with music spanning 120 genres.

Terms and conditions

The Musicmatch terms and conditions are fairly straightforward, but contain lots of information about who may purchase and use the software and when and how they will be billing you. For example, they'll put a hold in the amount of $1.00 on your credit card account as part of the process of verifying whether or not your credit card is valid, and they will bill $9.90 to your credit card when you begin purchasing tracks. They do offer a refund for defective tracks if you notify them within 30 days of the purchase.

Privacy policy

Like other sites, Musicmatch collects both personally identifiable and non-personally identifiable information for a variety of reasons, primarily to complete business transactions and for marketing purposes. Stating a copyright policy that most other legitimate sites adhere to, Musicmatch notes they're bound by the Digital Millennium Copyright Act (DMCA) to collect information about which tracks you receive from their streaming music services.

System requirements

To successfully download and utilize the Musicmatch software, the site suggests that you need a Pentium Class 300 MHz processor or better, Windows 98/SE/Me/2000/XP, 128MB RAM, and a minimum of 150MB of hard drive space. You will also need Internet Explorer 5.0 or later. At the time this book was written, there was no Mac version offered.

Software installation

You should find downloading the Musicmatch Jukebox (9.0 as of this writing) very easy. The basic player is free, and a Plus player is available for $19.95.

Getting Real with Real Network's RealRhapsody

You can find Real Network's RealRhapsody music download software at www. real.com/rhapsody, and the Real Network's online download service at www. real.com/musicstore. The online music store offers a library of more than 700,000 songs. Each song sells for just $0.99, or you can get most albums for $9.99.

Terms and conditions

As of this writing, RealRhapsody requires a credit card in order to sign up even for their 14-day free trial. After 30 days, a subscription costs $9.95 a month.

System requirements

The RealRhapsody requirements are pretty minimal; you only need to have a Windows PC with a 350 MHz processor and 250MB of hard drive space. Sorry, Mac users — although there may be a Mac-compatible version at some point, none was available when this book was published.

Privacy policy

Although RealRhapsody's developer, RealNetworks, does not have a special privacy policy for its RealRhapsody product, RealNetworks privacy policy applies to all of its services, including RealRhapsody.

In the Privacy policy section of its Web site, RealNetworks says that it "does not sell, rent, or share your personal information to a third party unless you consent to provide such information to a third party partner or content service." RealNetworks also prohibits partner sites and businesses (such as music companies that make songs available to RealRhapsody subscribers) from distributing information about you to their business partners without your knowledge and consent.

Downloading and installing RealRhapsody

To sign up with RealRhapsody, go to www.real.com/rhapsody/. Scroll down the page until you see the "Click Here To Try Real Rhapsody" link, shown in Figure 2-9. This link will take you to a series of screens where you will enter your credit card number and other information. After you complete your order, RealRhapsody will automatically install on your PC. Once it installs, you will need to reboot your PC in order to use the program.

Figure 2-9: The RealRhapsody download page

> **Note**   MSN Music and Sony Connect were not yet available as of this writing, but should be by the time you read this book. These services will be offered by major industry names and are expected to be very competitive with the existing services outlined here.

Connecting with Sony Connect

Sony Connect is a new digital music store from Sony Music, one of the largest recording companies in the world. You can listen to samples and download songs for $0.99 or entire albums for $9.99 and up. Currently, the service does not list the specific number of titles in its catalog, but it does claim to be one of the largest services for obtaining legal music.

Terms and conditions

According to Sony Connect's Terms and Conditions policies, you may not reproduce, distribute, or transfer any tracks you purchase from the site to anyone else. Although you can copy or transfer most music you purchase to an unlimited number of portable music devices, you can only transfer tracks released by Warner Music Group to a maximum of three devices. Also, you are not allowed to burn more than ten copies of any particular track you have purchased to a blank, recordable CD.

RealRhapsody and RealPlayer

It is easy to confuse RealRhapsody with RealPlayer. RealPlayer, also from RealNetworks, is both a software program that can retrieve and play music from Internet radio stations, and a tool to play music files you have downloaded to your PC. RealRhapsody, however, is more of a digital music store than a digital music radio station. Yet, once you have purchased songs on RealRhapsody, you can play them either on your RealRhapsody or RealPlayer software.

System requirements

To play music, Sony Connect it uses a utility called SonicStage (see Figure 2-10). The program is downloadable from www.connect.com.

Here are the minimum requirements:

✦ Windows 98 Second Edition or newer (Mac not supported)

✦ Internet Explorer 5.5 or newer

✦ Pentium II 400 MHz or higher

✦ 400 MB or greater of available hard drive space

Figure 2-10: SonicStage allows you to connect directly to its music store.

Privacy policy

Sony Connect's privacy policy is influenced somewhat by parent company Sony's status as an entertainment conglomerate with interests in movies as well as recorded music. This puts Sony in a unique position to cross-market its digital entertainment assets. Cross-marketing routinely involves frequent customer contact. When overly frequent, such as by constant e-mails touting a Sony movie that features a track you have bought from Sony Connect, this contact can make some customers feel that their privacy is being violated.

For those reasons, Sony's privacy policy is driven by two competing forces: the desire to cross-market its products and the company's awareness that if unchecked, these efforts can be considered excessive.

Sony Connect says it will not share the personal information you provide on the Connect Web sites with any other parties, except with other companies fully or at least half-owned by Sony. This contact will only be made with your consent, as you may have granted when you register with Sony Connect. With your consent, Sony will also share personal information about you with partner Web sites. What those sites do with the information they receive from Sony is covered by their own privacy policies.

Introducing MSN Music

In September of 2004, Microsoft introduced its own online music store, MSN Music, as shown in Figure 2-11. Although MSN Music is marketed through Microsoft's MSN Internet access service, anyone with an Internet connection can purchase and download legal tracks on MSN Music.

MSN Music is available either via the MSN Music Web site (`music.msn.com`), or by opening Windows Media Player 10 and clicking the Music tab (as shown in Figure 2-12).

The service offers some one million individual tracks for $0.99 each and an unspecified, but growing, number of full albums, most of which are available for $9.99 each. First, you need to register with MSN Music. To do so, point your browser to `https://signup.msn.com/pages/AccountInfo.aspx`. You will see a Create Your MSN Music Account page. Enter your billing information on this page. Click the Review your information tab on the bottom of the Create Your MSN Music Account Page. A Review And Accept The Agreements page opens. Scroll through the user agreement. Type your name in the box to the right of where your name appears in the User Agreement area of the page. Then click the I Accept button. A Please Wait While We Configure Your Account progress bar briefly appears. This step should just take a few seconds. Once your credit card is confirmed, the main MSN Music page will appear.

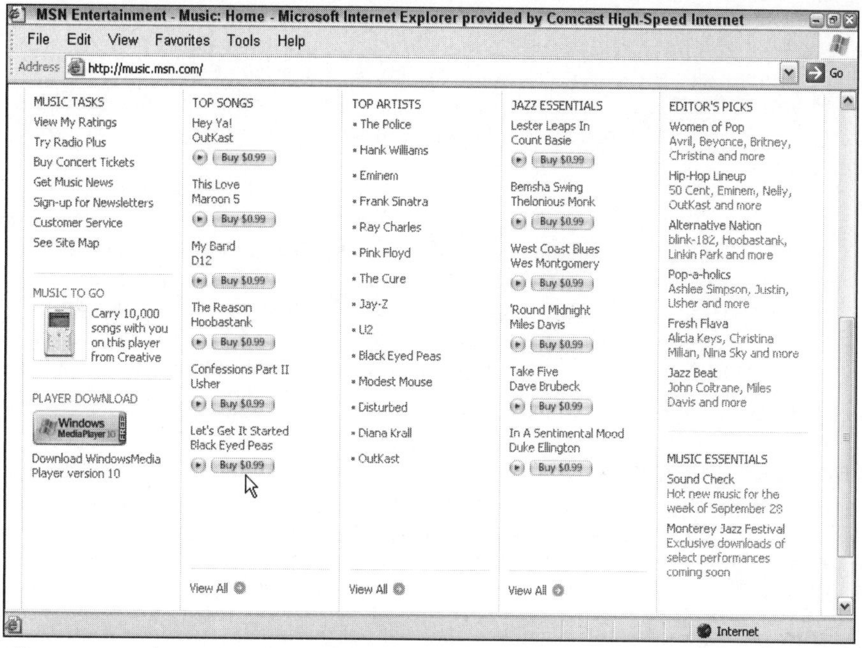

Figure 2-11: The main MSN Music Web page

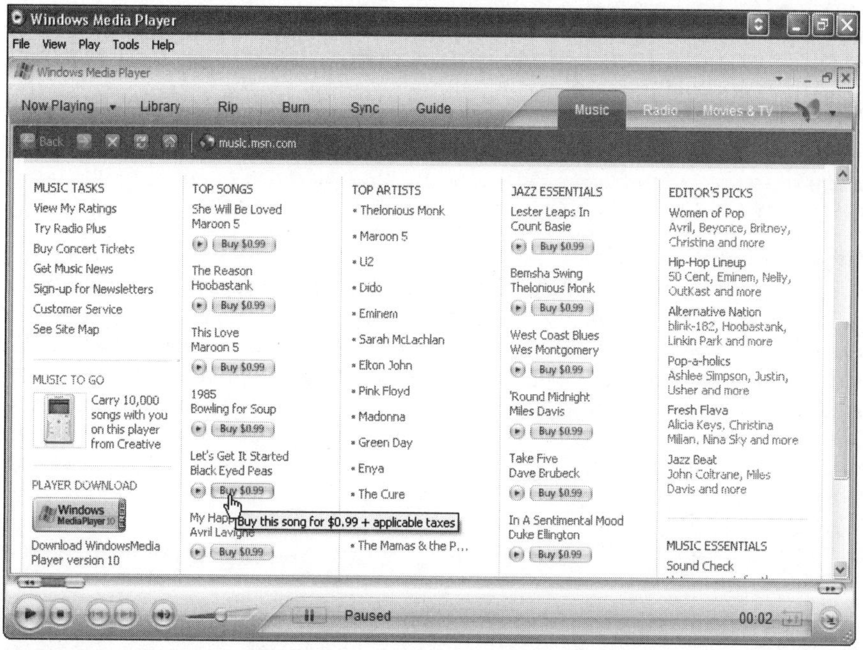

Figure 2-12: Accessing MSN Music in Windows Media Player 10

To purchase a track, simply click on the Buy tab next to the song you want to purchase. If you have registered on MSN Music, you will be asked to sign in. MSN Music remembers the credit card information you furnished when you registered. When you find a track you would like to purchase, click the Buy tab next to the name of the track. The song you have chosen will automatically download to your PC.

Caution

To ensure that the credit card you submit during your registration is valid, MSN Music, (as well as other sites including iTunes) will attempt to authorize a small test transaction on your card. The amount is usually $1. The authorization does not stay on your card as a purchase, though. Most credit card companies refund the authorized amount after a few business days. If the credit card you use to register with MSN Music is over its limit or past due, the test authorization will not go through. You will then be asked to submit another credit card to register.

Terms and conditions

At the time this book was published, Microsoft did not have a specific set of terms and conditions for how you can use the digital music tracks you purchase from the MSN Music site.

System requirements

Unlike most other legal online music stores, MSN Music does not provide its own software and user interface. The tracks you download, however, are configured to work best in Windows Media Player 10, the latest version of Microsoft's multimedia player software. The basic system requirements for Windows Media Player 10 include Windows XP, at least a 233 MHz processor, 64MB of RAM, and at least 100MB of available space for storing tracks.

A Mac-compatible version of Windows Media Player 10 should be released by early in 2005.

Privacy policy

Although there is no separate privacy policy for MSN Music, the service is covered under the MSN privacy policy. This policy indicates that MSN does not sell, rent, or lease its customer lists to third parties. MSN reserves the right, however, to contact you on behalf of external business partners about a particular offering that may be of interest to you. In those cases, though, your personally identifiable information (such as your e-mail, name, address or telephone number) is not transferred to the third party.

Top Ten Things to Consider when Installing and Using Downloaded Software

1. **Read your direct-download software application's installation requirements and instructions.** These requirements and instructions can typically be found on the Web site. Make sure you have the type of computer and operating system specified for the software you're going to download, and make sure you have enough RAM, hard drive space, and CPU power to run the software properly. For example, in the Musicmatch Jukebox software, the cache setting starts at 250MB. It helps keep music playing smoothly by downloading and saving the streaming music on your hard drive, but if you run out of room, your system may crash.

2. **Always save and back up your work while you're listening to streaming music or playing downloaded tracks.** Your computer's operating system, CPU, and hard drive work overtime to playback music smoothly, and they are constantly connected to the Internet when receiving streaming music, so experiencing a total system failure (the blue screen of death) is not uncommon. If you've been working all day to finish a project and you haven't backed up, you may lose all your work.

3. **Read the Terms and Conditions for using each site and its software, and follow them.** If you don't like their terms, don't become a member or install the software. The terms and conditions often contain restrictive policies that limit your rights to use what you've paid for, or to share files among computers or with other users.

4. **Read the privacy policy and marketing policy of each site.** Privacy policies nearly always start with phrases like "we respect your privacy," and then go on to detail exactly how they'll share your personal information among many other related entities, often without any further consent on your part.

5. **Read the software license before installing the software.** Some software items have very liberal conditions attached (liberal for them) that may allow complete access to your system without your knowledge. This means that the companies may configure their software to examine any part of your hard drive (including personal information) without your knowledge. Remember, these software packages constantly make connections to the Internet for legitimate purposes, but Internet connections can also be used to send information back to the company without your knowing what was sent or when it was sent.

6. **Make sure you've got plenty of space on your hard drive in which to store downloaded files.** You can check how much space you have by going into Windows Explorer and simply clicking on the C: drive (or the D: drive, if that's the one you installed the software on). You'll see a graphic image of the drive and some text that tells you how much space you have available. Keep in mind that when you install the software, you can install it with just barely enough room for the software, but when you download tracks, they tend to take up lots of room, and you can quickly run out of space.

7. **Watch out for fake or illegal download sites.** Just because a site claims to have music to download (and perhaps claims it is "100% legit, honest!") doesn't mean they have the right to sell the songs. And sometimes the songs are bogus too. Spend three minutes and run a check on the site with Google, using searches including the name of the site and perhaps keywords like "complaints," "features," and "billing problems."

8. **Get to know the user interface for buying tracks or albums, as well as the policy for returns, refunds, billing, subscription rates, free trials, and so on.** Knowing what you are paying for—and what you might end up paying for—is important. Many sites do not allow refunds. Each site is likely to bill a little differently. For example, even for a free trial you often have to submit a credit card number, so make sure you know when they will begin charging you. You really don't want to be billed improperly, and it is often a headache to straighten out later.

9. **Use a broadband Internet connection with the highest quality settings for the best streaming music experience.** If all you have is a dial-up Internet connection, the best speed you can get is about 45-50 Kbps (Kbps is kilobits per second, so 45 Kbps is 45,000 bits per second). This really isn't fast enough to get a great listening or viewing experience with streaming media, so at slower speeds, you'll be happier if you simply download and play back the tracks you buy. Playback from a saved file on your hard drive should be much faster and therefore much clearer than playback from a slow Internet connection.

10. **Know which player you want to use as your default player before beginning to download software.** If you prefer to stay with your current default player software, you may have to choose a custom installation (you should get this option during installation of any package) and deselect the "use this player as your default player for these file types" option. Each of the packages discussed in this chapter would like to be the default player for all file types, because when you're using their software, it's more likely that you'll buy tracks from them. But you're under no obligation to set them as the default player, and it won't hurt anything if they're not the default player.

Summary

In this chapter, you've read about commercial direct-download services. These services differ from free or open-source file-sharing services in that you must register as a member, they charge for their services, and they provide the files directly to you, rather than simply being a middleman running a server that allows you to find your files on other peoples' computers.

The services include offerings from Sony, Napster, Apple, and Real Networks. Before you are able to download and install software in order to access their offerings, these and other sites make you agree to their terms of service—which usually forbids you from redistributing copyrighted material you buy from them.

✦ ✦ ✦

Managing Your Risk by Choosing the Best File-Sharing Service

◆   ◆   ◆   ◆

In This Chapter

Understanding online file sharing and file-sharing protocols

Using file-sharing networks

Using file-sharing software and services

Getting to know file-sharing organizations

◆   ◆   ◆   ◆

File-sharing services are not all created equal; huge differences exist in the care they take in developing their software and checking the files available on their systems. Although even the best services can't totally prevent the unintended distribution of bad files, you can (and should) take some basic steps to derive the most benefit from them. In this chapter, I discuss the major file-sharing services, what makes them great fun or a pain, and what to look for in the future, as file-sharing services evolve.

Understanding How File Sharing Works

At the heart of file sharing, there aren't searing guitar licks of MP3 files but something quite a bit more technical: A concept called protocols. The term simply means hardware and software standards that govern data transmission between computers — in this case, your own PC and another computer connected to your file-sharing service with a hard drive that contains a music file you want. Like other forms of computer communications on the Internet (and on networks in general), protocols specify the format of bits and data for file sharing. Basically, protocols define:

✦ **The sequence of messages between computers.** When computers communicate across a network, they send requests and responses to each other in a specific sequence, verifying that communications are taking place as planned.

✦ **The sequence of bits in each message and what they mean.** Request and response messages between computers are commonly divided into headers and bodies; headers include such things as address, date, and time, and bodies include the message "payload".

Cross-Reference   Chapter 4 has a much more detailed discussion of file storage.

File sharing is not illegal. What happens when files are shared makes an individual file-sharing session legal, or not. If the file is not copyrighted and is being distributed over a file-sharing network, then it is most likely legal to do so. If it is copyrighted, and the law holds that distribution over file-sharing networks is not authorized, then that particular file-sharing exchange is most likely not legal. To put it another way, file sharing is not inherently legal or illegal. It is just a technological means to an end.

Still, to understand how file sharing works as a platform for actions both legal and not, it would be interesting to explore the history of this technology in relation to the downloading of copyrighted digital music files.

A Boston-area college dropout named Shawn Fanning developed one of the major file-sharing protocols, used for Napster, in the late 1990s. Napster was essentially sued out of existence because it directly facilitated the illegal swapping of music files, but many other file-sharing protocols were developed with similar capabilities and less legal exposure. The most popular services now available tend to avoid using any kind of central server, encrypt files being shared, and provide at least some anonymity to users. The content industry, led by the Recording Industry Association of America (RIAA) is still hard at work trying to shut down or scare off users, but whether the newer protocols will eventually make any such efforts impossible is still an open question.

The real problem is not technology; after all, anyone who wants to share a file, legally or illegally, can easily do so in many ways. And, since so many file-sharing methods are completely legitimate, massively used, and central to the workings of a modern society, a total ban on file sharing is highly unlikely to happen (and shouldn't even be considered). The real (and legitimate) problem for the content industry is that some services and software applications are making money by making it easy for their users to swap files illegally. But new file-sharing protocols such as Freenet are designed primarily to make sharing of any type of file fast, easy, anonymous, encrypted, and hard to detect or deter. This is a problem for which no effective technological solution may exist, and it is certain to continue making news and driving the creation of more laws.

Note I certainly don't encourage breaking the law or engaging in illegal file sharing, but if you're a user who has extensive and legitimate reasons for file sharing, you should keep up with the laws that are being passed and make sure your elected representatives don't remove your rights to communicate and work effectively in the name of protecting the RIAA or anyone else.

Using File-Sharing Networks

When you use any file-sharing software application, you are essentially advertising your presence on the Internet to anyone else using the same file-sharing software or to anyone whose file-sharing software happens to use the same file-sharing protocol.

A file-sharing network is any group of computers connected by and communicating through a shared protocol. When the protocol is *open*, it means that anyone can connect if he uses the protocol, and no legal or physical restrictions bar connections. It's like speaking a language: Anyone who knows that language can use it to communicate with anyone else who knows the language, and you can't effectively stop a person from doing so. This means two important things:

✦ You can find and use software that connects to any of the major file-sharing services' software/networks, unless they happen to operate through a central server and the service doesn't allow unauthorized connections.

✦ Unless you disable the ability for others on your file-sharing network to scan your hard drive for music at the same time your copy of the file-sharing network is scanning others' hard drives, you are exposing your presence and your hard drive to anonymous connections by anyone else out there who can make a connection.

The purpose of this book is to provide the knowledge you need to protect yourself, not decide for you whether or not to use file-sharing software. But be aware that any time you're connected to a stranger's computer or a stranger is connected to your computer, the potential for abuse exists. Even the best software can be hacked, and simply providing a means to connect to your computer is an invitation to hackers.

The Gnutella file-sharing network

The Gnutella network (the latest version is Gnutella2, or G2) is the major network to which many file-sharing services' software connects. The fact that Gnutella users communicate through a specific protocol makes Gnutella a network. If all users suddenly stopped using a particular file-sharing protocol, the network would cease to exist. It's not a physical or hardware thing; "network" in this case is simply what a group of users connected by a protocol is called.

In technical terms, Gnutella2 is a platform for peer-to-peer (P2P) connections over the Internet. Gnutella2 consists of a network architecture (the Gnutella2 network) and standards for applications attempting to communicate over the network (the Gnutella2 standard).

Many popular file-sharing applications, such as the legally controversial but quite popular Kazaa service, connect to the Gnutella2 network. While connecting to Gnutella 2, Kazaa and other applications adhere to a set of technical standards, or ways of doing things. The Gnutella2 standard is quite technical and of interest mainly to file-sharing application developers. It's interesting to read the standards if you program applications, but for the rest of you, the most interesting thing about the standard is that application developers cannot be forced to comply fully. Not that this is necessarily a serious problem; users gravitate to applications that conform to well-written standards. However, malicious programmers may decide to develop file-sharing applications that are capable of connecting to the network and yet don't play nice or cooperate with the rest of the users on the network.

The Freenet file-sharing network

The Freenet file-sharing network is based on an open file-sharing protocol and is considered to be very resistant to snooping and very defensible against the legal attacks aimed at other file-sharing applications. In fact, the Freenet protocol forms the basis for a platform rather than simply a software application, in that it specifies standards for communications, but does not actually do the work (various groups have created file-sharing applications that communicate using the Freenet protocol, just like KazaaLite allows communications using the Gnutella protocol).

Other file-sharing networks

Several other file-sharing networks exist, including the Overnet, BitTorrent, and iMesh, just to name a few. What they all have in common is the ability to allow users to connect to each other's computers in a P2P fashion for distributed file sharing. Some are optimized for privacy, some for security, and some for scalability. Many offer file-sharing applications designed for their protocols.

Overnet

Overnet is a distributed search network that peer-to-peer networks such as eDonkey use to find files. Distributed search connotes the ability of a network to search files on multiple computers within a network. It was invented as a standalone application but was enhanced by the developers of eDonkey to search large numbers of PCs simultaneously.

BitTorrent

BitTorrent is a protocol designed for transferring files. It is peer-to-peer in nature, as users connect to each other directly to send and receive portions of the file. Unlike some other file-transfer protocols; however, there is a central server (called a tracker) that coordinates the action of all users who are transferring files at a given time. BitTorrent's developers built this application with the intent that users should upload at the same time they are downloading so network bandwidth is utilized as efficiently as possible. As opposed to other file transfer protocols that either do not notice, or are slowed down by multiple requests for a certain file, BitTorrent is designed to work better as the number of people interested in a certain file increases.

iMesh

iMesh is a P2P file-sharing program that lets you simultaneously find, download, share, and publish audio and video files with other iMesh users who have agreed to share them. Files can be transferred directly from one desktop to another without the need for a server. Its main claim to fame is built-in support in the form of an advanced resume feature that ensures the automatic completion of all your requested downloads. That's a handy feature if you are on a dial-up Internet connection, have not disabled call waiting, and receive an incoming call during a music file download (made lengthier, of course, by the slow speed of your Internet hookup). iMesh's critics maintain the program is vulnerable to the transmission of adware and spyware that track the Web sites, pages, and ads that you click on.

Using File-Sharing Services

In this section, the major file-sharing services are discussed, and the particulars of installing their software and using their systems are reviewed. Note that the software offered by many of the different sites connects to the same network of users, and some of the sites offer software that actually just connects to the networks of users created by another site's software.

Shareaza

Shareaza began as a file-sharing application connecting to the original Gnutella network, but then sponsored the development of Gnutella2. Shareaza claims to be fully open source (meaning that all the source code for the application is publicly available).

You can find Shareaza at www.shareaza.com. The Web site also offers downloads, forums, support, and a variety of ways to access more information about installing and using Shareaza (see Figure 3-1).

You won't find a Terms and Conditions page on the Shareaza site, nor will you find a Privacy Policy page. This makes sense because the program does not collect any information whatsoever in exchange for the download, and it does not contain third-party spyware or other software.

Third-party software

According to the Web site, Shareaza includes no third-party applications, spyware, or advertising software in the latest release, 2.0. You won't find a "plus" or "pro" version for sale—you won't find any versions for sale at the site at all; every version is free. In fact, the site FAQ recommends asking for a refund if you paid for a copy on another site.

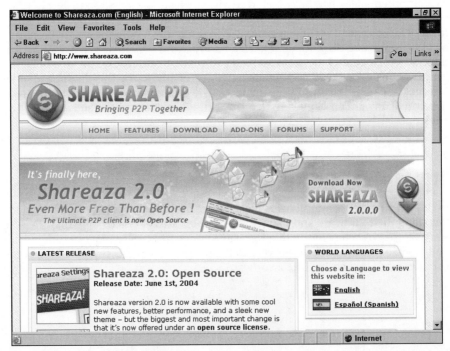

Figure 3-1: The Shareaza Web site

About the application

You can download Shareaza's file-sharing application from the site's download page. New users who don't have file-sharing software installed are asked to download from the direct-download area of the page, while users who already have some other file-sharing software (or are upgrading) are asked to download from the file-sharing area.

The application includes the ability to connect to several networks including Gnutella 1 and 2, eDonkey, and BitTorrent. It also offers fast downloads, a media player, chat capability, and the ability to block certain IP addresses for security.

System requirements

The software works only with computers running one of the common versions of the Windows OS, such as 95, 98, ME, NT, 2000, or XP. No Mac version is available.

A blurb at the bottom of the downloads page recommends that Windows 95 and NT users download a font that makes Shareaza's text look right, but there's no mention anywhere about how much hard drive space is required, recommended CPU speed, or that sort of thing.

Installation

After you've downloaded the application (it's about 2.5MB and takes only a few seconds if you have a cable modem or DSL connection), you can run the installation file. Follow these steps to walk through the setup process:

1. **Double-click the install file you downloaded.** You'll see a dialog box resembling Figure 3-2.

Figure 3-2: The Open dialog box of the Shareaza setup wizard

2. **Click Next, and choose the defaults you want.** The only choice of interest is the location to which you'd like to install the software, so you don't have much to do until after you have installed the software (most of the configuration settings are done in the software when it opens for the first time). After selecting your defaults, click Next to reach the screen shown in Figure 3-3.

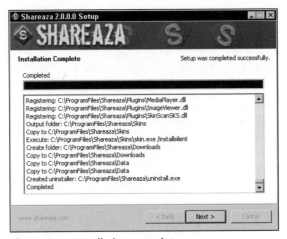

Figure 3-3: Installation complete

3. **Click Next past the final installation screen, and Shareaza should open.** You can close the little player application window and pick a language and then click Next.

4. **Configure your computer settings for Shareaza.** A series of screens will appear requesting your configuration choices. After you make your choice in a screen, click Next. In Figure 3-4, the screen for telling Shareaza about your Internet connection is shown; if you have a firewall and use Network Address Translation (NAT), you may have to set up port forwarding. If you indicate that you have a firewall, Shareaza informs you that you need to set your router or firewall to forward TCP Port 6346 to your local PC.

5. **Decide where on your hard drive to allow files to be shared or stored, and click Next.** The drive shown in Figure 3-5 happens to be formatted as an NT File System (NTFS) partition. NTFS partitions allow extensive restrictions on file permissions. You may want to add a folder to an NTFS partition on your hard drive if you happen to have this type of file system installed. Make sure you have plenty of room for files you'll download.

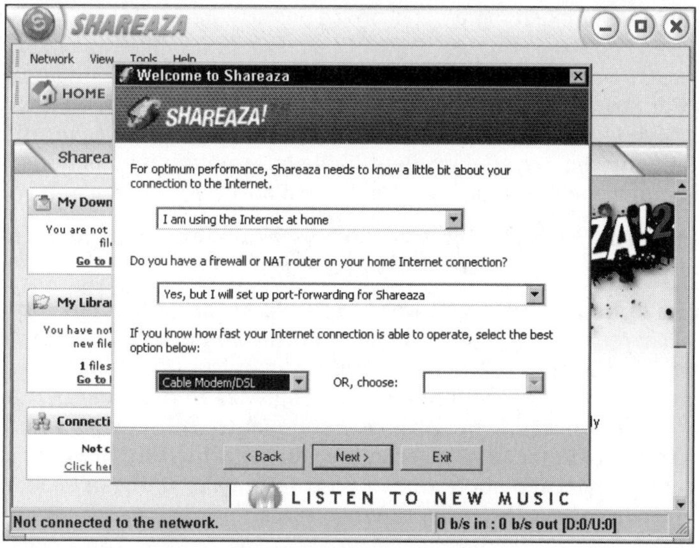

Figure 3-4: Setting Internet connection options

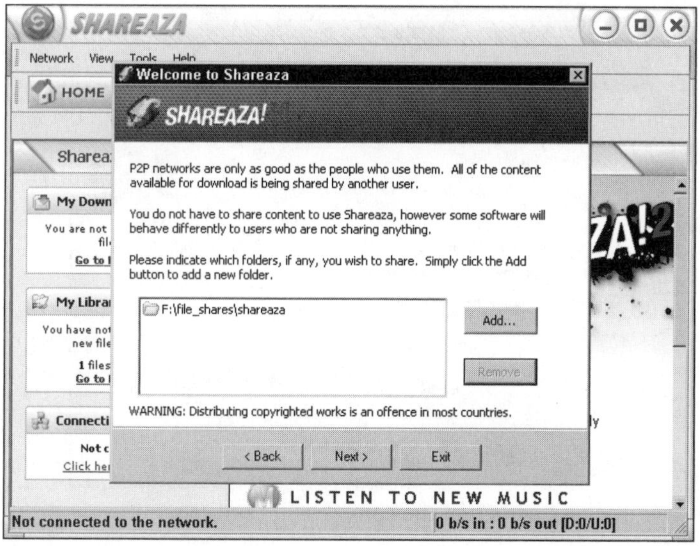

Figure 3-5: Set the folder from which you want to share.

Cross-Reference See Chapter 4 for much more detail on file permissions, users, and groups.

6. **Fill in the requested information, and click Next.** This screen asks for information you can give Shareaza that is non-identifying. Make sure that you don't give any personally identifiable information if you choose to provide any information at all; better safe than sorry.

7. **Choose which networks you want to connect to, and click Next.** You can connect to more than one network at a time.

8. **Select an option for how you want to run Shareaza, and click Finish.** The final screen (shown in Figure 3-6) informs you that Shareaza is ready and gives you several options for running Shareaza. You should uncheck all these options unless you really want Shareaza to run most of the time; you can always start the program and connect to the network when you're ready. Note that you can also rerun the QuickStart wizard anytime as well, so if you're concerned about one of your settings or it doesn't seem to work properly, you can easily try different settings.

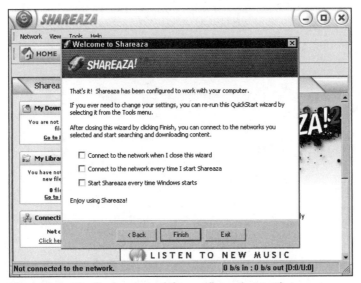

Figure 3-6: The final screen of the configuration settings

Shareaza tour

Shareaza has one of the nicest and easiest user interfaces of all the file-sharing applications available. The following information gives you a quick tour of the features Shareaza provides.

The Shareaza user interface, shown in Figure 3-7, is very user friendly. You'll find tabs for all the major functions of the application. It also has several buttons that enable you to manage your digital files.

Figure 3-7: The Shareaza user interface

The Library tab gives you a hierarchical view of your files, similar to what you might see in Windows Explorer (see Figure 3-8). Notice that clicking either the Folders button or the Organiser button located below the word Library on the left side gives you different views of your files. From here, you can group files by album, artist, and genre (such as Metal or Jazz).

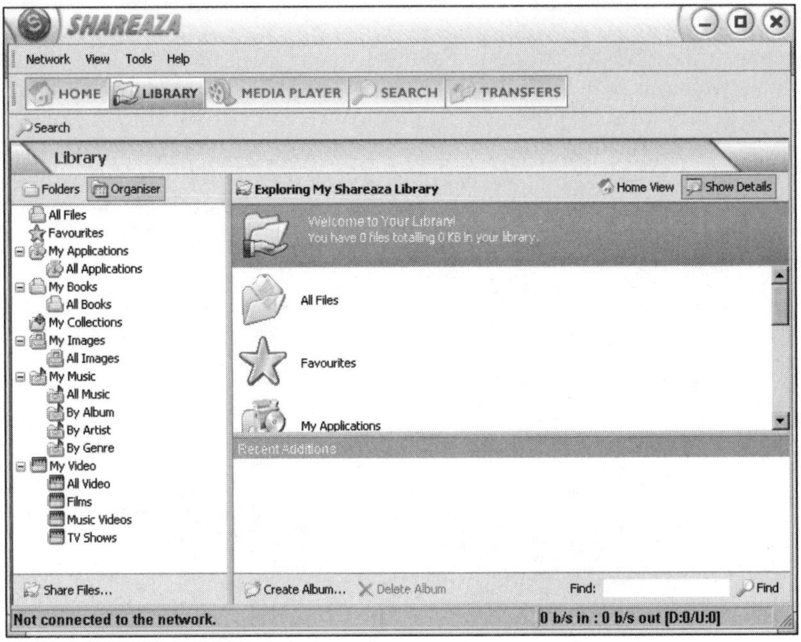

Figure 3-8: The Library tab

The Media Player tab displays the player application, as shown in Figure 3-9. The player controls are located at the bottom of the screen. Not only does it have the common controls, you also have the ability to create a play list.

Tip   If you unchecked the "Connect to a Network" check box during the initial configuration of Shareaza, you may need to choose Network ➪ Connect from the top-line menu before you try to download any files.

The Search tab displays the Search interface. Several search methods are available. You can enter a search term or add file types; you can even enter the entire name of the file you are searching for after you pick a file type. Figure 3-10 shows the results of a search for sci-fi video files.

You can download a file by right-clicking the file name from your search results and choosing Download on the shortcut menu. After you choose download, the Transfers screen appears (shown in Figure 3-11), and you can monitor progress here or choose a different tab; for example, you can conduct another search in the Search tab.

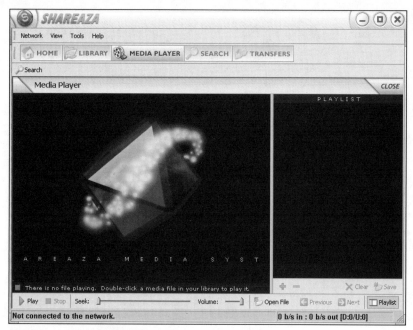

Figure 3-9: The Media Player tab

File	Type	Size	Rating	Status	Host/Cou
The Roswell incident footage - f...	mpeg	217.38 MB		✔	(185 so
Sci-Fi Battle - Star Trek n Star ...	avi	10.52 MB		✔	(164 so
Adult_Sci-Fi__Animation (funny ...	mpg	4.39 MB		✔	(33 sou
Adult_Sci-Fi__Animation (funny ...	mpg	4.39 MB		✔	(28 sou
Repo Man (1984) (Sci-Fi_Horror...	avi	634.12 MB		✔	(24 sou
[DIVX - ENG] The Butterfly Effe...	mpg	769.71 MB		✔	(12 sou
The Day The Earth Stood Still - ...	avi	698.28 MB		✔	(10 sou
Sci-fi.Ita.Cult.1957.Quatermass...	avi	727.04 MB		✔	(10 sou
[Documentary] The Roswell inci...	mpeg	217.38 MB		✔	(10 sou
David Lynch Sci Fi Channel - Nu...	avi	1.28 MB		✔	(6 sou
Sci-Fi Ita Cult 1967 La Morte Sc...	avi	664.96 MB		✔	(4 sou
{Classic Sci-Fi } Dark Star (John ...	avi	680.18 MB		✔	(4 sou

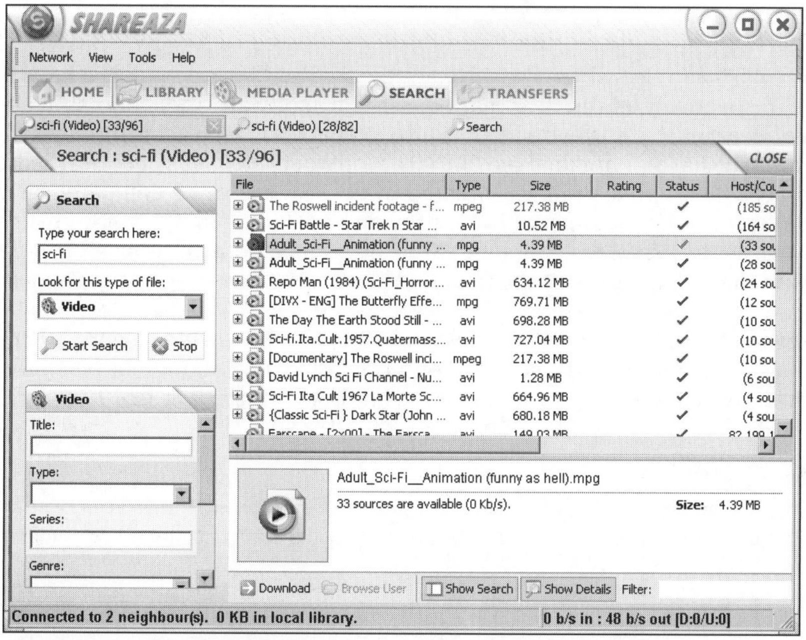

Figure 3-10: The Search Interface displays results, here with results from a video search.

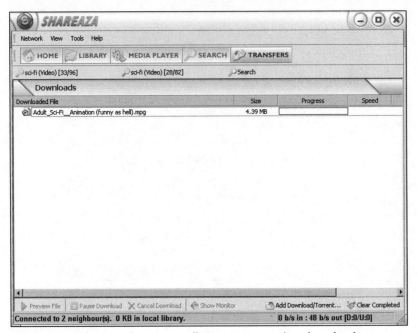

Figure 3-11: The Transfers screen allows you to monitor download progress.

BearShare

BearShare 4.5.0 and BearShare Pro 4.5.0 are the free and for sale ($3.99 a month) versions, respectively, of the BearShare file-sharing software application. An ad-free version of BearShare, BearShare PRO, is also available on a six-month renewable membership basis for a nominal fee of $3.99/month*, to help support BearShare development. This application was created by Free Peers, Inc., a company based in Florida, whose mission statement is "to provide free, high-quality, peer-to-peer software to our users." The Free Peers, Inc. Web site is located at www.freepeers.com if you want to read more about the company.

The software, however, can be found at www.bearshare.com (see Figure 3-12). You can also find a user guide, several FAQs (including one about P2P computing), an end-user license agreement, and a privacy policy statement at this site.

Third-party software

Unfortunately, BearShare 4.5.0 (the free version) does come with third-party software included when you install it. The third-party software claims to provide services, but it's actually aimed at tracking your browser use and sending you advertisements. While BearShare itself does not overtly slow down your computer or tax your PC's available memory, the adware it distributes can affect the performance of your PC if you are running numerous other applications.

About the application

BearShare 's Pro and free versions can both be downloaded from the BearShare Web site at `www.bearshare.com/downloads.htm`. The developers of this Gnutella-based application claim it has faster downloads than Kazaa, with a built-in digital file music library, where you can organize your digital files by artist, song title, or musical style.

Both versions of BearShare offer chat support. This means that while you are swapping files, you can chat in real time with other BearShare users, presumably about the merits of the files you are swapping.

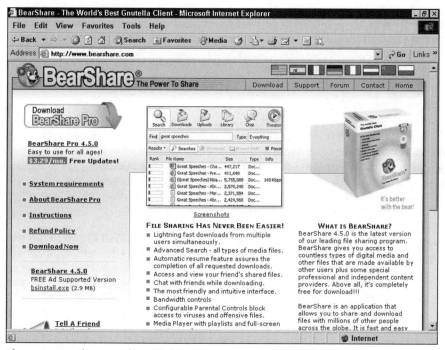

Figure 3-12: The BearShare Web site

Terms and conditions

The closest thing to Terms and Conditions on the site is the end-user license agreement. This license covers the usual restrictions about copying and using the software, but is unusual in that it specifically restricts several companies (MediaForce, Inc. and MediaDefender, Inc., to name two) from installing or using the software.

Privacy policy

The BearShare privacy policy contains the usual disclaimers, promising to never give away your private information or collect or use any personal information for anything other than legitimate purposes. But when the free version of the software is installed, it does install several other applications that snoop your computer and browser use and send that information back to a central site.

System requirements

BearShare 4.5.0 runs under Windows 98, NT, 2000, ME, or XP. You need to have a computer with at least 4MB of install space, 32MB of RAM, and a 166 MHz Pentium processor. Currently, no Mac version is available. Obviously, you want to have a good Internet connection too. The system requirements also include a caveat about file sharing from behind firewalls.

Installation

This section walks you through installation of BearShare. However, I did find after installation that the third-party software installed (the one tracking browser usage) crashed Internet Explorer Web browser several times. The installed version was removed, and the test machine seems to be back to normal now. This doesn't mean your computer will have the same reaction, but if you have problems after you've installed the free version, consider uninstalling it to see if that fixes the problem. Follow these steps to install BearShare on your computer:

1. **Download BearShare, and then double-click the install file to begin installation.** Click the check boxes and radio buttons to choose your options, and click Next after each. You'll see several typical install screens. The first one of interest is shown in Figure 3-13. At this screen, you have the option of starting BearShare every time Windows starts and also of completely closing BearShare when you're not using it (instead of the default, which is to leave BearShare running minimized). If you intend to use BearShare frequently, click Minimize to Tray. There's also a Family Filter for hiding most search results with adult content. You can also work with Preview/Play in Theater's radio buttons to make the BearShare application take up most of your monitor if you play a video obtained via the service.

Figure 3-13: Begin setting BearShare options

Tip

I do not recommend you let BearShare start every time Windows starts. This can slow down your PC by having your digital music files open for distribution even though you are doing something else on your computer

2. **Choose the speed of your Internet connection (such as DSL, cable, or dialup) and the directory on your hard drive where you want to install the software, (such as C: ProgramFiles\BearShare Pro), clicking Next for each screen.** The screen that follows these can be somewhat confusing (see Figure 3-14).

3. **Choose the location where you want to keep your files to share, and click Next.** Folders outlined in red show the file path you're sharing from (meaning that others are accessing this location on your computer). Folders with a check mark are the ones actually shared. You can click the Legend button at the bottom for more information about what the symbols mean.

4. **At the next screen, click Finish to complete the setup.** At this point, installation is complete and you can begin using the software.

Figure 3-14: Setting your share folders

eDonkey and Overnet

eDonkey 2000 is both a free and an enhanced, $19.95 eDonkey Pro file-sharing application that runs on the Overnet file-sharing network. The free version comes with software that spies on your Web activities, but the Pro edition claims to be free of such digital distraction.

Both networks and applications were built by MetaMachine in New York. Figure 3-15 shows the eDonkey2000 Web site located at www.edonkey2000.com. The Web site also contains contact information, FAQs for both eDonkey 2000 and the Overnet, some online technical support, and extensive documentation. EDonkey is most commonly used to refer to the application, with Overnet used to describe the file-sharing network on which eDonkey is built.

Privacy policy

The privacy policy statement contains the usual notices and disclaimers about privacy, and it's up front about the fact that companies that advertise on the eDonkey Web site use cookies to help capture information to better target their advertising. These companies may use information (not including your name, address, e-mail address, or telephone number) about your visits to this and other Web sites in order to provide advertisements on this site and other sites about goods and services that may be of interest to you. For example, if you repeatedly click on an ad for a single's dating service, you may receive a pop-up ad with an invitation to purchase clothing from another Web site.

About the application

eDonkey offers the requisite set of applications, including file sharing, a music library for organizing your files, as well as chat where you can talk to other users. It also has a proprietary feature called Horde, which looks for the fastest Internet connection among other users who have specific digital files you want to obtain.

System requirements

Unlike some other file-sharing services, eDonkey has versions for other operating systems besides Windows. Specific system requirements are: 64 MB RAM, and either Microsoft Windows 98, NT, Me, 2000, XP, Mac OS X 10.2+, or Linux.

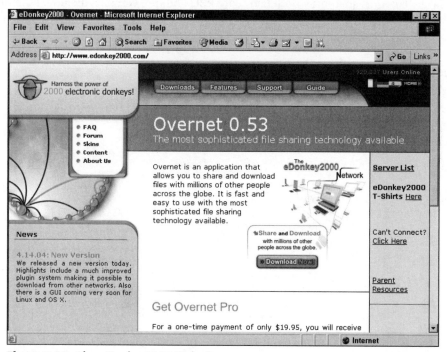

Figure 3-15: The eDonkey2000 Web site

LimeWire

LimeWire 4.0 claims to be "The Fastest P2P File Sharing Program on the Planet." Created by LimeWire LLC, a subsidiary of Lime Group in New York, two versions of the software are available for download: LimeWire PRO, which costs $18.88, and a free version. The free version is ad-supported. Figure 3-16 shows the LimeWire Web site at www.limewire.com. The Web site contains both versions of the application for download, online support, and a list of features. LimeWire connects to the Gnutella network.

You won't find a Terms and Conditions page on the site. And, the privacy policy statement contains the usual disclaimers about respecting your privacy, and like most other sites, it says the company will collect information for normal business uses.

About the application

LimeWire runs on the Gnutella network and claims it offers faster downloads than Kazaa. Features shared by both LimeWire PRO and free versions include: PC and Mac compatibility, an integrated library and audio player, and interoperability with iTunes.

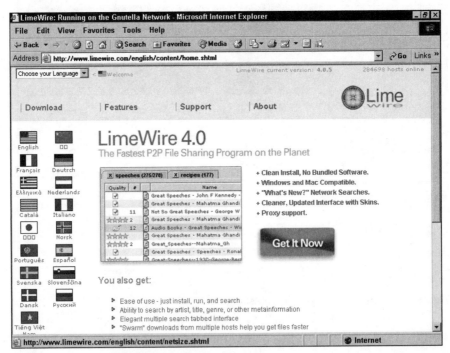

Figure 3-16: The LimeWire Web site

Configuring Your Firewall

A *firewall* is a device between your computer and the Internet. The purpose of this device is to allow you set restrictions on incoming and outgoing transmissions, thereby increasing your level of security. Firewalls use software to intercept and restrict communications, so you can run either a software-only firewall or a firewall that is embedded in a separate piece of hardware (routers commonly include firewalls).

If you connect your computer via dial-up modem, cable modem, or DSL connection directly to the Internet, you're probably not running a firewall (if you are running a software firewall on your computer, you probably are aware of it). But if you have a device (such as a router) that shares your Internet connection among several computers in your home or office, it may include a firewall.

Depending on the software provided with your router or firewall, you also have the option for restricting the types of incoming or outgoing packets and data that reach or originate from your computers.

Many types of hardware and software firewalls exist. As an example, the DLink 808HV router includes a firewall that you can modify to accept file-sharing services as shown in the following figure.

For $18.88, LimeWire Pro users get faster download speeds, no ads, live e-mail support, plus the ability to download and install a "skin" to change the appearance of the utility's user interface.

Installation

The site contains no apparent system requirements for the software, but versions are available for Windows, Mac (both OSX and Classic), Linux, and other operating systems. First, you need to download and install the LimeWire Installer from the LimeWire Web site at `www.limewire.com/english/content/ug_installation.shtml`. This Installer utility will actually open the LimeWire copy that you download. When downloading, you'll be taken to `www.download.com`, and there you'll find more system requirements information, plus reviews of the software by Download.com.

Morpheus 4.1

Morpheus would be just another file-sharing application, but it claims to connect to many of the popular file-sharing networks including Gnutella2, eDonkey, and iMesh. Morpheus is built by Streamcast Networks in California. The Morpheus Media Player, shown on Figure 3-17, can be downloaded from the Morpheus Web site at `www.morpheus.com`. The site contains some very short FAQs in support of Morpheus, some contact information, links to the parent company, P2P United's Web site, and a link to Morpheus Ultra (the for-sale version or Morpheus). Unfortunately, the free version contains adware.

Terms and conditions

On its Web site, Morpheus takes pains to point out that "the use of Morpheus for illegal activities, including infringement of intellectual property laws, may subject the infringing user to civil and/or criminal penalties." StreamCast, which has developed and distributes Morpheus, does not condone copyright, patent or other intellectual property infringement. Yet as with other file-swapping services, StreamCast maintains that "due to the nature of peer-to-peer software, (it) is unable to monitor or control the files searched for or shared using Morpheus."

Other File-Sharing Applications

File-sharing applications are fairly easy to make from code that is freely available to the public, so other file-sharing applications are appearing rapidly. Many more file-sharing applications exist than the ones listed here, such as Grokster and iMesh. They all have similar features and restrictions.

Figure 3-17: The Morpheus Media Player

Privacy policy

Morpheus states that it does not use or distribute spyware, nor share any personally identifiable information about the users on its network. Yet when I ran the free version of this application, my anti-spyware utility picked up numerous spyware files.

About the application

Morpheus offers as complete a set of capabilities as most any other peer-to-peer digital file service. It includes a built-in anti-virus download scan, Web search (for digital files not on the Morpheus network, user chat, as well as an integrated media player where you can organize and play your digital music files — even those that you did not use Morpheus to obtain.

Important for your security, Morpheus also has Blacklist and Proxy options. You can use Blacklist to block specific users and Web sites from access to your digital music files. The Proxy capability can be used to hide your computer's address from prying eyes. Once again, I'm not endorsing such steps: I merely point out that they exist, and are available to you.

System requirements

No system requirements are listed, but Morpheus is only compatible with Windows PCs.

Installation

Morpheus 4.1's initial download prompt is on the Morpheus site. Clicking this prompt takes you to a Morpheus download page at Download.com (www.download.com). To download and install Morpheus 4.1 from Download.com, perform the following steps:

1. **Click the Morpheus Download now link at Download.com.** Within a few seconds, a file called Morpheus.exe transfers to your computer. A File Download box appears with the name of this file.

2. **Click Save, and this installation file will be saved to the default directory on your hard drive (such as C:).** A Download Complete box opens.

3. **Click Open Folder, and Windows Explorer opens.**

4. **In Windows Explorer click on the file morpheus.exe.** A box appears, asking if you want to install the free or paid version.

5. **Click the radio button next to your choice, and then Next.** The actual Morpheus file will download to your PC.

6. **Click to approve the License agreement.** The Installation Folder opens.

7. **Select a directory to install Morpheus, and then click Install.** A Morpheus setup screen appears. Here, you can specify directories on your PC that you want to keep off-limits to other Morpheus users (Figure 3-18).

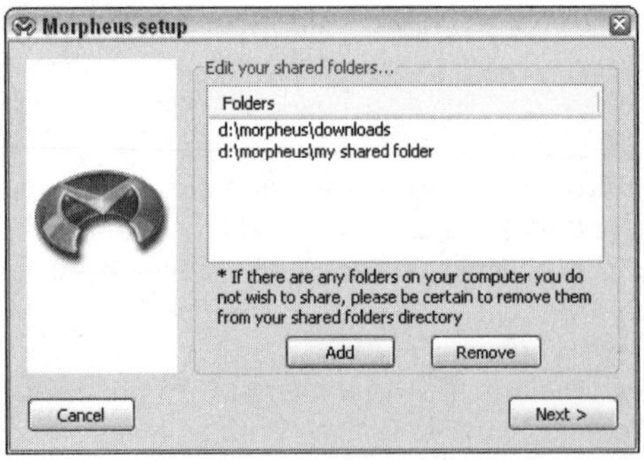

Figure 3-18: Morpheus lets you block certain directories from other Morpheus users.

8. **Click Next.** This setup screen has boxes that you can check to start up Morpheus when Windows does, and to make Morpheus your default media player. Make your choices and then click Next. An optional setup screen appears, asking you whether you want to reveal your location (country, city, and state, where applicable). The reason for this is to ensure faster downloads.

9. **Enter this information, and click either Next (if you enter this information) or Skip (if you don't).** This completes the installation process.

Kazaa

Originally created by programmers Niklas Fennstrom and Janis Friis, the software development for Kazaa is now supported by Sharman, an Australian company. The software packages of Kazaa Media Desktop and Kazaa Plus make Kazaa work. You can find Kazaa at www.kazaa.com, shown in Figure 3-19. Also at the Kazaa Web site, you will find the desktop applications and some online technical support. Advanced tech support is available to customers who purchase Kazaa Plus.

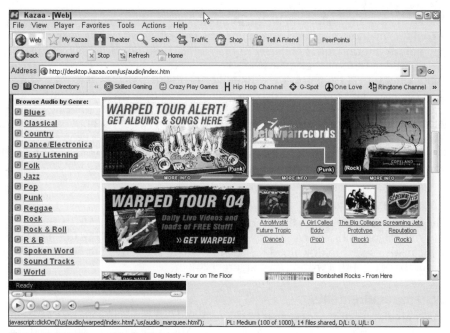

Figure 3-19: Kazaa Media Desktop

Third-party software

Kazaa includes third-party applications, spyware, and advertising software in the free version. Although the specific source of these applications and spyware are not spelled out, they are accepted by many of Kazaa's loyal users as a trade-off for the "right" to obtain music without having to pay for it. A worthy "lesser of two evils" or a deal with the Dark Side? You decide.

Terms and conditions

The closest thing to a Terms and Conditions page on the site is the end-user license agreement. This page informs you of your rights for using the software and includes many do's and don'ts as well. These include an admonition not to violate copyright laws. Interestingly, you'll note that several third-party software applications are included with the product, some for anti-virus purposes and some designed to deliver advertising to your desktop that is triggered by your computer usage or to send you to PerfectNav's Web page if you incorrectly type a Web address. These last two seem quite intrusive.

Privacy policy

The Kazaa privacy policy can be found by clicking the Privacy link on the Web site. It contains many of the standard disclosures and disclaimers. For example, at several points, information is collected (personal and non-personal), which might be distributed to third parties in a variety of ways. Kazaa seems to be very up front about what they do and how they do it, but the inclusion of third-party applications (and the attendant third-party privacy policies) makes privacy seem rather insignificant. Especially troubling is the amount of active information gathering that occurs while you use the software. The PerfectNav and Gain AdServer applications actually monitor your use of the software *as well as* your use of your own browser to perform their functions, which seem as much designed for benefiting Kazaa as for helping you accomplish your own tasks with Kazaa.

About the application

The free version of Kazaa's file-sharing software is called Kazaa Media Desktop, as shown in Figure 3-19.You can easily download it by clicking on the Get It Now link. You can also select to download Kazaa Plus, which is ad-free, but costs nearly $30 to purchase as of this writing (see Figure 3-20).

System requirements

Kazaa Media Desktop is designed to run on Windows machines with at least 20MB of spare hard drive space. You need Windows Media Player 6.4 or later, and your machine needs to be running Windows 98 or newer. The site contains no specs concerning processor speed or required RAM.

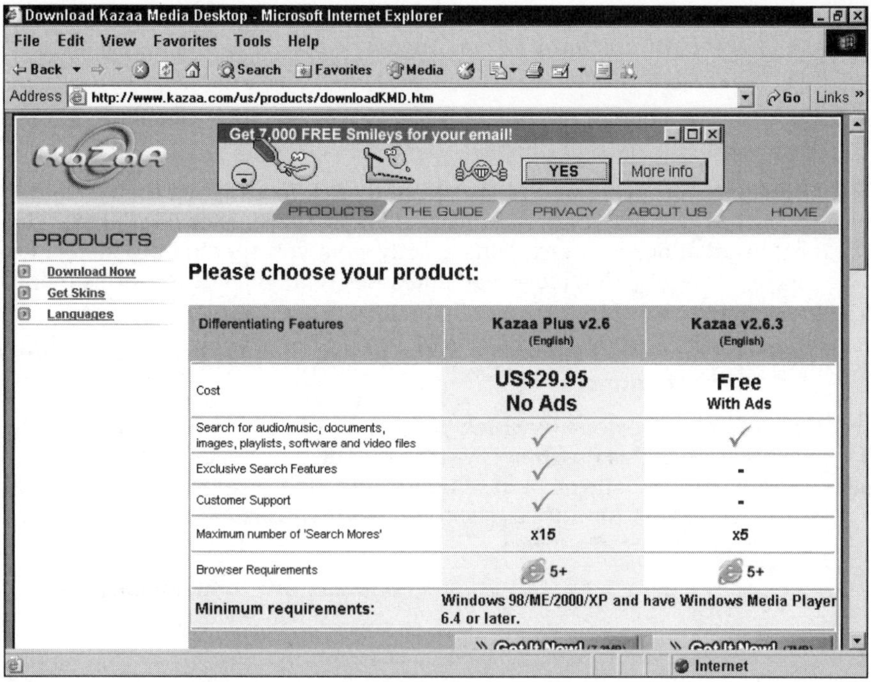

Figure 3-20: Choosing your download version of Kazaa

Installation

Installation involves downloading a small file (563KB) that then runs Internet Explorer to download the remaining files and perform the installation procedure.

To install Kazaa on your PC, perform the following steps:

1. **Go to the main Kazaa page and click the Get It Now link.** You are taken to a page where you can select either Kazaa PLUS or the free version.

2. **Click the Get It Now! button under the description for the version of Kazaa you want.** If you select KazaaPlus, you will need to fill out an order page. If you want the free version, continue by clicking the free version link. A File Download page opens with the file name kmd.exe.

3. **Click Save, and the filename is marked to be saved to a default directory on your hard drive.** After you click Save, the download of the actual Kazaa program begins. After the download finishes, a Download Complete box opens. To save the file to a different directory, click Save As, and a Save box will open. In the Save In box, click the pull-down menu until the Save In box shows the directory in which you want to save Kazaa. Click Save. The installation file will be saved to that directory.

4. **In the Download Complete box, click Open Folder.** Windows Explorer opens the directory in which the Kazaa program is installed. The actual installation file (`kmd.exe`) is highlighted.

5. **Click on the name of the file, and Kazaa will open for installation.** Kazaa Media Desktop Installer opens.

6. **Highlight your preferred language, and click Next.** When the Welcome screen appears with basic information about Kazaa, click Next again. The next installation screen explains exactly what you are about to install. Read this text carefully. You must read and agree to all the license terms before installing the software.

7. **Once you have read and agree to the terms, click the green check box and click the Next button.**

8. **Select to the directory in which you would like to install Kazaa and click Next.** The default is Program Files\Kazaa. The download progress bar displays (see Figure 3-21). The amount of time it takes to download the file depends on the speed of your Internet connection. When the installation completes, a launch Kazaa button appears.

9. **Click on the launch Kazaa button, and Kazaa will come up on your PC.**

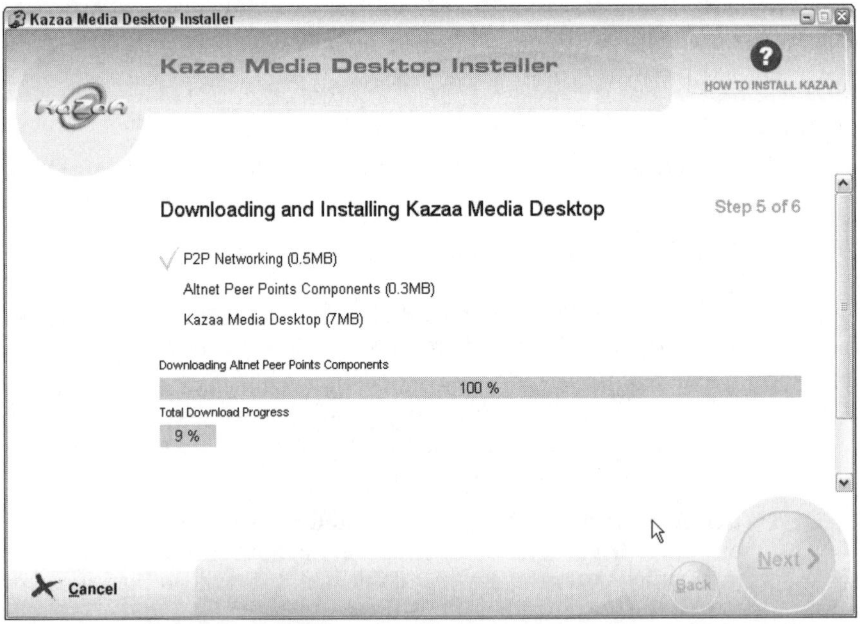

Figure 3-21: Kazaa is installing.

Deciding Which File-Sharing Application to Use

To share files, you should pick a file-sharing application (or perhaps more than one) based on the application itself, not the network, because the file-sharing protocols and networks that are available to you depend on which file-sharing application you use. The following list provides some guidelines for choosing a file-sharing application.

Network connections

For maximum connectability, you might want to use an application that connects to more than one network. For example, Shareaza and Morpheus both have the ability to connect to more than one network, and will likely incorporate the ability to connect to other networks that may become popular in the future.

Open-source software

Open-source software is free to use and develop, and the source code is available to everyone. In practical terms, this means that if you are capable of programming, you can create your own applications from the source code (source code is the uncompiled code from which any piece of software is built). Another advantage of open-source code is that many eyes in the software developer community view the code, and bugs and security holes are quickly found and fixed. Shareaza is open source.

Freedom from popup ads and spyware

The free versions of many file-sharing applications have third-party software included for the purpose of displaying ads to you. Sometimes, this software is also spyware tracking your browser clicks or scanning your system's installed software. These third-party applications can be annoying, insecure, and downright dangerous on many levels. To avoid this, select an application that doesn't have this kind of third-party software, such as Shareaza.

User interface

The user interface of your application is also an important consideration. Software that is otherwise great can be seriously handicapped by a user interface that is complex, unintuitive, or hard to use or learn. For example, the BearShare user interface is logical and intuitive.

Features

Obviously, the main feature you're looking for in an application is the ability to share files, but other features, such as a built-in player application, the ability to download from several locations simultaneously, or a rich search interface can also make one application better than others depending on your specific needs.

Documentation

Most file-sharing applications, especially the free versions, don't offer live support. Instead, online support (such as online documentation and e-mail support) is the norm. Even so, some of the Web sites are quite short on documentation. A well-documented, easy-to-navigate Web site is not only helpful, it is an indication that the software's designers don't take shortcuts. Make sure you know what kind of support you will have access to before downloading an application for use.

Top Five Things to Consider for Safe and Satisfying File Sharing

1. **Decide for yourself if you even want to share files with potentially millions of other anonymous users.** No matter how you look at it, sharing files is risky to some degree.

2. **Review the specifications on each type of file-sharing network.** Different networks potentially expose you to different risks or different levels of the same risk.

3. **Decide whether you want to pay for non-ad-supported software, or whether you'd like the free version.** Free versions of file-sharing software often come with third-party applications that collect data from your system and/or from your Web surfing habits.

4. **Set aside a folder to share to and from, and carefully set the permissions for that folder.** See Chapter 4 for more information about setting permissions.

5. **Keep up-to-date with news about lawsuits filed by the music industry against peer-to-peer networks.** News reports, searchable on sites such as CNET"s News.com, often mention what network the sued parties were using. If you see that a preponderance of lawsuits are filed against users of particular file-swapping peer-to-peer programs, then by all means stay away.

Summary

This chapter gave you the basic information you can use to decide which file-sharing application is right for you. Not only did it explain the concepts behind file-sharing protocols, it also explained the file-sharing network and what it really is. It also took an in-depth look at various applications, system requirements, whether third-party software is an issue, privacy policies, and even some basic installation information and software interface overviews. At this point, you should have a good idea of which of these file-sharing applications is right for you and your needs.

✦   ✦   ✦

Protecting Yourself Technologically and Legally

PART

✦ ✦ ✦ ✦

In This Part

Chapter 4
Behind the Scenes:
What Really Happens
When File Sharing

Chapter 5
Dangers of
Downloading or
Sharing Files:
The Nature of
the Threat

Chapter 6
Protecting Yourself
and Your Computer

Chapter 7
Protecting Your
Network

Chapter 8
Protecting Your
Privacy

Chapter 9
Protecting Yourself
from Illegal
Downloads

✦ ✦ ✦ ✦

Behind the Scenes: What Really Happens When File Sharing

♦ ♦ ♦ ♦

In This Chapter

Knowing whether
your system is
good enough
for file sharing

Understanding
operating systems:
Windows, OS X,
Linux, and more

Storing files

Understanding file
properties: Users,
groups, and
permissions

Managing and
organizing files

♦ ♦ ♦ ♦

File-sharing services make it easy (or at least easier) to find and swap music, video, and other files, but do you know what's actually happening inside your computer or across your network when you share or download files? File systems (the system that stores and manages your files on your hard drive) come in a variety of flavors, not just the familiar old Windows or Mac file systems you're used to. Although it's unlikely that you'll change your existing file system based on what you read here, knowing your options, and the benefits and drawbacks of the file system you're using, is worth the effort.

In this chapter, you'll find a primer on file systems, how file-sharing works behind the scenes, and how you can find out what's happening and protect yourself. I also review the basics of computer hardware and operating systems (OSs), because your hardware and OS play a big role in how effective your system can be at storing and playing back music and video.

Computer System Basics

If you're over 16, you probably drive a car. Do you *really* know how it works? Or do you just get in, turn the key, put it in drive, and work the steering wheel, gas pedal, and brake until you arrive at your destination?

Lots of folks use cars to get where they are going without knowing much about how they work, and that's okay. It's the same way with computers; lots of folks just turn them on, open their favorite program or file, and away they go. That's okay too. But for cars and computers, when something goes wrong or danger lurks, knowing more pays off.

So before you can realistically protect yourself and your computer from disaster, you need to have answers to some very basic questions. The first question is: What kind of computer do you have? To answer this question, you have to figure out what hardware you have and what operating system you're running. Let's start with the hardware.

Computer hardware

If you have a cool transparent case with lots of flashing lights, that's fun, but it doesn't make any difference when playing audio and video files. What really makes a difference is the hardware and software that does the work. If you have a small hard drive, slow CPU, tiny amount of RAM, dinky audio or video cards, or a slow network connection, you're in trouble.

You'll find two main types of personal computer on the market today: Windows PCs and Apple Macs. Which one do you have? If you don't know, look on the case; if it says Apple or Mac, you know it's from Apple, and most anything else (Dell, Gateway, or even a local brand) runs on the Windows operating system. Note that I'm talking hardware here; you can load the Linux operating system (OS) and many other near-unknown OSs on your Windows PC.

Note   Notebooks and laptops can be defined by the attributes listed here because even though they're smaller, they're still quite similar in features.

You know you have a mouse, a monitor, and case, but do you know what is in your case? Here is what your case likely contains:

Note   You're unlikely to find a reason to change your case, but you should know what your power supply is rated at (it's probably in the range of 300 watts) because if you add better audio or video cards, extra hard drives, and other components powered by the same power supply, you may approach its limits.

✦ **Motherboard, CPU, RAM.** These components usually come together, although upgrading your CPU and RAM is still common with most motherboards. However, doing so may not be as practical as you think; by the time you think to upgrade your CPU and RAM, you may be better off just buying a whole new computer. The main criterion by which CPUs are graded is clock speed. The newest Intel offerings run as high as 3 GHz (3 billion cycles per second). But you should know that clock speed isn't the only determining factor; chip architecture (the way the processing elements are designed to work together) is at least as important, and a chip with a slower clock speed may still perform some functions faster (processing music and video is one such function). For example, Mac CPUs often run at a slower clock speed than PC chips and yet perform music, video, and graphics operations more quickly because they are optimized for this type of work.

✦ **RAM.** Your random access memory, or RAM, is where your data is held while it's being processed (for the most part). Modern systems run from 128 to 1024MB of RAM. The important factors in RAM are how much you have (get at least 512MB) and how quickly it can talk to the CPU. After all, having lots of RAM doesn't do much good if it can't interact with the CPU quickly. Bus speed is the term used to denote communications speed between RAM and CPU; look for at least 400 MHz (some newer Intel chips run at 800 MHz bus speed).

Tip

You can purchase CRT and flat-panel monitors, but the criteria by which they should be judged are size (look for a 20-inch model at least), dot-pitch (how small the dots are; at least 0.3 mm), horizontal and vertical resolution (look for at least 1600 by 1200), and refresh rate (the better monitors refresh at a number of rates for better compatibility with your video card).

✦ **Video and audio cards.** These components come separate on better computers, but on some mass-produced machines their circuitry is embedded directly in the motherboard. Having your video and audio circuits on the motherboard is fine for day-to-day business use or balancing your checkbook, but not if you want to get the best video and sound out of your system. Why? If the video or audio circuits break, you'll need to replace your entire motherboard. Second, what if you want to upgrade? Again, you'd have to replace your entire motherboard. If your components aren't separate now, next time you purchase a computer, make sure to buy a computer in which these cards are separate components. Look for 64 to 128MB of RAM on your video card, plus all the typical compatibilities (like AGP). For your audio card, what's more important is the ability to deliver many different types of sound. For example, you need 2, 4, and 5.1 speaker support for all the different ways you might have your speakers set up. Although this is "under the hood" stuff, you might also want to look at your PC's spec sheet to see if your computer has the new Intel High

Definition Audio codec. A codec is either hardware or software that encodes/ compresses and decodes/decompresses audio and video data streams, reducing file size while keeping the audio and video intact. Intel's offering is a type of technology that delivers the features and high-end performance of advanced audio cards in the chip, rather than in a separate card. This codec is capable of playing back more channels at higher quality than previous integrated audio formats. If your PC has the Intel 925X, 915G or 915P Express chipsets, it most likely is armed with this new codec.

Tip   You are going to be downloading music, so don't forget your speaker system. For audio playback, good speakers and a good amplifier are just as important for your computer as they are for your home theater sound system. If you have a very good sound card and the rest of your computer is decent, the speaker system becomes the determining factor in how good your system sounds.

✦ **Network card and modem.** These devices allow your computer to connect to the world. Communications speed is the most important criterion. Dial-up modems are the most basic device, and the most recent improvement in download speed offers up to 56KB (56,000 bits per second). But that's old news; you should really get a cable modem or DSL connection. DSL speeds typically top out at around 1.5MB (1.5 million bits per second). DSL works best if you live 18,000 feet or less from a phone switching office. Recent improvements in cable modem technology achieve broadband download speeds up to 3.2MB (13.2 million bits per second). Upload speeds, however, are significantly slower, often no faster than 128KB (128,000 bits per second). Unless you create a lot of video and audio content, and have to upload it to a Web server, that shouldn't matter, though.

If you use a cable modem or DSL connection, or are connected to a Local Area Network (LAN), you'll need to have a network card installed. Regardless of which type of connection you have, you are limited by your cable modem or DSL connection as well as by the speed your Internet service provider makes available to you.

✦ **Floppy drive, hard drive, and CD/DVD drive.** Your computer probably has one each of these. Some PCs also have a Zip drive, which on most models can hold up to 250MB of data. Many newer PCs and most new notebook computers (which some people use for their main PCs) increasingly are not coming with floppy drives. Floppy drives are gradually falling out of use because they hold only 1.44MB and transfer data rather slowly (but, because this 1.44MB size is too small to hold even one MP3 file of decent quality, this isn't really a problem). CD and DVD drives originally were designed for file distribution rather than storage, but modern computers come with CD and DVD burners. You can buy both writable and rewritable disks of both kinds, so you can use rewritable CDs and DVDs as well as Zip disks for backups, storage, and other kinds of file sharing.

Now are you wondering what hardware you have? Turn off your computer, get out your screwdriver, open up your case, and pull out all the guts. Not! Although you can tell quite a bit (if you know what you're looking for) by examining the hardware (**never** open your case unless you know what you're doing), you can also choose Start ➪ Settings ➪ Control Panel. In Windows XP, you get to the Control Panel directly through the Start menu. Then, when you open the Control Panel in Windows XP, the default setting is a Category View. In the left frame of the Category view, click Switch To Classic View. The System box will open, and if you click the Device Manager tab, you'll see a list of the hardware that has been installed (as shown in Figure 4-1).

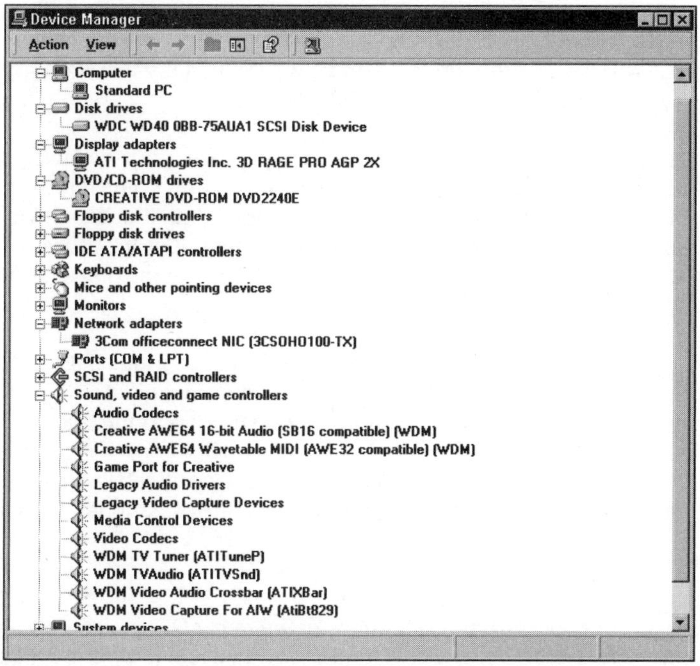

Figure 4-1: Hardware devices in Windows Device Manager

You'll find quite a bit of useful information about your hardware in here, including device names and even brand names. If you don't have the documentation that came with your computer handy (remember that big pile of manuals, books, and disks that came with the system?), you can always go online and find the Web site of the manufacturer of all those devices, and search their sites for your particular model. You can find the tech specs (such as how much RAM your video card comes with) on the manufacturer's site.

An easy way to document your hardware is to take screen shots of all the documentation you can find for your system's hardware, and then insert those images into a big Word document. The best way to do this is by clicking Insert ⇨ Picture ⇨ From File. When the Insert Picture box opens, Browse to the location of the image you want to insert and click on the filename, and click Insert. Following this procedure will come in handy later, especially when you're trying to figure out whether you have the right system components to handle music and video file players you'd like to install.

Operating systems

The big differentiator of systems after hardware is your operating system. The two main operating systems available are Windows and the Mac OS. You don't have to install Windows on a Windows-compliant PC (that's what's usually installed for you). If you buy an Apple, it definitely has the Mac OS on it.

The main functions of an OS are to coordinate the actions of all your hardware (so your hard drive talks to your CPU, which talks to your RAM, and so on), provide a foundation for your software applications (application programs like Word, Internet Explorer, or Apple's iTunes music player), and provide convenient file storage mechanisms (the files are stored on your hard drive, but your operating system does the work of storing them).

So it really doesn't matter which operating system you have, so long as it works well (all the major ones work well enough), runs your software, and stores your files. Linux, in its many incarnations, is becoming increasingly popular, partly because it's relatively inexpensive and partly because it works quite well. It does all the things expected of a major OS, has thousands of free application programs available (including lots of music and video players and editors), and isn't hard to install anymore.

Caution   Although most player software is made in several versions, one for each of the major OS brands, older but still popular versions of the major OSs may not be supported. Although you are probably safe with Windows Millennium, just because the player software is made for Windows does not mean it will run on Windows 95 or early versions of Windows 98. That's another good reason why you should read the system requirements carefully.

If you want detailed information about your operating system, and you are running some version of Windows (Windows 98, Windows Millennium, Windows XP, etc.), choose Start ⇨ Help and Support (Help in Windows Me). You'll see something like Figure 4-2.

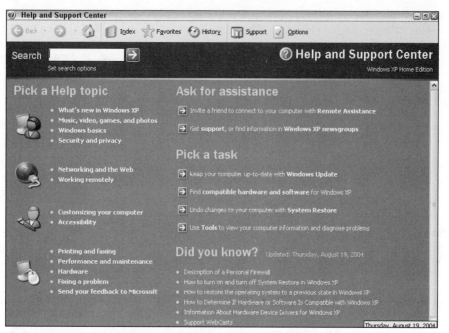

Figure 4-2: Windows XP Help and Support's main interface

If you have a Mac, check the Help menu for Mac Help to find out the version. Note that from OS 10 (OS X) on, the Mac OS has changed radically under the hood and works much more like Linux, even though the user interface (the part you see on your screen) has features similar to older versions of the Mac OS. By the way, if you have OS X, you probably already have the iTunes and iMovie player software installed.

If you're running Linux, you probably already know it. But you can find out more about it by checking Help (click the Red Hat symbol in the lower-left corner of your desktop if you're running Red Hat). Figure 4-3 shows the help manual for the KDE Desktop (one of the Windows-style interfaces you can install) in Red Hat's Fedora version of Linux.

Document the specifics of your operating system just like you document the specifics of your hardware, in the same Word document if you like. You definitely need to know which OS you're running (and the specific version) when it's time to decide which version of a music or video file player to download and install. Plus, operating systems have patches, upgrades, fixes, and so on all the time, so it's good to know exactly how well patched your OS is, to protect yourself against security holes. Go to the Web site of your OS maker and search for patches, updates, security bulletins, and so forth before you start downloading or file sharing.

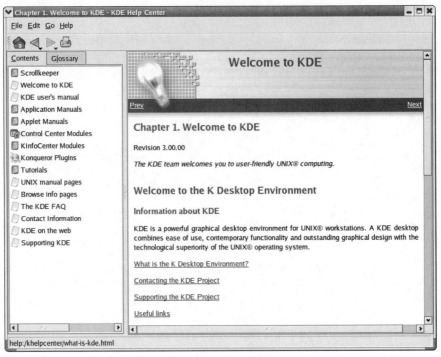

Figure 4-3: The KDE Desktop manual in Red Hat Linux

Drives and Files Systems

When you start your computer, software hard-wired into your motherboard runs first, performing a power-on self test (POST). This is a basic test that determines whether the hardware in your system is working. Then the basic input/output system (BIOS) software runs. This software checks out everything and establishes connections between your CPU, hard drives, and so on. In the BIOS are settings that tell your computer on what drive it should look for the OS. The OS resides on what is called the boot disk.

Caution You can easily examine the settings in your BIOS (with Windows PCs) by watching your monitor during the startup process, and then pressing the key noted on the screen (you'll see a message such as "press the Delete key to enter Setup"). This will discontinue the startup process and instead display the BIOS and BIOS settings. Although doing this once or twice to become familiar with the settings you'll find there (such as which boot disk to find the OS on) is a good idea, be careful! If you change any of the settings in the BIOS unknowingly or mistakenly, it could be difficult to figure out how to change it back properly. You'll usually find an option to reset everything to the factory defaults, but if your computer was specially configured at any point, the factory defaults may not be correct.

Boot disk

Your operating system resides on one of your disks, and the disk that holds the operating system is called the boot disk. You can actually run software that lets you switch among various operating systems (if you have more than one installed) when your computer starts up. But most folks stick with one OS.

If you happen to have a problem with your operating system, you may have to start your computer and operating system from a floppy disk or CD. For Windows PCs, a setting in the BIOS allows you to start from the A: drive (the floppy drive in most cases), or from the D or E: drive (the CD drive in most cases). Just be careful when changing your BIOS settings.

Hard disk drives and partitions

You're probably familiar with the fact that you can have one or more hard drives on your computer. Windows PC users tend to think of the primary drive on the computer as the C: drive. Historically, the primary drive has been labeled C:, the floppy drive has been A:, and other drives added to the system then take on the next letters in the alphabet (D:, E:, and so on).

FAT File Systems

The acronym FAT stands for file allocation table. A hard drive partition must contain some record of the clusters into which the partition has been divided. The record consists of the addresses of each cluster. When a file is saved, a record is made of the address of each cluster containing a piece of the file and the order, so the file can be reconstructed from the pieces. The record includes a number for the address of each cluster. The numbers are written in ones and zeros, leading to the names of the two older Windows file systems: FAT-16 and FAT-32.

The far older FAT-16 file system makes use of 16-bit numbers to describe the address of partition clusters. There can be only 16^2 (16 squared, or 256) binary addresses with a 16-bit number, placing a limit on the number of clusters possible in a FAT-16 file system. For example, on a 1-2GB partition, the clusters would be 32KB. Another limitation imposed by the number of cluster addresses is a 2GB limit on the size of the hard drive partition that can be addressed with FAT-16.

Also getting a bit long in the tooth, FAT-32 file system (on the same 1-2GB partition) has the ability to create 32^2 (32-squared, or 1024) addresses. Thus number of clusters can be much higher and the size of the clusters much smaller (4KB). This means that much lest space is wasted. It also means that FAT-32 file systems can use much larger drive partitions, because even with smaller clusters the file system can still address much larger hard drive partitions.

But a single drive can be formatted so that it is split into *partitions*, which are logically separated areas on the drive that are treated as separate drives, each with their own letter showing up in your file manager. Each individual partition can then be assigned its own drive letter, even though several partitions may actually be on the same drive.

When you split a drive into partitions in this way, you can format each partition with a different type of file system. For example, you can format one partition as FAT-32 (which means File Allocation Table 32-bit) and another as NTFS (which means NT File System). Of course, doing so is a good idea only if the OS you're using can read files formatted in this way (older versions of Windows 98 can't work with NTFS files).

Fragmented files

The file system format you choose for a partition affects how much data it can hold, because when you choose a file system you are also choosing how finely divided the drive is. You see, each disk partition, in its raw state, is simply a long track of bits ready to be set. Before you can write any data, you must divide the partition into segments (called *clusters*), and each segment must have an address.

This makes sense, because when you write out a file onto the disk, you never know how many bits the file will take. Therefore, to find the file again, you have to have an address for each cluster of the file written. For example, if you have a file that is 96KB, but the partition is divided into clusters 32KB in size, your file would be stored in three separate segments. You'd never notice this file segmentation, because your OS, file system, and hard drive would take care of all the details.

But suppose your file was only 70KB in size? It would still take up 96KB of space, because the last 32KB cluster would still be devoted to the last 26KB of your file, even though the cluster still takes up a full 32KB. Store enough odd size files (and most files are odd sizes) and you can lose a lot of hard drive space.

So why not just store all the files end to end? Data files change size constantly as you work on them and modify them. If you removed something from a file in the middle of all the rest of the files, you'd have to rewrite all the files again so they were end-to-end each time you saved a file, and that would seriously degrade the performance of your computer. Blocking partitions into clusters is simply the best mechanism so far for storing files.

The reason for all this discussion is that the file system you choose (or happen to have) may divide your hard drive into smaller or larger clusters, thereby increasing or decreasing the amount of usable space you have, as well as affecting your computer's ability to find and play back tracks.

FAT-16 and FAT-32 file systems also have the drawback of not providing for sophisticated assignment of users, groups, and permissions, which are discussed in more depth later.

Safely defragmenting your hard drive

Many utility programs are available for defragmenting your hard drive, but your operating system probably came with one installed. For example, Windows has Disk Defragmenter. The recommended procedure is to analyze volumes (hard drive partitions) first and then to defragment the ones that need it. The Analyze Volumes utility provides a report that tells you how fragmented the files on a particular volume are, allowing you to choose which partitions really need it.

In Windows XP you can get to Disk Defragmenter by choosing Start ⇨ All Programs ⇨ Accessories ⇨ System Tools ⇨ Disk Defragmenter (from your Start menu). Figure 4-4 shows the Disk Defragmenter utility as it analyzes volumes for fragmentation.

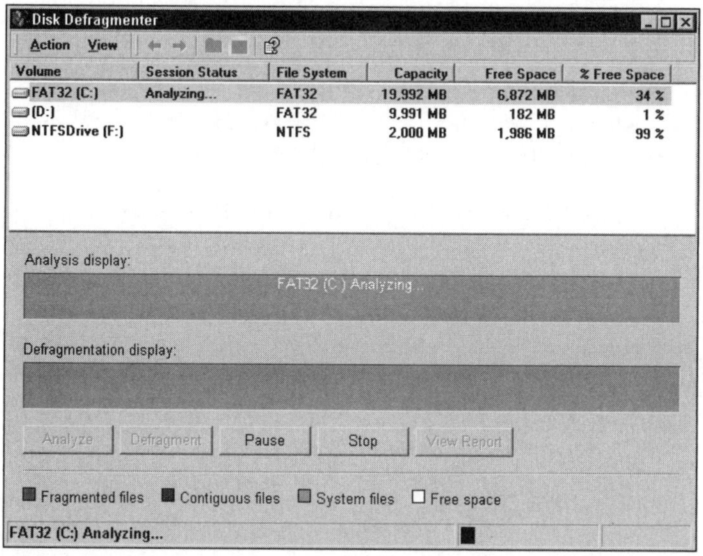

Figure 4-4: Disk defragmenter analyzing FAT-32 C: drive

After you decide which drives to defragment, be prepared to leave your computer running for quite a while. You shouldn't shut down the computer unless absolutely necessary during defragmentation, because doing so could lead to a breakdown of your file system. Power outages can also cause serious problems if they occur during defragmentation, so be sure to back up your critical files first. In fact, since you probably need to defragment only once or twice a month, you should schedule defragmenting your drive so it follows a backup.

Understanding File Basics

Now that you know what hardware and OS you're running, take a closer look at exactly what's happening on your system when you download files. The subject of this book is how to protect yourself when downloading music and video files from the Internet, so to be thorough, you should take a very quick look at what that means, how it applies in any situation, and what the real risks are. I'll start from the most basic definitions of what files are and proceed through to music and video file types and downloading methods.

Cross-Reference I just briefly cover the subject of downloading methods in this chapter; you can find out much more in Chapter 6.

Bits and bytes

All information on computers is stored as bits. Bits are very tiny spots on floppy disks, hard drives, CDs, or in the transistors in the chips inside your computer that are either on or off. The bits on a floppy disk or hard drive are magnetic areas in metal, while the bits on a CD or DVD are really just very tiny blemishes on plastic, and the bits in your computer's chips are formed by the flow (or no flow) of electricity through a transistor. It doesn't matter how bits are formed or what medium they live on (or in). What matters is that your computer can read them.

A series of seven or eight bits forms what is called a byte. Because of the way data is stored in computers, one byte is often sufficient to contain one character (such as A, B, or C, or a number, or a punctuation mark). One thousand bytes roughly equals one kilobyte (KB), and one kilobyte is enough to store about 1,000 characters of plain text.

One thousand kilobytes roughly equal one megabyte (MB), and one thousand megabytes roughly equals one gigabyte (GB). A typical hard drive on a modern computer may be able to store 100-200GB of data.

Caution The difference between text data (with characters such as A, B, and C making up most of the data) and music, video, or any digitized media files is huge. Although a text document may have 1,000 characters per page (and may therefore require 1-2KB of storage space on your computer), a music file sampled in 16-bit sound at 44,100 samples per second may contain 100KB of data per second (each 16-bit samples is 2 bytes, times 44,100 for 88,200 bytes per second, plus a little overhead). You can see why media files take up so much space so quickly as you record.

Files

So what are files? Basically, two types of data are stored as files on your computer: the files making up programs that process data and the files containing your data. Your operating system, word processor, spreadsheet, virus-protection, browser, and other applications are all examples of programs that process data. Music, video, images, text, spreadsheets, and so on are all examples of data files. Applications perform work, while data files are the result of performing work with applications.

Tip   The terms program and application are basically interchangeable. The terms folder and directory are also interchangeable.

Folders are also files. Folders are simply special files that can hold other files, to make it easier for you to store your files conveniently.

File extensions and file types

When you use Microsoft Word to write a letter, you may be aware that the file is saved with a name that includes what is called an *extension*, in this case the letters "doc" for "document." If you know how to view all the files on your hard drive and can't see the extension as part of the filename, try resetting your view of your files. To reset your view in Windows XP, follow these steps:

1. **Open My Computer.**

2. **Choose Tools ⇨ Folder Options from the main menu.** The Folder Options dialog box opens.

3. **Click the View tab (shown in Figure 4-5).**

4. **If the "Hide file extensions for known file types" box is checked, uncheck it.** All files displayed on your system should now show their file extension as part of their name.

If you've been using computers for more than a few years, you may recall the day when Windows (and Microsoft's predecessor operating system DOS) restricted filenames to eight characters plus a three-character extension.

Nowadays, filenames can be very long and can have long extensions as well, but in most cases file extensions are still three to four characters. Another aspect of extensions is that they are always preceded by a "." (dot). So for the filename "myimage.jpg," you know that the extension is "jpg" because those letters follow the dot at the end of the filename.

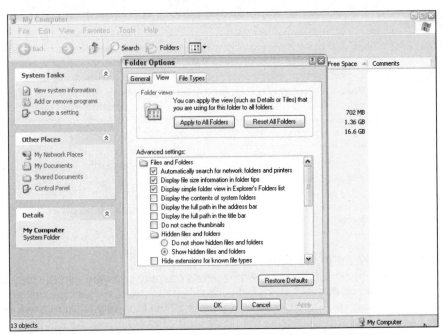

Figure 4-5: Folder Options dialog box in Windows Explorer

But you can name a file any name you like, and you can make the extension anything you like as well, or even leave the extension off entirely. Why is it important to know this? Well, filename extensions indicate to your programs how the data in the file is formatted. And if a filename has the wrong extension (for example, if you renamed a Word document so that the extension is "jpg" rather than "doc"), trying to open it probably wouldn't work, because the program opening the file wouldn't be able to read it correctly.

And this brings us to file types. File type is determined by how the data in a file is formatted and structured, *not* by the filename or extension of the filename. In fact, for many file types, more of the file's space is taken up by formatting and structures than by the data you've entered into it.

Caution   Just because a file has an extension you've seen (such as .jpg), don't assume the file is actually that type. Malicious file-sharers and hackers sometimes modify file extensions so the wrong program will attempt to open the file, and the file contains code that then crashes the program and perhaps even takes over your computer.

File type is very important for music and video downloads, because not all music or video player programs can play all file types. Also, some file types can be downloaded directly, while others can only be streamed (downloaded as a continuing stream rather than a single file) but not saved. And some file types are smaller than others or are compressed, and compressed files need to be reconstituted when you're ready to use them.

Connecting files and player software by file type

In Windows, files are connected to software applications by file type, based on the filename extension. This means, for example, that you can associate all files ending in ".wav" with the Windows Media Player application, and then whenever you double-click a file with this extension, the file will automatically open in Windows Media Player.

When you install software, the software often asks you if you'd like it to be the default application for this file type. It is actually asking you if you'd like the connection between file type and the installing application to be created (and any existing connections between this file type and other applications to be deleted). Essentially, the software is asking if you'd like to allow it to take over running files of this type. Generally, it doesn't hurt anything if you change default applications for a given file type, but you may be surprised the next time you double-click one of your favorite files and a strange application automatically opens up. Leaving the default application setting alone is usually best; change it deliberately when you need to, not the first time you install an application. You can always open files in any application that can handle that file type, and you can reset the association between file types and applications manually as well.

To reset the association between file types and applications in Windows XP, follow these steps:

1. **Choose Start ⇨ Control Panel to open the Control Panel.**

2. **Click Switch to Classic View, and then double-click Folder Options to display the Folder Options dialog box.**

3. **Click the File Types tab, and then scroll down to WAV (as shown in Figure 4-6).**

4. **Click the Change button to select another application as the default player for WAV files.** The Open With dialog box appears, and you can scroll down and select the program you want to use to open WAV files by default. Of course, the program you select must be capable of playing WAV files. (In Figure 4-7 you can see that both QuickTime and Real Player are installed and available on this computer.)

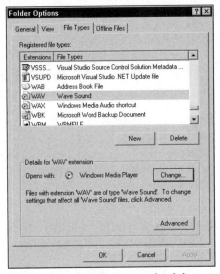

Figure 4-6: The File Types tab of the Folder Options dialog box

Figure 4-7: Selecting a player application

You can use the same procedure to associate any file type with any application, but keep in mind that only one application can be the default for any given file type.

So now that you have a clear idea what files are, what file types are, and how they are stored on your computer, consider your file system, file permissions, and sharing files.

Understanding File Systems

A number of file systems are available for Windows, Macintosh, Linux, and other operating systems. If you have a choice, look for a file system that allows the assignment of user, groups, and permissions. These days, the only file systems that don't allow users, groups, and permissions are found on older Windows and Mac machines; Linux, OSX, and Microsoft's Server OSs (NT, Me, and XP) have always provided advanced file capabilities.

Each OS and file system stores files in its own way. A music file stored on Linux or OSX cannot be directly opened and played on a computer running Windows 98 with a FAT-16 or FAT-32 file system.

So how can you download a music file from a Linux server (most Web sites run on Linux servers) and play it back on your Windows system? When you download a file from a Web site, you use the File Transfer Protocol (FTP). Whether you are downloading via your browser or directly using an FTP application, your FTP program is smart enough to automatically convert the file from its original format to the one your computer is running.

Managing Your Files

Downloading and playing back music is great fun, but you may become a little frustrated if you can't find that great tune later from another program when you want to burn it to a CD for a friend. File management is the key, and the first step in managing your files is becoming proficient at copying, moving, renaming, and finding your files.

Most operating systems come with file manager utility programs. You may have thought yours was part of the operating system because file management is such an integral part of using a computer. But no, they are utilities. In Windows XP, My Computer is the easiest and the Mac and Linux machine have their own file manager utilities as well. as well. Handy file management tools display files and folders in hierarchical format or as a series of windows. I prefer the hierarchical format, as that's what I'm used to, but some people like their files displayed in a series of windows, with each folder in its own window. Either way, you can navigate among your files with ease using My Computer. And you can also find out about file properties and drive properties (such as how many gigabytes of space you have left for more music and video).

To get to My Computer in Windows XP, just click Start and then My Computer. Once you are there, take a look. You should see a list of File and Folder tasks arranged in a hierarchy down the left side, and if you click on a folder, you'll see any files in it (including subfolders) displayed on the right side of your screen (as shown in Figure 4-8).

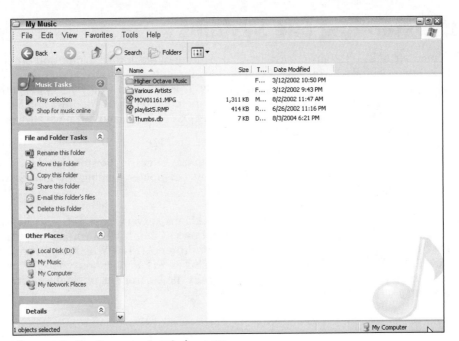

Figure 4-8: My Computer in Windows XP

A single click displays the contents of a folder, and a double-click (or a click on the plus sign next to it) opens the folder. Double-clicking on a file opens the file, unless the file is not connected to any known software application.

Click on a file and drag it over a different folder, and you'll move the file if the current location and new location are on the same drive. Drag a file to a folder on another drive and the file gets copied over. If you want to copy a file to a folder on the same drive, you need to hold down the Ctrl key while dragging.

Caution   You may want to be careful when you move files that have been stored in a music software program's library. If you switch digital music software players, your new player may not be able to find these files, and you will have to load them into your new software's library manually.

Right-click on a drive or folder, and a shortcut menu appears. Click Properties on the shortcut menu, and a variety of attributes appear, including the amount of free space available. This is important because when you save files (or install software, for that matter), you have to make sure that your computer has enough room.

And when you access another computer via a Local Area Network, such as an office setup where several computers are linked together) the computer you connect to is assigned a drive letter, even if you're connecting only to a single folder on that computer, rather than the entire drive. Again, these drive letters show up in your file manager, and you can navigate across the files and folders you have access to just like any other files and folders.

Files and folders

Folders are files; they are just special files designated as folders. Folders are displayed with the folder icon so that you can tell they are folders, but on your disk they are still files. They are special because they are structured so they serve as a sort of little database containing markers to the files they hold.

One thing common to file systems is that folders may contain files and other folders, and no folder may contain two files with exactly the same name.

File properties

On just about any file system, you can establish properties for files. The name of a file is one property; the time and date a file was created or changed is another property. The owner of the file (generally the user who created it) and the file permissions are also properties of the file. If you right-click on a file, a shortcut menu appears. Click Properties from that shortcut menu, and the properties of the file appear in a dialog box (similar to what you see in Figure 4-9).

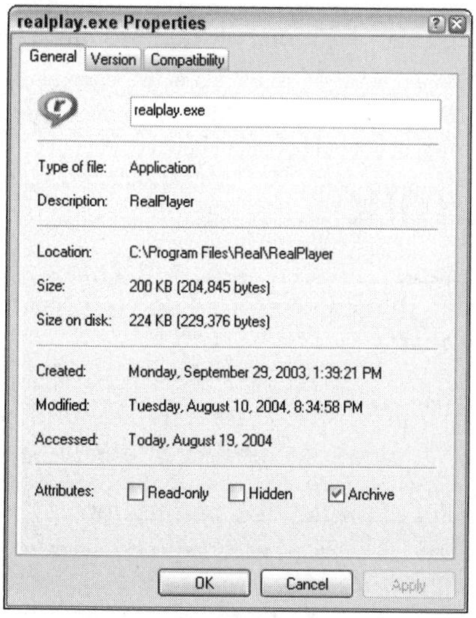

Figure 4-9: The File Properties dialog box of RealPlayer

FAT-16 and FAT-32 file system properties

For FAT-16 and FAT-32 file systems, file properties include the name, size, and date created, as well as whether the file is archived, hidden, or read-only. As mentioned, you can view the File Properties dialog box for these file systems by opening My Computer, navigating to the file, right-clicking it, and choosing Properties from the shortcut menu. The archived, hidden, and read-only properties can be changed from this dialog box.

NTFS File system properties

On NTFS, file properties are called attributes. These attributes include the filename, the security descriptor (lists the owner of the file and other access parameters), the data in the file, and the datestamp of the file (when the file was created or changed).

You can view the properties of NTFS files by opening Windows Explorer, navigating to the file, right-clicking it, and choosing Properties from the shortcut menu. The dialog box displayed shows basic file properties such as name, datestamp, and so forth, plus a Security tab that displays which users have access to the file. The amount of access any particular user or group has is dependent upon the permissions allowed to that user or group.

Linux file system properties

The Mac OS X and IBM PCs with Linux installed have very similar file properties and permissions that can be set. File properties include the filename, datestamp, owner, and permissions. If you're using the command-line interface (the non-graphical, non-windows user interface), you can navigate around directories using the cd (change directory) command (cd plus the name and path of the folder); when you're in the desired folder, you can use the ls-a (Linux System Administrator) command to display all files and their properties.

Permissions, Users, and Groups

If you're a long-time Windows user, you may never have encountered a file system with restrictions attached to the use of any file that can be found on your hard drive. So imagine for a moment a file system that:

✦ Knows who you are by your login

✦ Knows all the files you've created

✦ Restricts access to files according to a set of predefined permissions

Linux, Windows NT, 2000, and XP, Mac OS X, and some other operating systems provide file systems that allow the use of permissions. In Windows XP Service Pack 2, which was released in September 2004, permissions have been tightened, not allowing anyone but authorized system administrators from granting or denying access to types of files. That may sound restrictive, but shouldn't be a problem for home users — who, in most Windows XP setups, automatically become "administrator" of their own computer.

What are permissions?

Permissions define what a user may do with a file. For example, if you have read permission for a file, you can read it into a program in order to find out all the data in it. But if you don't have write permission for the file, you're not allowed to make any changes to it. And if you don't have execute permission for a file, you may be able to read from or write to the file, but not run it as a program.

Windows NT, 2000, and XP use the NTFS file system, so you may be able to establish an extensive structure of users, groups, and permissions on your hard drive. The big advantage, of course, is that you can set aside a drive, partition, or folder on your hard drive specifically for downloads and sharing, and then maintain more control over what those files may do.

NTFS allows you to establish the following permissions for folders:

✦ **Full Control.** Take ownership, change permissions, delete subfolders and files, and all other activities that may be performed in the file system.

✦ **Modify.** Delete the folder, as well as all other activities permitted by Write or Read & Execute.

✦ **Read & Execute.** Navigate through the folder to other folders and files, as well as all other activities permitted by Read or List Folder Contents.

✦ **List Folder Contents.** View the names of files and subfolders in the folder.

✦ **Read.** View files and subfolders in the folder, and view file ownership, attributes, and permissions.

✦ **Write.** Create new folders and files in the folder, change folder attributes, and view file ownership, attributes, and permissions.

NTFS allows you to establish the following permissions for files:

✦ **Full Control.** Take ownership, change permissions, and all other file activities that may be performed in the file system.

✦ **Modify.** Delete or modify the file, as well as all other activities permitted by Write or Read & Execute.

✦ **Read & Execute.** Execute (run) the file as an application, as well as all other activities permitted by Read.

✦ **Read.** Read the file and view file ownership, attributes, and permissions.

✦ **Write**. Write to the file, change file attributes, and view file ownership, attributes, and permissions.

Users and groups

Permissions are closely tied to the concept of users and groups. If your operating system requires a login before use and restricts file access with permissions, this means that the system recognizes you by your user ID and allows access to files according to the permissions you have as that user.

Whenever you must login, whether to your computer, a network, or an application (whether it's a desktop application or an online application), you are establishing your presence as a user, so you're familiar with the concept of being a user.

More advanced systems extend the concept of users to include the concept of groups of users. When groups can be established, file permissions can be assigned to groups, and then users assigned to groups. This practice is primarily designed to make the system administrator's job easier; instead of individually assigning access to each file every time a new user is entered into the system and given a password, the system administrator simply assigns the appropriate file permissions to a named group just once and then assigns new users to that group (or another group with different permissions). As a user within a group, you inherit all the access permissions of all groups you are assigned to, thereby allowing you to do any work you need to with those files or programs that are the responsibility of your group (or groups).

Altogether, the concepts of permissions and users and groups form a good solution to maintaining order and security on a computer and across networks.

Top Ten Techniques for Mastering Your System

1. **Examine your computer and determine what hardware you're running.** You should already know whether your computer is a laptop, notebook, or desktop, and what kind (Mac or Windows PC). Check CPU model and speed, total amount of RAM available, how many hard drives you have, and how much free space is available. Pull out those manuals you got with the system (if you still have them), or go online to the manufacturer's site, both for the entire system and for the maker of each individual component. Find out what kind of audio and video cards you have, how much RAM the video card has, and how many ways the audio card can output sound. Check your monitor

and speaker systems to make sure they're high quality and working properly. Document what you find so you can check it later when you're installing player software.

2. **Figure out what operating system you're running.** If you have a Mac, you are most likely running either OS X (a version of Linux specially optimized for the Mac) or one of the older Mac operating systems (nothing to do with Linux). If you have a Windows PC, you're probably running one of the newer versions of Windows, such as Me, 2000, or XP. Again, document what you find.

3. **Check the file system type and capabilities your system allows.** Check specifically to see if you can set permissions on files and folders, and whether you can set up users and groups. Review your current settings to find out which users are already established on your system, whether you're logging in as the root or administrator of your system, and which drives or folders are already shared.

4. **Open the default file manager program that came with your computer (the default file manager program for Windows OS is usually My Computer).** Work with it a bit, until you're familiar with how to copy, move, save, and rename files. Learn all about how to use it to navigate and manage your drives, network places, folders, and files, as well as how to display file-name extensions.

5. **Use your file manager application to check file properties and permissions.** Experiment with it until you're proficient at setting and changing file permissions. Understand what happens when you set a file to be executable or read-only.

6. **Set up a plan and schedule for backing up your files.** You're going to spend quite a bit of time searching for, downloading, and cataloging music and video files on your hard drive, so you should take the time to back them up. Learn how to use the default defragmenter utility application that came with your OS. Know how to safely defragment your hard drive, and how to restore backed up files if you need to.

7. **Know how to find files on your system.** Your file manager probably has a Find function, and often you can use wildcard characters (such as the asterisk or the question mark) to extend its search capability.

8. **Review the programs that have already been installed on your computer.** Most likely, you have multiple player applications already installed (especially if you followed through with Chapters 2 and 3). Some of them may play the same file types, and you may actually have set your system to have one or the other application become the default player without remembering which one is correct.

9. **Learn how to associate file type (by file extension) with an application.**

10. **Because you'll be using your browser to download files quite a bit, open your browser and check its settings.** Learn how to make your browser automatically open or save specific file types.

Summary

This chapter is designed to provide the information you need for a complete under-standing of your own computer, operating system, and peripheral devices, so you can get the best storage and playback of any files you download, whether by direct download or file-sharing.

To that end, this chapter included a short primer on computer hardware, including a quick look at modern CPUs, RAM, hard drives, monitors, and speaker systems. You also reviewed the three main operating systems and their associated file system types. The most common OS is some version of Windows (such as Windows XP or older). You also learned a bit about the basic input/output system (BIOS).

You should now understand how data is stored on a computer, specifically the structure of files and folders. And you should know much more about file types, file properties, and file permissions, as well as how to navigate with your file man-ager, how to create shared folders, and how to set folder and file permissions.

✦   ✦   ✦

Dangers of Downloading or Sharing Files: The Nature of the Threat

◆ ◆ ◆ ◆

In This Chapter

Understanding your
level of risk

How hackers,
crackers, and scam
artists invade your
computer

Detecting hackers

Viruses, worms,
Trojan horses,
and spyware

Recognizing Web
site threats

◆ ◆ ◆ ◆

Up to this point, you've had lots of fun. You've learned about all the riches to be had on the Internet — nearly unlimited music and video, plus many other file types, and a plenitude of player software, much of it free. But you've also learned that your system is vulnerable and that dangers lurk out there. In this chapter, you learn all the various kinds of dangers, how they operate, how they try to sneak into your system, and how they try to hide themselves so they can do their dirty work behind the scenes or even make your computer a slave for their ill-conceived ends.

Understanding the Threats to Your PC

One good way to start defining the threat is to categorize the types of threats you face by intention. A good person who means you well can unintentionally cause you harm by delivering an e-mail with an attachment, by giving out your password, or even by spilling coffee on your computer. A person with malicious intent can harm you by doing these things deliberately. Ordinarily, it's up to you to use good practices to protect yourself from both types, but of course the good person is a little easier to defend against. For example, not giving out your passwords unless someone really needs to know them, not responding to "too good to be true" e-mail offers, and keeping your computer in a safe place with your files backed up can all help you avoid unintentional damage, or recover from it more quickly.

Another good way to categorize the threat is to divide threats into online and offline. Offline threats can come from taking floppies or CDs and DVDs from unknown or unreliable sources and inserting them into your computer. There's also at least some element of risk in allowing people to access your computer who are unfamiliar with your PC or how your files are named and structured. Again, whether or not the person has malicious intent, protecting yourself against these kinds of threats by securing your computer, using an operating system (OS) that requires a password, not letting just anyone have login access, and by logging yourself out whenever you'll be away from your computer for a lengthy period are all good ideas.

Online threats are by far the most insidious, because with the dramatic increase in always-on, broadband capability, your computer can be used against you without any knowledge on your part. Although I discuss how to avoid or mitigate all the threats at the end of this chapter, the rest of this chapter focuses on online threats (also known as remote access threats).

Remote Access Threats

Any program that can communicate with your computer (either with you voluntarily accessing it or not) can be the source of a virus or worse. Most of you communicate on the Internet constantly, at work and at play, via e-mail, Web browsing, instant messaging, or downloading and sharing files, so you're constantly exposed to threats. It's helpful to review why computers are at risk and what makes them valuable targets.

You always face the possibility that your computer will experience hardware failure. As with anything electronic, computer parts sometimes burn out or become damaged. But, for the most part, a good working computer that has been working for a while will continue working well.

In addition, even if your computer suffers a hardware failure, chances are good that you can remove the hard drive and place it into another machine, and then recover your data. Hard drives are quite well made (at least the major brands are) and tend to last as long as or longer than most other electronic components in your machine.

But this points to an important fact: Your data is probably worth much more than your hardware, especially if you have a month or two worth of work stored on your computer. So think of your computer and its parts as semi-disposable, and think of your data as your irreplaceable resource. After all, you created your data, but someone else built the computer! With this in mind, you can see that backing up your data is critically important. If you're afraid of being without computer access for a short time, just get a CD, DVD, or Zip drive and back up your key files once in a while. That'll take care of both needs.

Now, why not meet the bad code and the bad people (often interrelated) who would just love to gum up your PC, and everything associated with it.

Evil software

A bad program is any program that does something that you didn't intend to happen. Bad software programs are not always written by hackers; sometimes well-intentioned programmers inadvertently create a program that crashes your hard drive, and with a severe enough error may destroy your data files or otherwise cause problems. I cover the subject briefly here and go into more detail in Chapter 6. Take a look at the various types of bad programs that are common.

Malfunctioning software

It's a known fact that even the best software contains bugs. Bugs come in two types: bugs that blow up the software application, and bugs that allow the application to continue working but produce the wrong answers or otherwise create problems (such as making a security hole).

If a software application crashes your system all the time under specific conditions, you can easily tell that it's a bad program, and I would hope that you could just remove the application. If your system crashes only under very unusual conditions or intermittently, determining which piece of software is the bad actor is much harder; therefore, figuring out how to fix the problem is much more difficult.

Sometimes the problem is not the software, but the music or video files. This is especially true with music and video files downloaded for free from a file-sharing service. These files are likely to have been created by file sharers from original copies on a CD or DVD — with varying degrees of expertise. Files can be corrupted (lose bits or get mangled during download, for example) and therefore be hard to play, or they can be in a format that the player software has trouble playing. Either of these conditions can cause your system to freeze or crash.

So when you download a player application and it crashes or does not do what it is supposed to do, is the problem due to the player application, corrupted or bad files, or perhaps even your OS? For faulty music players, you can also diagnose the problem by going to the customer support or Help pages on the Web sites of these products. Once there, you can do a search for a description and remedy appropriate for your specific problem. In one example, if you go to RealPlayer's Web-based help resource at `http://real.custhelp.com` and enter "cannot burn CDs" in the search box, you will come up with an explanation of the problem and why it exists, as shown in Figure 5-1. Similarly, Microsoft's Support site at `http://support.microsoft.com` offers help for Windows Media Player technical issues, as shown in Figure 5-2.

Another good way to stay current on known bugs and incompatibilities (as well as workable fixes) is to visit sites that provide news about software patches and fixes. One of the best is aptly named VersionTracker (`www.versiontracker.com`). Here, you can search or browse for patches for that balky software that has been causing you consternation.

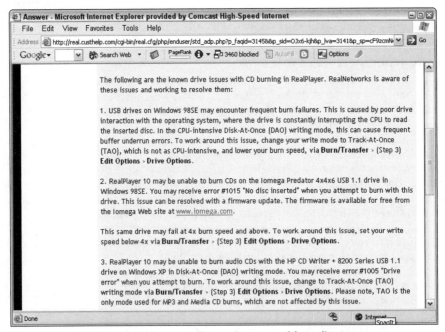

Figure 5-1: RealPlayer's Help area offers software problem diagnoses.

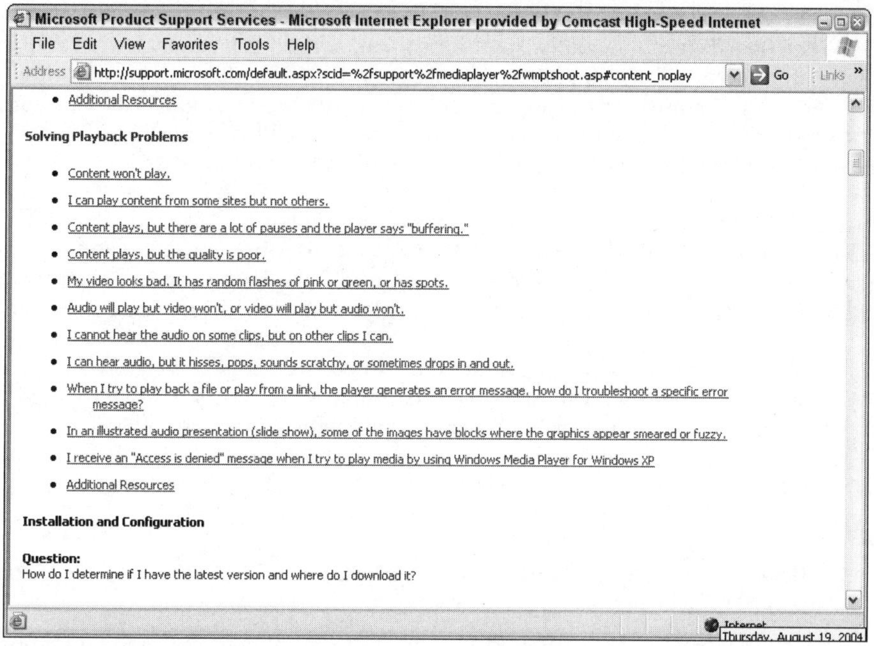

Figure 5-2: Windows Media Player won't load that file? Microsoft Support's Web pages may have the answer.

> **Tip** Another useful site that offers patches and fixes is The Software Patch (www. softwarepatch.com).

Viruses

Viruses are programs that you install unknowingly and that wreak havoc with or destroy your files. They are called viruses because their programming includes methods to replicate themselves to external media or files that might be transferred from one computer to another. The damage they do can range from harmless to complete destruction of all your data files, program files, and operating system files. You can find more information about viruses and how to remove them at the sites of the major anti-virus solution makers (such as Norton and McAfee), but many smaller anti-virus makers that often provide basic anti-virus protection for free.

> **Tip** AVG Anti-virus (www.grisoft.com) has a free anti-virus program that is as capable and functional as most of the better-known anti-virus utilities. It scans your incoming e-mail and examines your programs and files as you open them.

Note that viruses can also be Trojan horses or worms, and that sometimes the terms are used interchangeably. Just to be clear, a virus is a program that replicates itself automatically. A Trojan horse is a program that appears to be something that it is not, usually something you want (such as a free music or video file). A worm is a program that spreads itself across the Internet, usually via your e-mail client and its address book. Some software has all three of these components.

Viruses depend on system resources to do their work and to spread. They infect by exploiting known weaknesses in operating systems or application programs, and they operate by hijacking common functions that legitimate programs need to do legitimate work (such as the ability to write files to the hard drive or send e-mail).

No two viruses are the same, but their removal process is generally pretty similar. Most anti-virus programs will remove a great majority of viruses. I use the example of the popular McAfee Virus Scan program to explain this procedure.

To remove viruses from your PC with McAfee Virus Scan, perform the following steps:

1. **Choose Start ➪ Programs ➪ McAfee Virus Scan.** The program opens, and the main interface shows.

2. **In the main interface, click My Computer, and check all the Scan Options boxes (see Figure 5-3).**

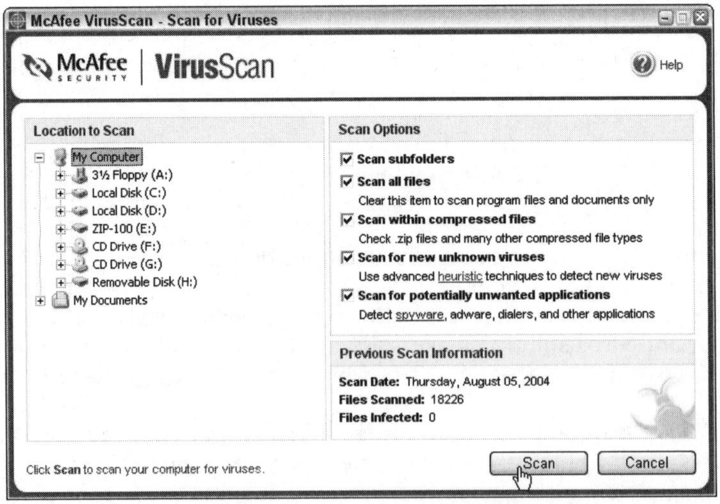

Figure 5-3: McAfee Virus Scan is being prepped for a virus checkup.

3. **To start the scan, click the Scan button.** McAfee Virus Scan starts scanning your computer (see Figure 5-4). If it encounters a virus, it will catalog it in the utility's List of Detected Files area, remove it automatically, or place it in a "quarantined" section of your hard drive where it will do no harm.

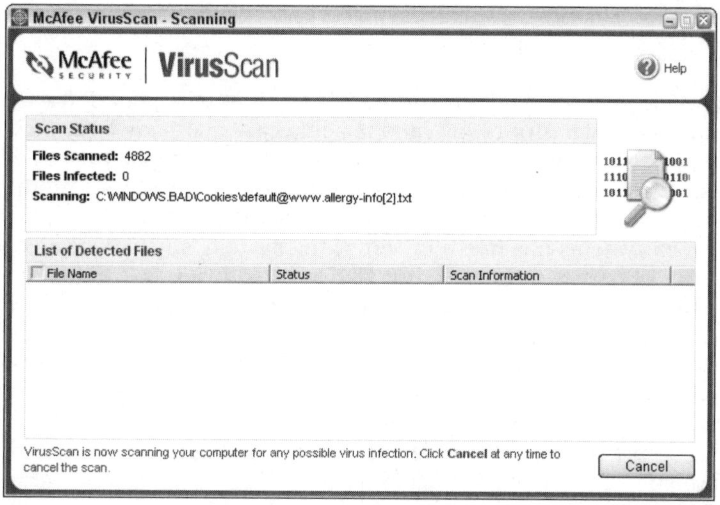

Figure 5-4: McAfee Virus Scan is examining this PC for computer viruses.

Tip

Because new viruses are introduced on the Internet all the time, be sure to update your anti-virus software on a regular basis. In fact, many anti-virus utilities offer this option to you when you install the program. You will not have to do any work, because at various intervals, your anti-virus fighter will query its parent, corporate Web site for new anti-virus "definitions" (code that will delete the virus), and then download it into your version. The next time you run your anti-virus utility, protection for that file will already be included.

Worms

Worms propagate via e-mail or networking protocols. They mainly attempt to replicate themselves, sometimes so much so that they clog a network's ability to communicate.

Although worms and viruses can be harmful to computers, worms are not the same thing as computer viruses. Viruses are often spread en masse, such as through e-mail messages or bad coding on a Web page, retrieved by a Web browser without the proper anti-virus safeguards. For example, e-mail viruses that spread through attachments replicate by automatically mailing themselves to everyone in your recipients e-mail address book.

A worm moves slowly from PC to PC. A worm that spreads via e-mail will activate itself when it finds e-mail servers that have security holes. It copies itself on such servers, and then uses that server to search for other servers to replicate.

Spyware

Spyware is a particularly insidious form of virus, although major software makers are in the process of incorporating (and in some cases, already have incorporated) some spyware features into legitimate software. Spyware doesn't try to damage your system; it spies on your activities and then communicates surreptitiously with its owner about you (hence the "spy" part of the name). Because software on many Windows systems has free rein across the system, spyware often can track not only every keystroke you make, but also what software is installed on your system (and what music files you've downloaded), and then report this information back to its maker. That company then sells information about your Web page visiting habits to marketing services or advertisers who might be interested in knowing this information.

Cross-Reference

In Chapter 8, I discuss how to use anti-spyware utilities to remove this pesky stuff from your PC. Odds are high this information will be helpful to you, because some of the major direct-download sites' software spies on you, and they tell you right in their privacy agreement that they're going to. In fact, a recent Kazaa installation I performed—without any file transfers, mind you—was quickly followed by a PestPatrol session that found no less than 380 spyware files!

Popups and services

You've probably noticed that when you visit some Web sites, additional windows of Internet Explorer will open with advertisements. These windows may not have the usual Internet Explorer controls, may be hard to close, and may give rise to even more windows. This annoying practice is common.

These popups are possible because Internet Explorer is capable of running JavaScripts, and JavaScripts are capable of spawning additional instances of Internet Explorer. The concept here is not bad and actually can be helpful in many circumstances (this is often how you can click on an image and have a larger version of it appear in its own little window). But it can be abused, and it's quite a nuisance if unending windows keep appearing until you shut down the computer or your browser is crippled.

Several free pop-up blockers are available. Some are part of toolbars where additional functions, such as search and one-click access to other services, are available. If you are running Internet Explorer, the Yahoo Toolbar (`http://companion.yahoo.com/`) and Google Toolbar (`http://toolbar.google.com`) are two of the best.

After you download these utilities, each will automatically itself into Internet Explorer. Then, when you run IE (but not other browsers), and you encounter a meddlesome pop-up ad, your new pop-up blocker will prevent it from appearing on your screen (see Figure 5-5).

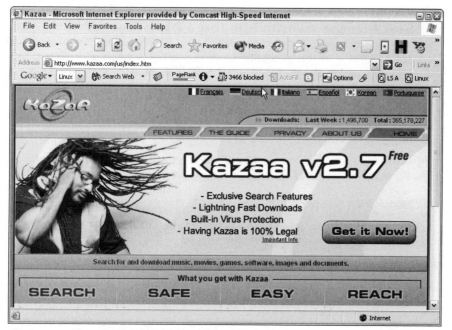

Figure 5-5: The Google pop-up blocker is doing its job.

Did you know that most recent versions of Windows also automatically run a service named Messenger, and Messenger constantly listens for outside communications? Some folks take advantage of this fact to send you popup messages, but not Internet Explorer popups. Messenger popups are gray and look just like those little boxes that popup when you use a piece of ordinary software and you do something questionable like try to save a file with the same name as an existing file (see Figure 5-6).

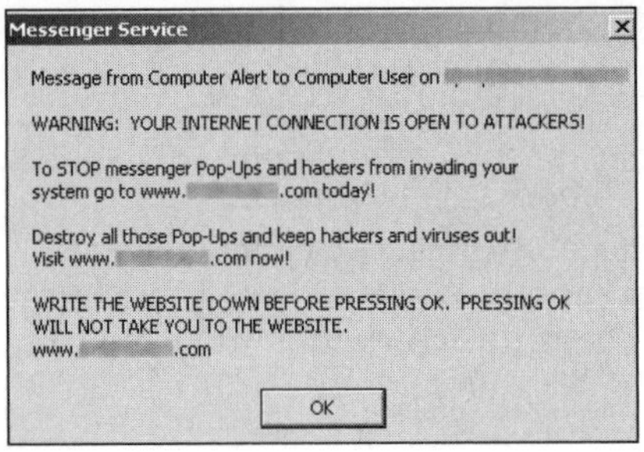

Figure 5-6: A Messenger popup

The Messenger service was designed to make it easy for a network administrator to send a message to everyone on a network, and because many networks use IP addresses to identify users, the ability to send messages via IP address was added to Messenger. This has the unintended side effect of allowing software developers to easily write software that spews out millions of advertisements to anyone with an IP address who hasn't disabled Messenger service. Disabling Messenger is easy enough, but for unsophisticated users, having to figure it out can be quite frustrating, not to mention scary.

There's a way to turn off Messenger in XP and some other versions of Windows. Follow these steps to turn off Messenger in the popular XP Home Edition:

1. **Choose Start ⇨ Settings ⇨ Control Panel.** The Control Panel opens.

2. **Click the Windows Category view link in the left frame of the Control Panel.** The Windows Category view opens.

3. **In Windows Category view, choose Performance and Maintenance.**

4. **Click the Administrative Tools link.** The Administrative Tools menu opens.

5. **Double-click Services to open the Services menu.** Scroll down the list to Messenger.

6. **Right-click Messenger, and then choose Properties.** The Messenger Properties dialog box opens.

7. **In the Service status section of the General tab, click Stop.** This signals that you want to disable MSN Messenger. The Startup Type Scroll bar appears.

8. **Choose Disable from the Startup Type scroll bar, as shown in Figure 5-7.**

9. **Click OK.** Messenger is gone!

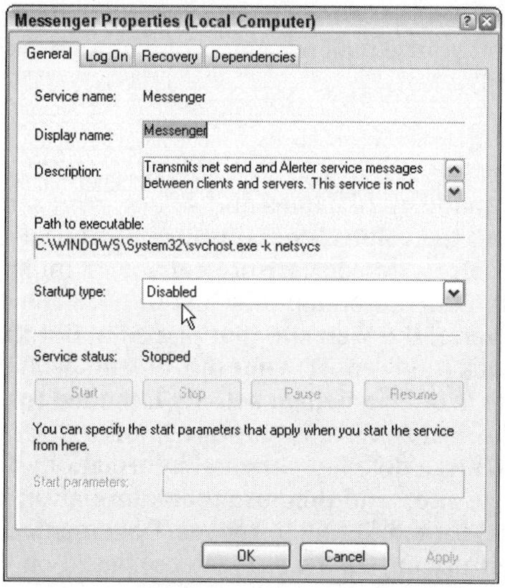

Figure 5-7: Messenger is being disabled.

E-mail

The world seems to revolve around e-mail these days. In just a few short years, the entire communications landscape has changed, and few people in the modern world try to conduct their lives without an e-mail address (or multiple e-mail addresses).

E-mail messages are plain text, and e-mail clients are fairly good about maintaining security. But e-mail messages can carry attachments, and those attachments can contain viruses or other disturbing material.

And even though e-mail messages are plain text, instances of a plain text e-mail message spreading infections without even being opened in the normal sense have been documented.

The arguably larger problem is junk e-mail called spam. Some authorities estimate that spam now constitutes more than 50 percent of all e-mail traffic, and it's growing at a tremendous rate. Although diligent application of spam filtering software (at both the server and client levels) helps stem the tide, some experts fear that the amount of spam sent and received will, at some point, simply overwhelm the ability of users to find legitimate mail, thereby rendering e-mail useless. If you think that's not a serious problem, just try turning off your e-mail (or your company's e-mail) for a couple days and watch the reaction.

Cookies

Cookies are simply short strings of text made up of names and values. For example, a cookie might be named "username" and the value it contains may be your user-name on a particular Web site. By themselves, cookies are not capable of inflicting damage to your system because they don't do anything; they just provide the contents of the cookie back to the Web server of the Web site that placed it. But this is enough information for a Web site to track (and report) your movements while on that Web site. Tracking your movements is often a benign activity intended to enhance your user experience at the site. But some sites capture information about your movements, combine it with much more detailed personal information (if, for example, you ever bought anything at the site), and then use that information internally (or sell it to third-party companies) for marketing purposes. Documented cases exist of companies modifying their pricing (increasing prices) based on their Web server detecting a cookie that tells it the user has little resistance to higher prices!

Some cookies are short lived, and some last essentially forever. You can eliminate existing cookies by clearing them out of your cache, but the next time you visit a particular site, it will probably place the same cookie again unless you turn off cookie acceptance in your browser.

Cookies have some security risk, but in fact, they can be helpful. Say you register with a legal music download site. Cookies save your user ID, password and other informantion such as credit card number, even your music preferences. You may get a bit more privacy turning them off, but in doing so, there are inconveniences. For example, you will have to reenter all your personal informantion each time you log on or attempt to make a purchase. It is your decision: If you keep cookies around, your computer's security may be slightly more vulnerable, but you may have to jump through extra hoops to remember that password you need to log on to that digital download site.

Trojan horses

The term Trojan horse identifies a method for inserting a virus rather than a piece of evil software. Like the ancient story of the Greeks winning the Trojan War by hiding in a hollow wooden horse and sneaking into the city, a virus spread by a Trojan horse sneaks into your computer masquerading as something benign, like a simple Web page. When you visit the Web page, the virus uses common capabilities of your browser (such as Internet Explorer) to infect your computer.

How the Bad Stuff Gets to Your PC

Unless you happen to be running some sort of server software on your computer, it's unlikely that a virus could sneak in simply by sending input to you. But even desktop operating systems are increasingly running server software (services) that listens faithfully for outside communications. If these services are running and listening, ill-intentioned hackers and crackers can take advantage of that to "ping" your system and possibly invade it. And, when you connect to the Internet or other computers on a network, you are initiating communications that may make your system vulnerable. So consider the ways in which your computer makes itself available to other computers on the network.

Meet the Bad Folks

Hackers, hoaxers, scam artists, and identity thieves are as prevalent in the online world as in the "real" world. These sections describe their nefarious exploits, and how you can stay clear of them.

Hackers and crackers

Not every programmer is a hacker, not every hacker is a cracker, and not all those who inhabit the world of computer viruses have evil intent. In this section, you'll look at some interesting ways in which hackers view themselves, which should give you more insight as to how to protect yourself.

The term hacking applies to many arenas, not just software and computers. Hacking, in its present form, means experimenting with any subject (physical, theoretical, or purely intellectual) and discovering ways to take the subject beyond the subject's presently understood limits. For example, there are folks who specialize in hacking digital cameras for better images.

Software hackers like to know everything about how the software they use works, what the software's weaknesses are, and what it can do that wasn't intended by the developers. This includes finding and documenting security holes. But for hackers, the fact that a security hole exists is amusing, not cause for criminal action.

Crackers are not respected by hackers, because crackers don't really know much about software, they just abuse toolkits and scripts for the thrill of illegal entry to private computer systems or for making illegal long distance calls. They also often end up causing serious damage, paying hefty fines, or even spending time in jail.

Scam artists

Scam artists online are the same as scam artists anywhere. They seek to defraud unsuspecting folks by constructing an elaborate lie (the scam) in which the "mark" (you) will receive a windfall in exchange for helping the scam artist. One common thread of scams is that you will receive a large amount of undeserved money; scams appeal to greed.

A common Internet-based scam is the e-mail from a Nigerian general or some other figure in authority in a small African country. The proposition varies, but is based around the notion that a very large sum of money is waiting to be claimed and that the general can't claim it due to being a government official, and he needs a third party (you) to provide a bank account number so the proceeds can be claimed by you and deposited in your bank account. You turn over the money to the general in exchange for a sum that he pays you for your assistance.

Of course, after they get your bank account information, they empty the account, and you never hear from them again. Like other scams, this one relies on your thinking that you'll receive a large amount of money that isn't really due you. The moral of the story is, never give out personal information unless you're sure there's a legitimate reason, and don't believe everything you hear, particularly when it sounds too good to be true.

If you get a message that you suspect may be a scam, look for these things:

✦ **Misspellings and/or poor punctuation and poor use of English.**

✦ **A message that promises that you can make a large amount of money in a short period of time, without doing anything (see Figure 5-8).**

✦ **Nothing that identifies the sender of the message with a name, place of origin, or normal contact information.**

✦ **The "greed" hazard.** For example, an e-mail message may imply that you are not rightfully entitled to the money it mentions, so it asks you to keep the message secret until they verify your information.

✦ **The owner of the domain name it originated from.** Check the header information of the e-mail message in question to see what address it came from, and then check that address.

Tip   To check header information in Microsoft Outlook, right-click the message's subject line when the message is closed. The information displayed should identify the real sender.

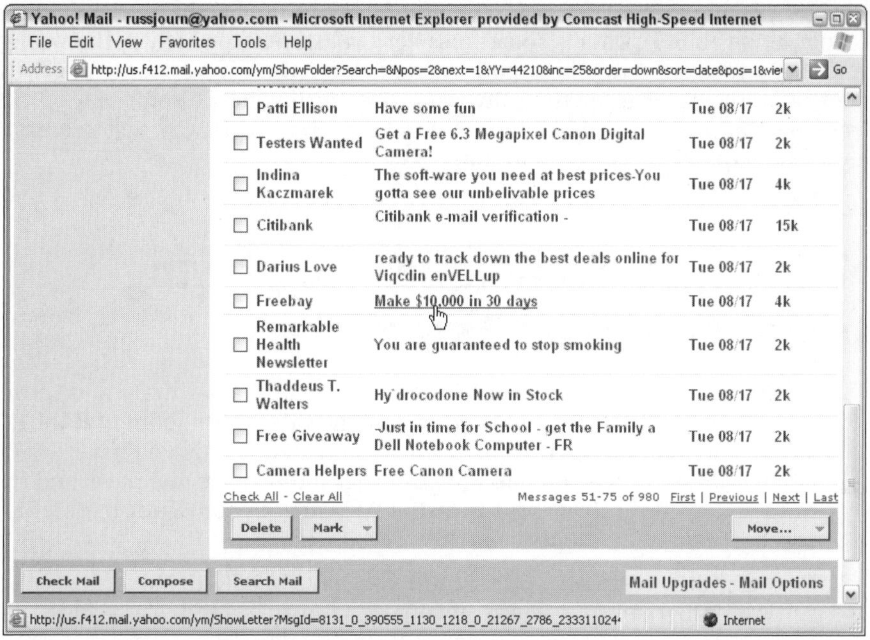

Figure 5-8: $10,000 in 30 days? Well, show us the money.

Identity thieves

The Nigerian general (or Nigerian letter, as it is sometimes called) is a scam that attempts to get personal information for illegitimate and illegal purposes. As such, it is related to another problem of greater proportions: identity theft.

The problem of identity theft, overall, is more than just someone abusing your credit cards or bank accounts. An unscrupulous person can do many things if they know enough of your personal information. For example, they could possibly trick a friend or relative of yours into providing even more information either about you or them, which furthers the damage done.

But the main problem with identity theft remains the abuse of your finances. With the right information, a crook can gain access to your credit cards, and order 500 songs from your iTunes account. Not fun.

Speaking of data, that's what makes your computer a target (that and more recently, its computing ability). Data is sometimes very valuable, especially in the wrong hands. You don't want to lose it, and you don't want the wrong people to gain it. And here's something else you really want to know: If you lose some of it or the wrong person gets access to it, you want to know that right away, just in case there's something you can do about it.

Eight Essential Techniques for Staying on Top of Computer Threats

1. **Document your hardware and OS.** Make a list of the hardware and OS you're running, especially the speed and type of the CPU, the amount of RAM, the size of your hard drive, the type of video and audio cards you have and how much RAM they have, the monitor and speaker systems you have, and the settings you're currently using. Check the Web site of your OS for updates and patches, especially security patches, regularly.

2. **Document the software applications you have installed.** Make a list of your software programs and where on your PC they are stored. Many anti-virus programs will only search your main hard drive by default, so if the problem is in a program on another drive (such as D: drive), you will want your anti-virus utility to search that area of your PC as well.

3. **Keep your executable files handy.** These files, marked .exe, typically are the main files for software and other utilities you have downloaded and purchased over the Web. If a virus or worm corrupts your version of these programs, you can usually re-install them from the .exe file.

4. **Know how to use your file manager program.** Know how to change where files are saved when you're finished creating one. (Do you save everything in your My Documents folder?) Know how to find your files later; independent of opening the most recent documents or the program you created the file in.

5. **Know what kind of Internet connection you have.** Figure out how it works, and try the reverse lookup for your IP address to see if Web sites you connect to can identify you. Start by going to a site such as `http://remote.12dt.com/rns/` and doing what is called a reverse DNS lookup. This online service gets your current IP address from your browser, and then searches a database of IP addresses to tell to whom that address is assigned. If you're on a DSL line, you may see your own name appear; if you're on a modem or cable modem, you'll see the name of your ISP. Then go to a site that displays a list of what your browser sends to the server to find out what the server knows about you (one such site is `http://www.lib.washington.edu/asp/browser/servar.asp`). A quick test could reveal that the server knows where you came from (the REMOTE-ADDR), as well as the type of browser you're using (the HTTP_USER_AGENT), and quite a bit more information as well.

6. **Learn to search the Internet safely and efficiently.** Find and put in your Favorites list sites that have music and video files, and sites that review new releases or provide news about sites that have music and video. Learn the terms and industry jargon about the file types you seek.

7. **Learn about bad software, software incompatibilities, viruses, worms, and spyware.** Two useful sites are anti-virus software maker McAfee's `www.mcafee.com` and Symantec's Security Response page at `http://securityresponse.symantec.com/`.

8. **Stay abreast of laws affecting your downloading and use of music and video.** Things are changing pretty rapidly still. Two useful news sites to keep up with the latest developments are Wired News (`www.wired.com/news`) and CNet's News.com (`www.news.com`)

Summary

In this chapter, I discussed the nature of the threats facing your computer and how spyware, viruses, worms, and other evils that can be transmitted through digital downloads and file-sharing can afflict your PC. By introducing you to the tactics of scam artists and crackers, I also discussed the "human" face of PC threats. Most importantly, you had the opportunity to review some effective countermeasures available—ranging from inexpensive and easy-to-use software to a good dose of common sense.

✦   ✦   ✦

Protecting Yourself and Your Computer

◆ ◆ ◆ ◆

In This Chapter

Creating a prevention strategy

Configuring spam-fighting software tools

Learning how to outsmart the spammers

Adjusting your operating system's security settings

◆ ◆ ◆ ◆

When you set out to download or share digital music or video files, there are many avenues by which your computer and your personal data can be compromised. That's why you need to be aware of additional ways to protect your PC.

Ways to Protect Yourself

Not all entry points to your computer involve Internet access or inserting disks into your computer. Protecting yourself involves knowledge of the tricks used to invade your privacy, and then outsmarting your unseen adversaries. In previous chapters, we have explored the problems and solutions for such privacy and security abuses such as spyware, identity theft, and computer viruses. In this chapter, I cover additional steps you can take to make your own computer more secure and the best techniques for making sure you remain secure.

Although you can often repair damage done by viruses, it is far better to prevent damage in the first place. For each threat to your computer, there are preventive measures you can take that are very effective, though not perfect. Downloading or sharing music and video files can be quite fun and rewarding, as you've seen in previous chapters; taking a few preventive measures is a small price to pay for peace of mind as you add to your collection.

As you are now aware, the threats to your computer evolve over time, so, unfortunately, protecting your computer is not a matter of simply installing some software or a firewall and forgetting about it. The development of a prevention strategy is ongoing and involves active participation on your part.

Start by taking a look at what you can do to protect yourself from one of the most prevalent methods of spreading viruses these days — your e-mail.

Securing your e-mail

Some file-sharing services, especially those that do not charge you for sharing and downloading files, are notorious for selling your e-mail contact information to third parties. Many such services say they refrain from doing so without your consent, but based on my personal experience, there seems to be a direct conduit between these services and the third party marketers with which they do business.

These third parties, in turn, are not likely to be the shining lights of private-sector innovation. These entities are more the type that will flood your e-mail inbox with pitches for fishy investment schemes, body enhancements, and so forth.

Even legitimate digital-download services sometimes sell your e-mail contact information to third parties. The companies they do business with are somewhat more on the level, but let me put it this way: We don't all want to be bombarded with pitches for the latest fashions and vacation packages.

Is there a happy medium? Can you derive intended benefits from music download sites *without* being besieged by spam? Yes, you can, and in the next section, I'll tell you how.

Spam

Spam, of course, is the common name for unsolicited commercial e-mail. Spam actually started as off-topic newsgroup postings when the Internet was still young, but a few enterprising individuals quickly invented methods for spreading spam via e-mail, and now e-mail is the most common form of spam.

The term spam has broadened to include e-mail spam, newsgroup spam, and even search engine spam, which is the practice of employing HTML coding or keyword tricks to gain an unfair ranking on search engines.

The tough thing about spam is that it's very difficult, in the final analysis, to pro-grammatically determine what is spam and what isn't. Although you all know it when you see it, you have the advantage of being human and being able to quickly recognize things. Computers, on the other hand, still have quite limited recognition capability. Computers are very good at recognizing well-defined things, but rather poor at recognizing "fuzzy" things.

There's an easy solution that would stop all spam, all junk mail, and telemarketing calls as well. If everyone just stopped responding completely, these things would dry up and blow away. It's those few suckers who respond that make the telemarketers and spammers continue, and the dollars the relative handful of overly trusting recipients shell out pay for all the hassle the rest of us face.

So why do you have to be so careful about spam? First off, spam may eventually degrade your ability to communicate by e-mail to the point that you're forced back to some less effective, more costly method. Second, if you don't read the privacy policy or terms and conditions of music and video Web site services you've sub-scribed to (or use), your e-mail address may be passed around like a bad penny. And third, some spam contains viruses, worms, and other malicious software.

Anti-spam software

Your most effective anti-spam software policy will be to install spam-fighting soft-ware on your computer. If you download or swap files on a site that required you to fill out a registration form with your e-mail address, then downloading and installing one of several spam-battlers will save you lots of time perusing through your inbox—separating the legitimate communications from the garbage.

If you use e-mail for business and are interested in receiving e-mail from a variety of sources (especially repetitive, marketing-oriented e-mail newsletters that may resemble spam quite closely), your best bet may be to simply make sure that all anti-spam software is set to mark suspicious messages as "suspected spam."

You can use the filtering capabilities of most e-mail clients to automatically set aside suspected spam in a folder all its own. Then, if you think you might have missed an important e-mail, you can always look in that folder and quickly scan down the subject lines for the missing message.

A quick search on Google for "anti-spam software" reveals a number of packages designed to clean or filter your e-mail and thus protect your system as well as relieve you of spam overload. The MailWasher Pro package is appealing, as well as is the Email Remover package.

You can find the MailWasher Pro anti-spam application at `www.mailwasher.net` (see Figure 6-1). It is made by a company named FireTrust in New Zealand and has received some great testimonials.

After installation, the application checks your e-mail (you can set up multiple e-mail accounts in the package) before your ordinary e-mail client does, and it removes spam while fixing or deleting viruses from the mail. It also has an archiving facility to forward suspect e-mails instead of deleting them, just in case. And the site claims that the program contains no spyware or tracking software and that they don't share your personal information with anyone. The program is free for a 30-day trial, after which time it costs $37 US to purchase.

The software is simple to install. You simply download the install file (`mailwasher_pro41.exe`), which is a little under 3MB. After you download the install file, you double-click it and some install screens appear. These screens are very basic, providing the license agreement and the location to which the application will be installed. You can click through without changing the defaults if you like.

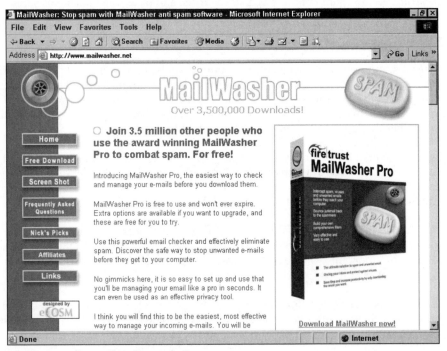

Figure 6-1: The MailWasher Web site

Tip   You should always read the license agreement whenever you download software, but with MailWasher, the agreement includes information about a subscription service called FirstAlert! to which you can subscribe for $7 per year. Apparently, you can forward spam messages to the service to be included in its database so everyone using FirstAlert! can be warned of spam messages.

After you're finished with the install screens, the setup screen (see Figure 6-2) appears. Several steps to perform are outlined on this screen, starting with identifying e-mail accounts you'd like it to check.

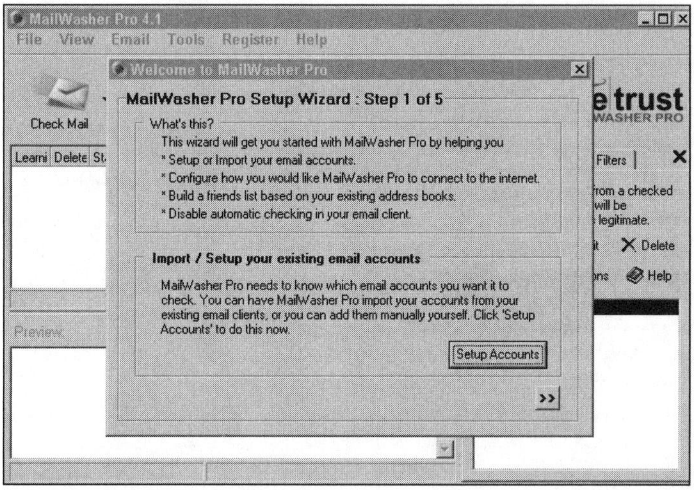

Figure 6-2: The MailWasher Pro setup screen

To setup the e-mail address to check, click the Setup Accounts button. You'll see a dialog box in which you can add accounts to MailWasher Pro, as shown in Figure 6-3.

When you click the Add button, another small dialog box (shown in Figure 6-4) appears asking you to choose which type of e-mail server you have (POP3 is very common; if you don't know for sure, you can often check your own e-mail client to see which server you currently have set up). Enter the type of server (such as POP3), the name of the server (such as my_email_server.com), and your username and password. Then click over to the Bounce tab, disable bouncing, and close the dialog box.

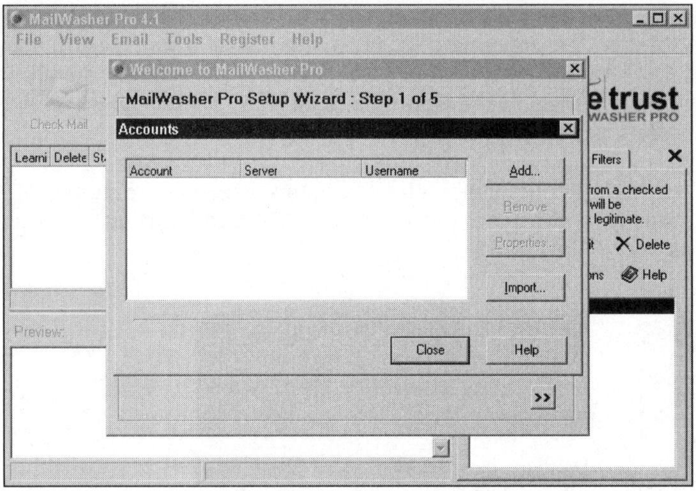

Figure 6-3: The Add Account dialog box in MailWasher Pro

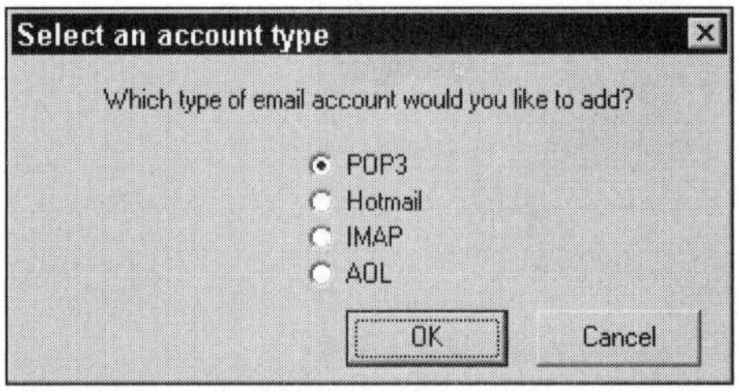

Figure 6-4: Choosing your e-mail server type

Next, a screen appears allowing you to select whether the application should assume that you're online or dial in (or not) when checking e-mail. Choose the appropriate option, and click the right arrows to go to the next screen.

The application next offers you the opportunity to import your address book so it can begin maintaining a list of "trusted" e-mail addresses (see Figure 6-5). Import your address book if you want to, and then click the right arrow again.

The next screen, shown in Figure 6-6, offers you the option of archiving e-mails (in case of accidental deletion, for example). To enable this option, enter an e-mail address to send archived e-mails to and the name of your sending e-mail server (the SMTP server). Click the right arrow again to proceed.

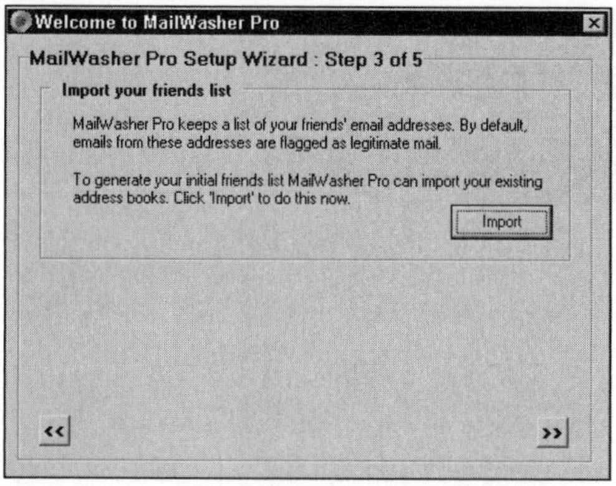

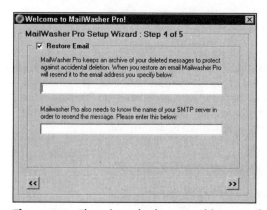

Figure 6-5: Importing your address book

Figure 6-6: Choosing whether to archive e-mails

The final screen contains a link to the firetrust.com site on one of the tech support pages showing you how to disable automatic e-mail checking in your e-mail client so that MailWasher has a chance to pre-filter and clean the mail before your e-mail client does. If you have automatic e-mail checking enabled on your e-mail client, turn this feature off using one of the procedures outlined on the tech support page.

You should now be at the main MailWasher screen. You can click the check mail button to begin the process of screening and filtering your e-mail. If you have entered a valid e-mail server name and e-mail address, the checking process should proceed smoothly; if either one is not correct, you'll see the screen shown in Figure 6-7.

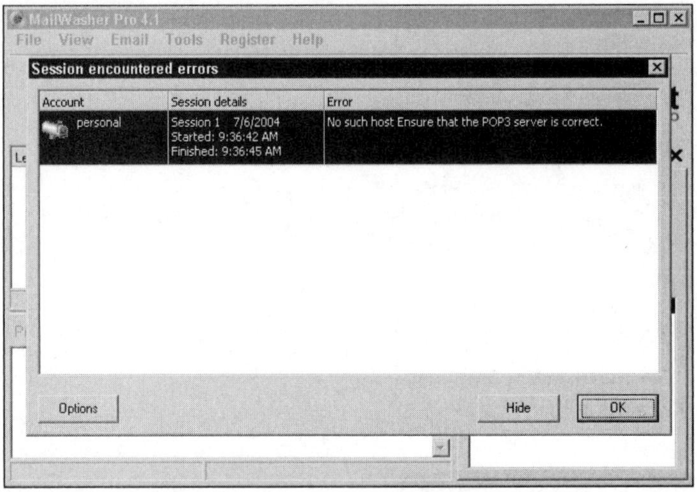

Figure 6-7: MailWasher Pro session errors log

After checking e-mail, you can view the Statistics screen (choose Tools ➪ Statistics from the menu), shown in Figure 6-8. As you can see from the figure, you'll find complete statistics about all the e-mail and spam that has been sent. The application applies a Bayesian Filter, a cool technique that catches spam messages that try to avoid detection by altering the spelling of known spam words.

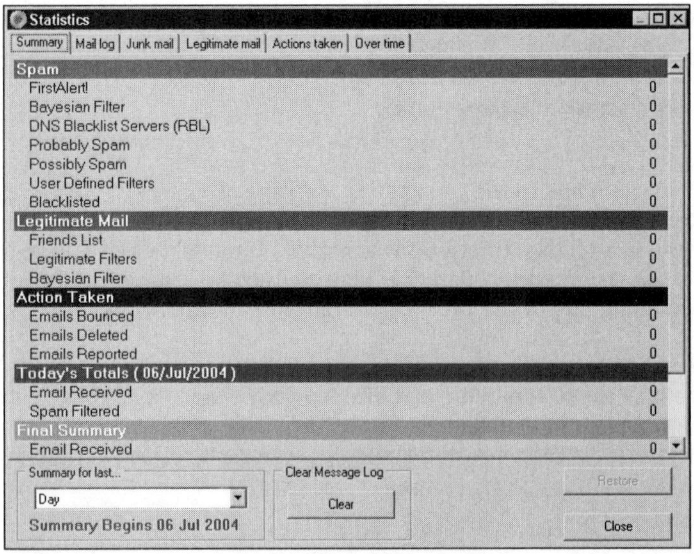

Figure 6-8: Spam Statistics in MailWasher Pro

What does this mean for the digital downloader or file-swapper? Well, if you have downloaded tracks from heavy metal acts, music industry and advertising demographers may assume that you are in your late teens to early twenties, are male, and like to party hearty. Perhaps you do: That's your business. Yet if some "business" that obtained your e-mail address from one of these file-swapping services tries to send you an e-mail message with a topic line of "che!ap sof!ware" or "corny babs" (instead of the more explicit terminology) well, then, that Bayesian Filter will get right on the case. If, for whatever reason, the Bayesian Filter does not intercept the suspect e-mail, just go ahead and delete the message.

File-swapping services, as well as the Web sites from which you download these programs and individual digital music and video files, are notorious for security holes. These holes can leave you vulnerable when you click on these Web sites, or when you receive e-mail from the file-swapping service itself, or when third-party "businesses" are in cahoots with the file-swapping companies whose software you've installed and are using. In this next section, I discuss further strategies for keeping your Web-browsing and e-mail sessions clear of privacy and security gremlins that can be planted on your PC by or via unscrupulous digital download sites.

Web-browsing security

File-swapping services, as well as the Web sites from which you download these programs and individual digital music and video files, are notorious for security holes. These holes can leave you vulnerable when you click on these Web sites, or when you receive e-mail from the file-swapping service itself, or when third-party "businesses" are in cahoots with the file-swapping companies whose software you've installed and are using. In this next section, I discuss further strategies for keeping your Web-browsing and e-mail sessions clear of privacy and security gremlins that can be planted on your PC by or via unscrupulous digital download sites.

In Windows, you can adjust your Security settings from the Internet Options dialog box. You can display the dialog box for setting Internet Options by choosing Start ⇨ Control Panel from the desktop and then going to Classic view. Then double-click the Internet Options icon. The dialog box in Figure 6-9 appears.

Click the Security tab, as shown in Figure 6-10, and you'll see all the security settings available. Security settings are divided into zones, and you can change the settings for any of the zones individually. Click the Custom Settings button to view and/or change settings for the zone you select.

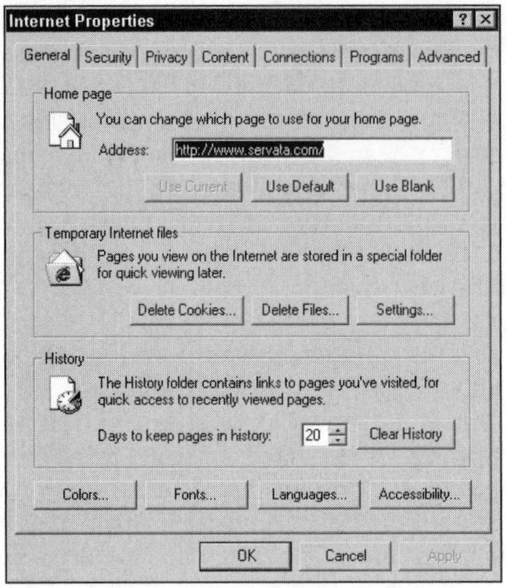

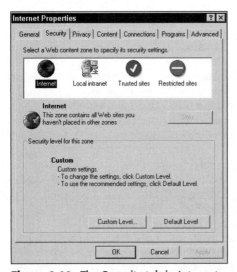

Figure 6-9: Internet Options in Windows

Figure 6-10: The Security tab in Internet Options

The default setting for the Internet zone may not be restrictive enough for you. These settings may be of concern to you:

✦ **Download signed ActiveX controls.** ActiveX controls have the ability to perform actions that may not be desirable. This setting is set to Prompt by default, but you may want to set it to Disable.

✦ **Active Scripting and Scripting of Java Applets.** You may want to set these to Disable. Be aware, though, that if you take this step, you will have additional security, but your online experience may suffer. Disabling Active X and Java may cause your PC to have difficulty displaying some of the animations and interactive features that some digital music sites offer. Again, this is your choice.

On the Privacy tab, you have several options for controlling how cookies are used to collect information about you. For example, the High setting blocks cookies that do not have a compact (well-defined) privacy policy and thwarts cookies that use personally identifiable information (such as your e-mail address) without your consent.

Although the Highest setting blocks all cookies, some cookies are helpful. To balance your privacy concerns with the usability you expect from digital download and related Web sites, I recommend that you choose the Privacy tab's High setting. To apply this setting in the Internet Options dialog box, click the Privacy tab, move the slide bar to High, and then click Apply (see Figure 6-11).

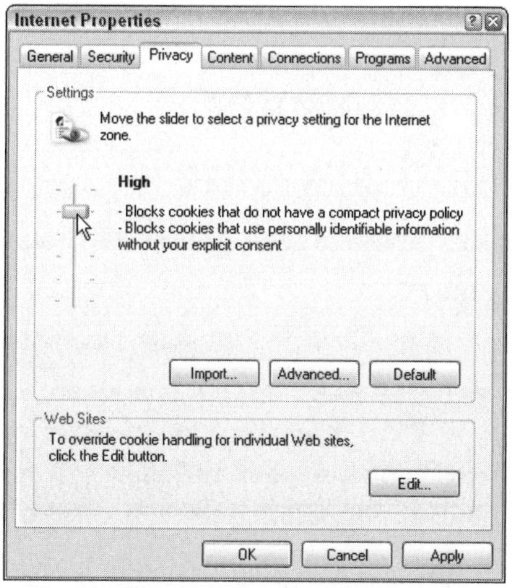

Figure 6-11: Setting the Privacy level to High

On the Advanced tab are several more Security options that you can enable or disable if you like. Some are directly related to your online digital music or video experience. If you click the Advanced tab and scroll down the Internet Properties box with the slider, you will encounter a Multimedia area (see Figure 6-12). It would be an excess of caution to disarm some of these necessary features, such as the ability to play sounds, animations, or video in Web pages. It's perfectly OK, even preferable, to leave these options on. To do so, simply click on the check box next to each of these options.

Figure 6-12: The Multimedia options in Windows XP's Advanced Security tab

Ten Ways to Protect Your Computer from Suspicious E-mail and Spyware

1. Understand the type of e-mail server you use to send and receive e-mail.

2. Install spam-fighting software on your PC.

3. Configure your anti-spam software to flag all suspect messages as spam.

4. Set up your anti-spam software to group all suspect spam in a separate folder.

5. Import your e-mail program's address book into your anti-spam software program, so your program will be able to recognize legitimate e-mail addresses you use regularly.

6. Understand that some spammers try to get around spam filters by sending messages with deliberate misspellings.

7. Familiarize yourself with your operating system's security settings.

8. Set up your operating system to disable automatic loading of Active X controls.

9. Set up your operating system to disable active scripting of Java applets.

10. Set your operating system's Privacy level to high.

Summary

In this chapter, I've covered how to protect your desktop computer system from common threats. You especially should be aware of the threats to your system and take steps to protect yourself when you download or share files with others. Music and video files are common sources of problems, especially when they are shared.

E-mail and instant messaging software now provide an avenue for spreading viruses, Trojan horses, worms, and other dangerous or malicious software. You can stop spam and filter e-mail messages using anti-spam software, and you can detect and clean viruses from your machine with anti-virus software. Often, you can find suitable software for these purposes for free or at very low cost, and they run quite nicely.

You can also prevent the installation of spyware by installing anti-spyware programs. But be aware that doing so may impede your use of some common file-sharing programs (although you may want to switch to programs that don't load your computer with spyware or adware in the first place).

A key part of protecting your system is setting up good housekeeping procedures in the first place: organizing your files, cleaning out unused files, turning off unnecessary services, and regularly backing up your files and practicing restoring files.

✦   ✦   ✦

Protecting Your Network

✦   ✦   ✦   ✦

In This Chapter

Understanding communication protocols

Examining network types

Recognizing weak points and attacks in networks

Preventing and recovering from attacks

✦   ✦   ✦   ✦

When you download or swap digital music or video files, many of you now perform these actions on a network. These networks can be at home, at school, or even at work. The Internet that you use to access these files is, of course, a network as well.

Because so many of your digital communications occur on or via networks, some basic information about network and Internet security will be useful to you as you endeavor to keep your PC safe from harm that lurks either on PCs connected directly to yours, or on the biggest of all networks—the Internet.

Being online implies a network connection of some kind. Whether you have a cable modem or a dial-up, DSL, LAN (local area network), or WAN (wide area network) connection, or are connecting wirelessly via a hotspot, in all cases you are connected to other computers and use some network protocol to effect communications.

In this book, I'm primarily interested in communications producing a downloaded music or video file, but the coverage I give to the subject of the Internet as a network will show you how to protect your PC from the hazards of this global network.

Understanding How the Internet Functions

Whether you are talking about the Internet, or just a local network that ties together a few of your PCs at work or school, all networks share a powerful commonality. All networks allow connections between computers via a physical link (this includes wires, optical fibers, and radio waves) that is used to send and receive bits. The physical portion of the network is not much different than any other common communications medium.

One thing that sets computer communications apart from broadcast radio and television, for example, is that signals are sent digitally. Digital signals can be switched, unlike analog radio and TV signals, which have no efficient switching capability built in.

The bits in a digital network signal are arranged in a specific pattern of headers and footers that help utility programs in your computer, servers along the way, and the receiving computer sort out which signals to receive and how to reconstruct them into the actual data payload.

For example, an e-mail message sent to you might consist of the actual text message, plus headers that tell the sending and receiving e-mail servers where the message came from, what time it was sent, who it is addressed to, and so on (see Figure 7-1).

When the e-mail message is broken down into packets, additional header and footer bits are added to tell forwarding servers which packets are part of the same e-mail, what sequence they go in, how long to keep relaying them if no receipt is acknowledged, and so on.

Physical connections

A network is often made up of hundreds or thousands of computers, and sometimes entire networks are connected to each other, creating *inter-networks* (the Internet is the largest inter-network). The speed and security with which your data packets travel between your computer and the server or personal computer on the other end are the responsibility of your ISP (and others). But that does not mean you are absolved from responsibility for the security of your own network-connected PC. Your primary concern is the speed and security of your direct connection to the Web sites to which you connect.

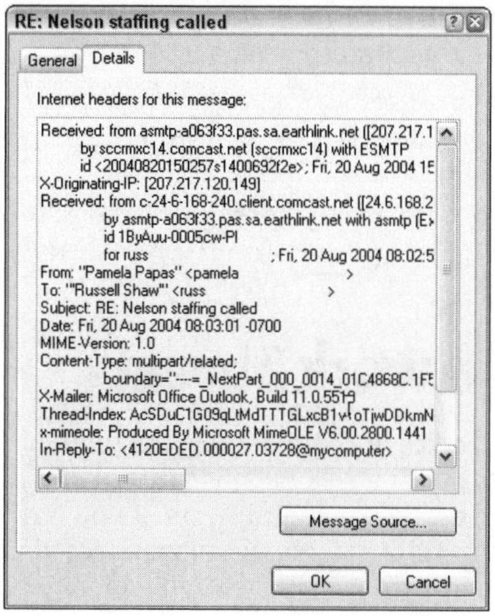

Figure 7-1: An Internet message header

The Internet as a network

The Internet is simply a large, interconnected network that uses a combination of TCP (transmission control protocol) and IP (Internet protocol) for communications. This set of protocols allows communications among a variety of computers and is decentralized, relying on no single central computer to manage the whole thing.

Here are the protocols that you use when you send and receive digital files, e-mail, and other information via the Internet.

✦ **TCP/IP.** Transmission control protocol/Internet protocol forms a communications foundation on top of which other protocols can be used for specific purposes. In short, this is the superhighway on which the cars (Web sites) and the people within them (the information) travel around the world, and to your PC.

✦ **HTTP.** Standing for hypertext transfer protocol, HTTP comprises Web servers and Web browsers sending and receiving Web pages and their associated files.

✦ **FTP.** File transfer protocol is used for transferring files, often directly between your computer system and another. When you send files in this manner, for example, this transmission may be occurring not through a Web site or e-mail, but from a directory on your hard drive to a directory on a company's computer system set up officially for that type of transfer.

✦ **SMTP.** Simple mail transport protocol actually is a TCP/IP protocol that defines the message format and the type of e-mail software (such as Outlook Express) that sends and receives e-mail. SMTP servers route messages through the Internet to mail servers at the recipient.

Understanding Internet Network Threats

Whatever network you happen to be connected to at the moment (and you may be connected to several, including the Internet) poses a risk because it provides an access point for malicious connections, viruses, hackers, and so on. If you have a dial-up Internet account, at least you have the ability to remain disconnected until you request a connection, but broadband connections (such as cable modems and DSL) remain connected whenever the computer is running.

And because traffic on connections is digital, there can be multiple connections to different hosts, ports, and applications running at the same time. Only your firewall can manage incoming and outgoing packets, and then only if it is properly configured.

Recognizing file-sharing security risks

In order to share files, you must allow external access to a portion of your hard drive. Although you can technically share files in many ways, for the purpose of this discussion file-sharing means creating a space on your hard drive that external users can read (and possibly write to or execute applications from as well).

Shared drives or folders broadcast the fact that they are shared to other users on the network. It's possible to limit these broadcasts, limit the permissions other users have to the shared space, and impose username and password requirements as well as user and group requirements on any user attempting to discover or use a shared drive or folder.

That said, if several users have access to a network-connected PC that you own or manage, you might want to ensure that your other users (family members or co-workers) have their own passwords and cannot find out yours. To do so, you will use Windows XP's User Accounts Management features.

In Windows XP, to manage the computer access of other users on your PC or network, perform the following steps:

1. **Choose Start ⇨ Control Panel ⇨ User Accounts.** The User Accounts box opens (see Figure 7-2).

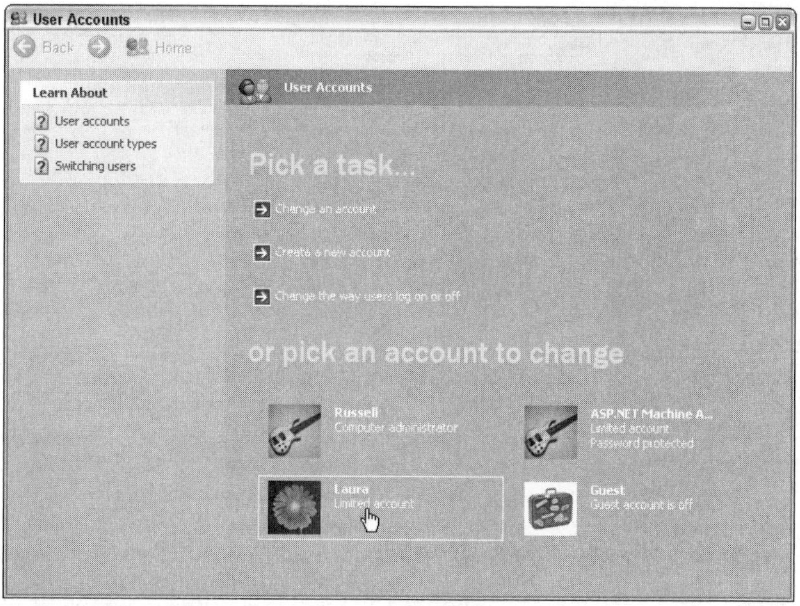

Figure 7-2: The Windows XP User Accounts box

2. **In the User Accounts dialog box, click the icon next to the name of the user you want to change settings for.** An account box opens, asking what you want to change about this user's account.

3. **In the account dialog box, click Change the Password.** A Change the Password dialog box opens.

4. **In the Change the Password dialog box, type a new Password and then type it again to confirm the new password.** You can also fill in the "Add a Password Hint" box.

5. **Click Change Password.** The user password is changed as shown in Figure 7-3.

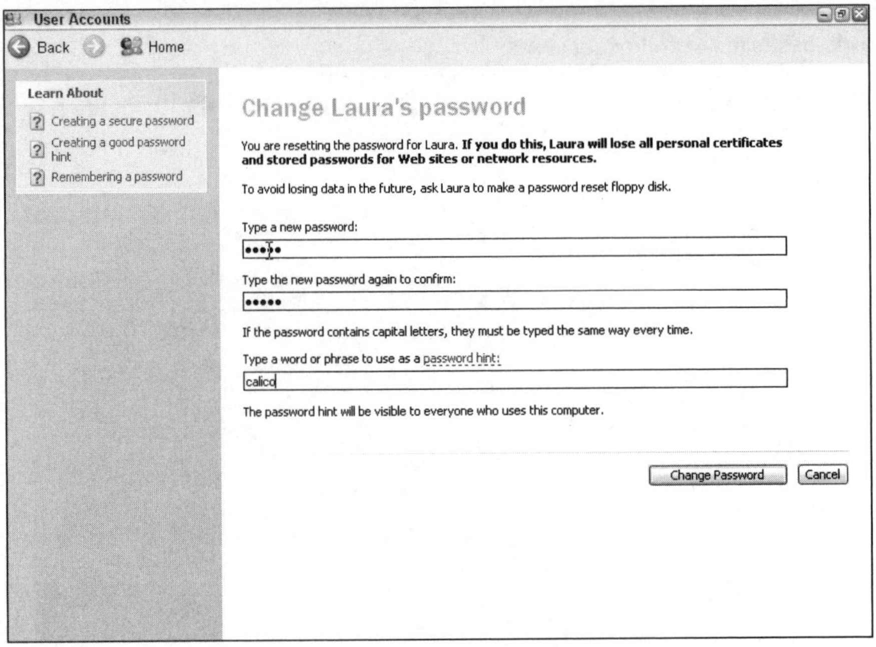

Figure 7-3: Changing the Password of another user on your PC or network

Server exploits and attacks

The term exploit refers to a method for attacking security vulnerability. An attack is the use of the exploit technique to gain access to the system (or at least try to). The first step in hacking into a computer system is to explore it for weaknesses. This is done by contacting the target system and waiting for its responses. If the target machine responds to queries on a particular port, it's very likely that a known service is running and listening to that port. Further queries can determine the identity of the service and whether it might have a weakness to exploit.

Exploits are known by a variety of interesting names and are discussed here.

Default or blank passwords

After you install an operating system, such as Windows XP, you may have several users who seek access to your individual or networked PC. You may forget to change the password for each user. If each user has the same password, even the same user name, they will be able to access each other's files and perhaps violate the privacy of family members or colleagues.

When you set up your Windows XP PC for multiple users, be sure to give each one his or her own password.

Password cracking

The simplest way to crack a password is to try all the combinations. It may take some time, but success is guaranteed in the long run. In fact, many encryption algorithms depend on the time it takes to try all the combinations for security. After all, if it would take uncounted numbers of years using all the computers currently available in the world doing nothing else but trying to crack your personal password, it's pretty unlikely to be broken (but random chance still offers a possibility).

But many folks still use simple, easy-to-break passwords based on known words or names. Making a password easy to remember is almost a guarantee that it can be broken easily.

Password cracking attacks include brute force, guessing, dictionary attacks, and some other more specialized techniques. Defenses against password cracking include limiting the number of times a password can be tried before the system enforces a timeout, or assigning passwords rather than allowing the user to choose them.

Do not give yourself a password that will be easy to guess, such as the numbers of your birthday or the name of your favorite pet. A string of seemingly nonsensical letters and numbers works best.

Spoofing

The term spoofing refers to the practice of inserting a fake return IP address or a fake return e-mail address into the header information sent with packets or with e-mails. Legitimate applications don't make it easy to do this, but there are many software tools available that allow the construction of any kind of packets or header. Such software actually has legitimate uses (mainly for network engineers trying to debug or resolve network and software problems), but unfortunately malicious users have also obtained it (or written it themselves).

Spoofing is a key part of many attacks, because it increases the difficulty of determining where an attack (or spam) is coming from.

Many spoof attacks come via e-mail. These often come in the form of messages that tell you either great news (you are entitled to a refund) or bad news (your account is overdue, and you must pay immediately). Often, the goal is to obtain your financial information—data that could be used to steal your identity.

Two of the easiest ways to spot spoof attacks are by gauging the tone of the message and checking for spelling errors. To go for the maximum impact, spoofers may add a note of urgency to your e-mail subject line. Spelling mistakes can indicate one or, possibly, two things. Either the e-mail was sent from a nation where excellent English spellers are not in abundance, or the spelling of a come-on word was changed to avoid spam filters. For example, a subject line might say "delinquant accownt" (instead of "delinquent account").

Sometimes, spoof e-mail can also carry a link to a Web site with an address that sounds just like the legitimate site it purports to be. If you are suspicious, open your Web browser and type in the "real" Web address. If this address does not match the one you were sent in an e-mail, then someone has tried to spoof you.

Securing Your Network: Keeping the Bad Guys Out

Security on a network (or even on a single computer) is difficult because although you want to keep the bad guys out, you also want to make sure that the system doesn't become unusable for the good guys. You could make a perfectly secure system, but no one would be able to use it at all. Anytime you open up a system or network to even one user, there's a chance that an unauthorized user could gain access.

So what to do? A comprehensive strategy, including running properly configured firewalls, good anti-virus, anti-spam, anti-popup, and other software while keeping passwords separate and hard to guess, will make your system less likely to be cracked.

Cross-Reference   Firewalls, plus anti-virus, anti-spam, and anti-popup utilities are discussed at length in Chapters 5 and 6.

Be safe by visiting encrypted Web sites

Encryption is the practice of encoding data such that only an approved receiver (one with the key) can decode the data. Encryption methods vary; some are more difficult to break than others, and they all create some overhead as data goes through an extra processing step at each end. But modern encryption schemes are considered to work quite well, and if enough bits are used, they are considered to be unbreakable (at least within the next few billion years).

The whole point of encryption is to disguise your data as it passes through networks, so that even if it is intercepted, the unauthorized receiver will not be able to make use of it. For example, when you use a Web site running Secure Sockets Layer (SSL), the data you submit in a Web page form is encrypted and then decrypted by the Web server on the other end.

Because of the safeguards involved in this procedure, it's very unlikely that anyone who happens to intercept your packets will be able to make sense of them.

Note   When an SSL session is started, the server sends its public key to your SSL-enabled browser, such as Internet Explorer. Your browser then uses the public key to send a randomly generated secret key back to the server in order to have a secret key exchange for that session.

It's easy to tell an encrypted Web site from a non-encrypted one. In Internet Explorer, for example, sites that encrypt their data display a lock on the bottom toolbar (see Figure 7-4). If you are considering using a Web site for any commercial purpose whatsoever — even to order a 99-cent music track — look for the encryption lock.

Physical security and firewalls

In an office or school computer network, firewalls are hardware and software barriers structured to keep unauthorized users or hackers out. On your own Internet-connected PC, software firewalls are useful for much the same purpose. They keep prying digital eyes away from snooping in on your network, planting viruses, or even extracting information that could be used to send you spam or, far worse, to steal some of your personally identifiable information.

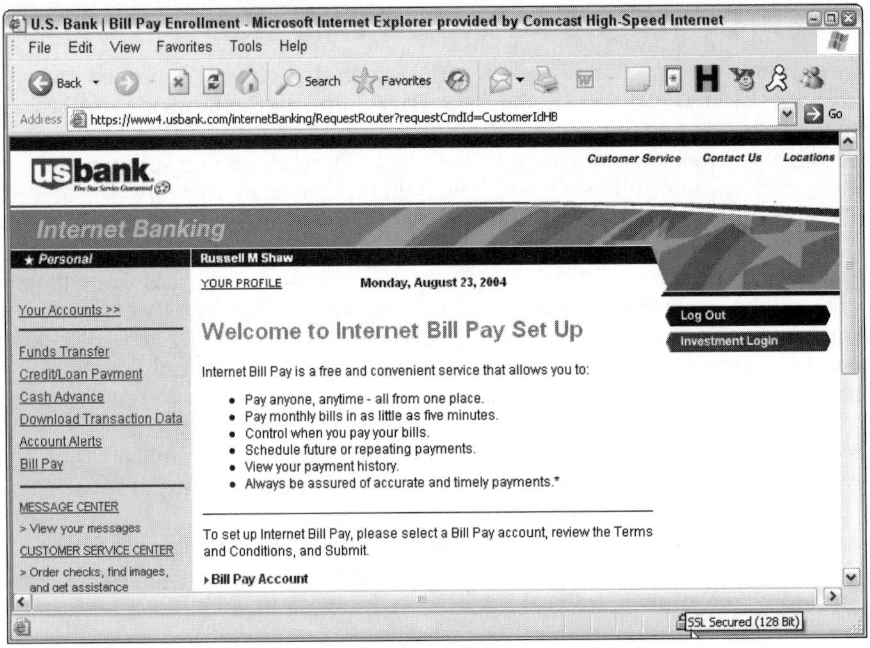

Figure 7-4: The lock on the bottom toolbar indicates that this site uses SSL encryption.

Configuring a software firewall for your Internet-connected PC is easy. Several commercial programs are available, including Norton Personal Firewall (`www.symantec.com/sabu/nis/npf/`) and McAfee Personal Firewall (`www.mcafee.com/myapps/firewall/ov_firewall.asp`). If you are one of the many PC owners who use Windows XP, then you will be pleased to learn that the free Windows Service Pack 2 update, which you download and install on your PC, has a built-in firewall.

Follow these steps to configure Windows XP SP2's built-in firewall to protect your PC from Internet and other network attacks:

1. **Point your browser to the main Microsoft Windows Update page at** `http://windowsupdate.microsoft.com`. Accessing this page automatically allows Microsoft to check your PC for any available upgrades that you do not already have. If you are running the original Windows XP, or XZP SP1, you must install SP2 before you can complete these steps. Reboot your computer after the download completes.

Note

It can take almost an hour to download SP2 even on a fast connection. But the new built-in firewall that is part of SP2 makes the download process time well spent!

2. **Choose Start ➪ Control Panel, and click Windows Firewall.** The Windows Firewall opens (see Figure 7-5).

3. **Click the General tab, and click the On radio button.** This blocks all outside sources from connecting to your PC, except for those sources you specify when you are in the Exceptions tab view.

4. **Click OK, and then click the Exceptions tab.** The Exceptions tab view opens.

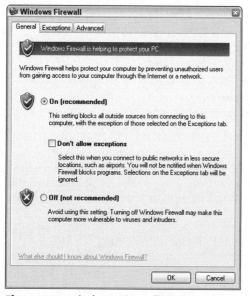

Figure 7-5: Windows Firewall opens

5. **Click the check box next to those applications that you do not want your firewall to block.** Because some music file services will not pass through firewalls, you should always check music file-sharing services in the group of applications you want your firewall to let through (see Figure 7-6).

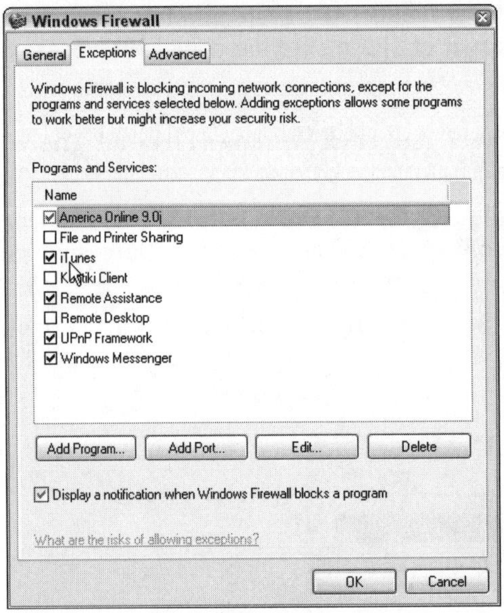

Figure 7-6: Setting up Windows Firewall to allow for unimpeded iTunes access

6. **Click OK.** You can also click the Advanced tab to make further modifications in your firewall. Because Windows XP's firewall settings are usually on the mark, the chances are slim that you will need to use any of the options available in the Advanced tab view. Click OK or Cancel depending on whether or not you made changes.

Your Windows XP firewall is now set up and is protecting your PC.

Ten Useful Ways to Protect Your Network

1. **Understand the protocols involved in sending and receiving files over the Internet.**

2. **Familiarize yourself with e-mail protocols.**

3. **Learn how to manage computer access for other users on your network.**

4. **Give each user on your network an individual password.**

5. **Don't make your password obvious.**

6. **Learn how to spot potential e-mail "spoofs."**

7. Learn how to recognize Web sites that encrypt sensitive information.

8. Consider installing a personal firewall.

9. If you run a Windows-enabled PC, upgrade your operating system to Windows XP Service Pack 2.

10. Learn how to use Windows XP Service Pack 2's built-in Windows Firewall.

Summary

In this chapter, I've covered the concept of the Internet as a network and how to keep your PC safe from attacks delivered over this and other networks. You have learned how to recognize file-sharing security risks, as well as server attacks on networks you may be using to download digital files. Finally, you have learned some safety measures you can take, and utilities you can install, that can make your downloading and Web-browsing experience a secure one.

✦　　✦　　✦

Protecting Your Privacy

✦ ✦ ✦ ✦

In This Chapter

Understanding modern life and online privacy

Protecting yourself from personal invasions

Knowing your privacy rights

Protecting your privacy on e-mail

Basic privacy housekeeping

✦ ✦ ✦ ✦

Like the problem of illegal downloads, protecting your privacy goes well beyond hardware and software issues with your computer. Every time you make a purchase (such as music ordered through an electronic commerce site) or conduct a business transaction online, you are potentially granting a third party unlimited rights to use your personal information in any way they see fit, and to share it with whomever they like. As you conduct more business online, the threat grows. In this chapter, I discuss how to protect your online identity from curious eyes.

Living in a Fishbowl: Modern Life and Privacy

When you log on to the Internet, you automatically become a "wanted" man or woman. There is a bounty on you, because you are wanted for your personally identifiable information.

Each day, companies that do business online pay for information about people such as you. In the overwhelming vast majority of instances, they are not doing this with malicious intent, but so they can effectively market their products and services to you. Indeed, companies are valued by the stock market in part on how many customers they have, and if your contact information and profile are in a company's database, so much the better for it.

The data that companies may have collected about you include your direct contact information, such as your e-mail and postal addresses, phone number, age, parental or marital status, income, occupation or profession, and even hobbies. Often this information is obtained by means of a registration form that you fill out in order to obtain access to a company's Web site or through shipping information that you entered when you ordered something online.

This information about you is not necessarily a bad thing for a site to have. If, for example, you have told a weather site the zip code where you live and that you like to ski, the next time you visit the site you may automatically see the current conditions and forecast for your area, as well as an advertisement for a ski resort.

The problem occurs when you start to receive e-mails or phone calls from that ski resort without your permission. The chances are good that your favorite weather site sold your contact info to the ski resort, and the ski resort may be peppering your e-mail with all sorts of interesting offers.

Receiving emails with 20 percent discounts on ski season weekends is not necessarily a bad thing. Yet what about a site that, unbeknownst to you, installs a bit of software code on your computer and notes that you have been visiting pages where information about new automobiles are offered for sale? How about a newspaper Web site that, via this code, can tell that you have been reading articles about arthritis? You may indeed look forward to e-mail updates about autos or about anti-arthritis treatments available in your area. Pretty soon, your e-mail box will clog up with messages for everything from get rich quick schemes to all types of interpersonal invitations (see Figure 8-1).

Some may find this info useful, but that is not the point. Whether you receive this bulk e-mail should be up to you. That's why the most ethical Web sites have privacy policies in place that let you, the site user, make the determination about whether information collected about you can be sold to third parties.

Getting to know you: The good and the bad

A good Web site should tell you in clear and unambiguous language just what information they are collecting from you and how this data will be used. Do they or do they not sell, or intend to sell, customer lists to third parties? The law does not require this clarity, but companies that want a business relationship with you owe you this degree of honesty.

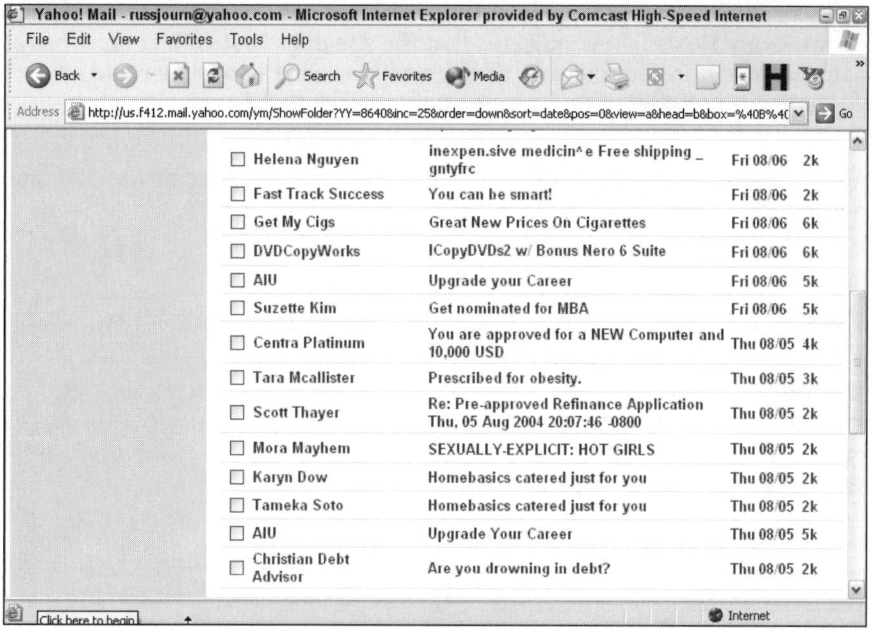

Figure 8-1: Here is an e-mail inbox full of spam.

The worst privacy offenders on the Internet fail to notify you when they are collecting, using, and reselling information about you. The release of this information should never be outside your control. You should be able to "opt out" of this arrangement. The best way to do so is to go to a site and instruct them to turn off the referral option for your name and contact info to be furnished to third parties. This process needs to include easy-to-spot icons, check boxes, and e-mail contact addresses that enable you to reach the site. Ideally, this degree of clarity should also be provided when you register with a site, or you buy or sell something from a site.

The Web site's privacy policy statement should, and will, contain information about what type of information is collected about you and what is done with that data. Often, a link to the Web page with the text of that policy is provided on the site's home page.

As an example of an electronic commerce site that collects information, the privacy policy of Sony Music U.S.A. indicates that the site does "not collect personally identifiable information about you on this site without your knowledge, and all such information is collected directly from you" (see Figure 8-2).

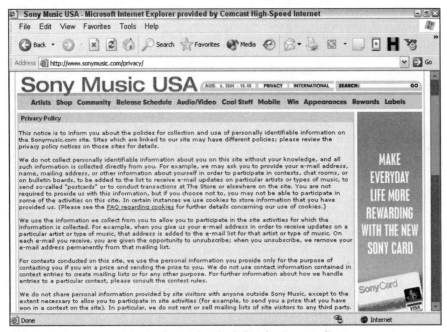

Figure 8-2: Sony Music's site has a clearly defined privacy policy.

Privacy services that look out for you

Although any Web site can claim to follow "appropriate" privacy policies, who's to say what is appropriate and what is not? Fortunately, there are several voluntary organizations that certify a Web site's privacy practices as being in order, or falling somewhat short of that mark. When a site's privacy policies pass muster and few, if any, contradicting claims have been logged against it, the site is likely to receive a certification of compliance. On sites with appropriate privacy policies, that honor is indicated by the appearance of a seal from organizations such as TRUSTe and the Better Business Bureau.

Note   For more information about TRUSTe or the Better Business Bureau, check out their Web sites at www.TRUSTe.com and www.bbbonline.org.

On its Web site, TRUSTe describes itself as "an independent, nonprofit privacy organization whose mission is to build users' trust and confidence on the Internet and, in doing so, accelerate growth of the Internet industry." The group, which includes corporate sponsors such as AT&T Wireless (to be part of Cingular Wireless later this year), Microsoft, and Intuit (both of which use e-mail to market their products to millions of customers), touts its leadership in privacy policy disclosure, informed user consent, and education programs to promote privacy awareness and protection on the part of consumers.

Web sites that collect information about their visitors and customers apply for the TRUSTe "trustmark," a seal that upon approval of TRUSTe can be displayed by those sites (see Figure 8-3). The certification process is fairly rigorous.

   Figure 8-3: The TRUSTe trustmark

Some of the more determining criteria for a TRUSTe trustmark include the following practices that Web sites must follow:

✦ Adoption and implementation of a privacy policy that takes into account consumer anxiety over sharing personal information online.

✦ Notice and disclosure of information collection and use practices.

✦ Choice and consent, giving users the opportunity to exercise control over their information.

✦ Data security and quality and access measures to help protect the security and accuracy of personally identifiable information.

In the eyes of TRUSTe, meeting these standards dictates that sites must disclose the type of personal information they gather about you, how this information will be used, and what other businesses and institutions the information will be shared with. Safeguards must be put in place to protect your personally identifiable information from loss or misuse. Additionally you, the customer, should be able to contact the Web site to correct inaccuracies in the information they store about you.

And the children shall click

You may consider yourself a savvy consumer, careful about the information you reveal on and to Web sites. Despite the fact that children, grandchildren, and others close to you may have sophisticated computing skills, this does not necessarily mean that they are mature consumers. With this in mind, TRUSTe has established a Children's Seal Program to safeguard privacy of those under 13.

Thankfully, the majority of Web site privacy breaches directed at children is likely not to be of the sordid variety, but is more likely to be an attempt to extract information that could then be used to market products or services to adults. For example, a nine-year-old girl may be enticed to give her age and e-mail address. Then, assuming that she shares an e-mail address with their parents, Mom or Dad could receive an unwanted e-mail pitch for products likely to appeal to their nine-year-old daughter.

The most rigorous prohibition in the Children's Seal Program prohibits the collection of online contact information from a child under 13 without "verifiable parental consent" or an opportunity for the parent to prevent the release of this data. Additionally, Web sites may not, according to TRUSTe, "entice a child under 13 by the prospect of a special game, prize, or other activity, to divulge more information than is needed to participate in such an activity."

BBBOnline: A seal of approval

BBBOnline is the Web presence for the Better Business Bureau, a group of 300,000 businesses that promote "fair and honest" standards for how these firms operate. Consumers may be familiar with the BBB's long-established process for submitting complaints against companies that may not be following these criteria.

The Better Business Bureau's BBBOnline Privacy Seal is the 92-year-old organization's official seal of approval for companies with appropriate online privacy policies. According to BBBOnline, businesses that receive this Seal must post an online privacy notice meeting rigorous privacy principles. These principles include allowing consumers access to all the information held about them in the Web site's database, as well as the opportunity to request that this information should be changed or removed if it is outdated or incorrect.

BBBOnline does not maintain a separate policy or offer a distinct seal for children's privacy, but folds its overall Privacy Seal policies into practices similar to those that TRUSTe insists upon.

Since online privacy is more of a business-practices standard than legal doctrine, your ability to protest to organizations such as the Federal Trade Commission is somewhat limited. All that unwanted e-mail spam you have been receiving may or may not encompass online privacy issues, but you can register a complaint with the FTC. Go to www.ftc.gov/ftc/consumer.htm, scroll to the bottom of the page, and click the File A Complaint icon. The resulting page will have a Tell Us Your Complaint pull-down menu of possible issues. Most will not relate to online privacy violations. If you feel you do have an online-related complaint, click an appropriate category, such as "Privacy," "Children's Advertising," or "Computers/Internet Services."

How and where to complain

If you think your privacy rights have been violated by a Web site that displays the TRUSTe trustmark or BBBOnline Privacy Seal, you can file a complaint with either organization. They will investigate and either remove the seal or convince the alleged offender that it is in their best interest to change their privacy policies to fix the issues in question.

TRUSTe posts its complaint procedure via a form on the File A Complaint Web site at `www.TRUSTe.org/users/users_watchdog_new.php`. Complaints can take any of several forms, including accusations of collecting unauthorized information from children, sharing personal information, sending spam, as well as making it difficult or impossible for users to change personal info, close their account, or unsubscribe from the site.

BBBOnline's File A Complaint page, as shown in Figure 8-4 and available at `www.bbbonline.org/consumer/complaint/`, is the launch point for grievances filed through that organization. According to BBBOnline, the grievance should allege that the site in question has "engaged in actions or practices with respect to the information collected from the individual online that are at variance with the BBBOnline privacy guidelines applicable to that Web site."

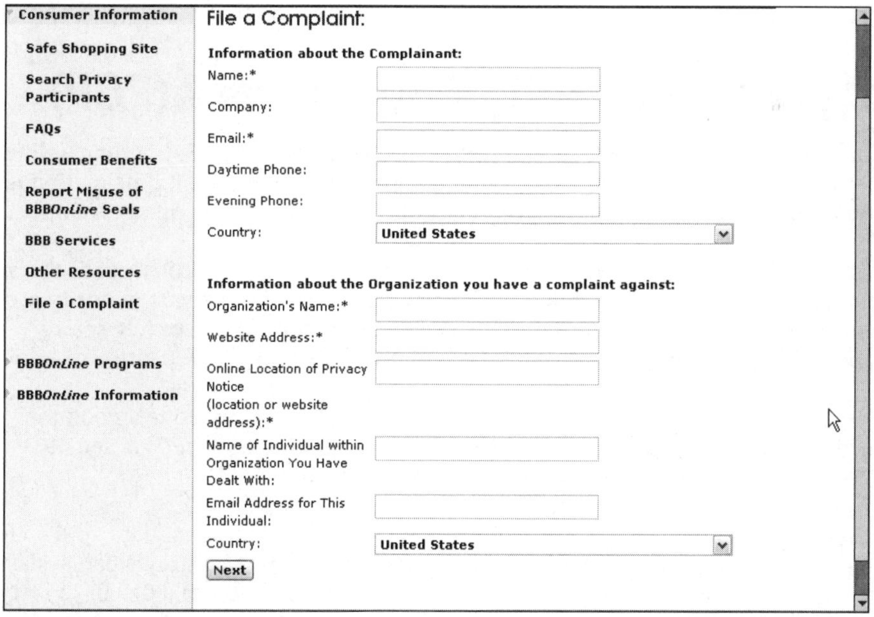

Figure 8-4: BBBOnline's File a Complaint page

If a Web site does not bear a TRUSTe trustmark or a BBBOnline Privacy Seal, it does not necessarily mean that the site does not safeguard your privacy. Some sites have scant online dialog with consumers. For them, privacy policies are not something they need to think much about. Other sites may be new or belong to small companies that may not be aware of privacy policy advantages. Regrettably, though, some sites do not display the TRUSTe or BBBOnline imprimatur because they have not earned it or because their privacy policies are under serious question.

Unfortunately, TRUSTe and BBBOnline do not post specific complaints. TRUSTe Watchdog Advisories are listed and linked from `www.TRUSTe.org/news/padvisories/index.html`, but no new entries have been posted since 2001. This does not mean that both organizations are inactive: In March 2004 alone, TRUSTe received 158 privacy-related complaints from consumers. From October through December 2003, BBBOnline received 422 complaints, 19 of which were deemed "eligible" for further investigation. All 19 of these grievances alleged that the "Company refused to timely process requests to be removed from mailing list or to be deleted from company's database."

Given the reluctance of privacy-certification sites to name offenders, the best course of action for you to take would be to regard the absence of a privacy seal with suspicion, but not necessarily as a mark of guilt that the site does not care about your privacy.

Encryption and Pretty Good Privacy (PGP)

The purpose of encryption (at least when you're browsing and shopping online) is to make sure that sensitive information is hidden while in transit. Encryption is common and easy to set up, so you really shouldn't shop at a non-secure site.

But after your information is delivered, how do you know it's still secure? You're trusting the retailer you're doing business with, and while the vast majority are honest, a few are dishonest or employ dishonest people or are purely scams (operating no business whatsoever behind that cool-looking Web site).

Even if the business is honest, has the Web hosting company done a good job securing the server on which your sensitive information is stored? Is sensitive information removed and stored offline frequently, or at all?

One way to protect yourself from online spying, theft of personal data, and so forth is to encrypt all your communications and data. Numerous programs can assist with this task, and some are open source or freeware. In this section, I discuss Pretty Good Privacy (PGP), which is a set of algorithms designed for strong encryption that are incorporated into several applications.

First, I want to talk about encryption and how it can be made to work with e-mail and other Internet communications, as well as with data stored on disk.

Encryption is a process for coding and decoding data. When communications are encrypted, if someone intercepts the data, he will find it nearly impossible to decode, thus your communications are quite secure. However, since the data is decoded when received, it may not remain secure unless it is encrypted again when stored.

Many different types of encryption exist, but of course they vary in how difficult to decode they are and how easily they can be used. One of the best types of encryption is called public key encryption. It relies on two keys (long alphanumeric strings) to encode and decode data.

Public key cryptography works by allowing the receiver to create two keys: one that remains in the hands of the user and is secret (the private key), and the other (the public key) that is typically published on the Internet. Thereafter, anyone can use your public key to encrypt data to send to you, but only you can decrypt it with your private key. Because no one else has your private key (unless he or she has direct access to your computer or you handed it out to someone), no one else can decrypt messages encoded with your public key.

The strength of public key encryption rests on the lack of any known method for breaking the code except brute-force (trying every combination). Because the possibilities are almost endless, it has been calculated that even using all the computers known to exist running at top speed, all the combinations could not be tried before the end of the universe as you know it. But someone could still get lucky. The main advantage of such encryption is that most people wouldn't be foolish enough to even try to break it.

The number of possible combinations is the main source of strength, so the higher the number of bits the larger the number of combinations, which means that the larger the number of bits the higher strength the encryption algorithm is.

Staying Clear of Spyware

Spyware works by recording the Web sites and pages you have been to and then monitoring your keystrokes while you were there. Theoretically, spyware could use these capabilities to steal your credit card numbers and even your account expiration dates.

The problem with spyware gets worse on public Internet terminals. In one well-known incident, a hacker surreptitiously installed spyware on Internet terminals in a New York-area Kinko's. Before he was caught, the crook captured more than 400 usernames and passwords, using them to access and even open bank accounts online.

How to stay clear of spyware

You can keep your identity from being hijacked by spyware in one of two ways. First, on your home or notebook PC, make sure that you have a software program that can examine your hard drive and look for spyware. Ad-aware (see Figure 8-5) and PestPatrol (see Figure 8-6) are two of the best such utilities. At periodic intervals — even daily — it can look through your system and identify and remove known spyware that has been installed on your computer.

And secondly, on public Internet terminals, the advice is obvious: Do not open a Web site from the body of an e-mail message, or enter any specific financial information on any Web site. The problem is the sheer number of anonymous users who often are not even required to sign in. If you're on the road and have forgotten to pay your bill, wait until you get home, or at the very least, use the PC in your hotel's business center. With sign-in and ID likely required for user access, you are much safer.

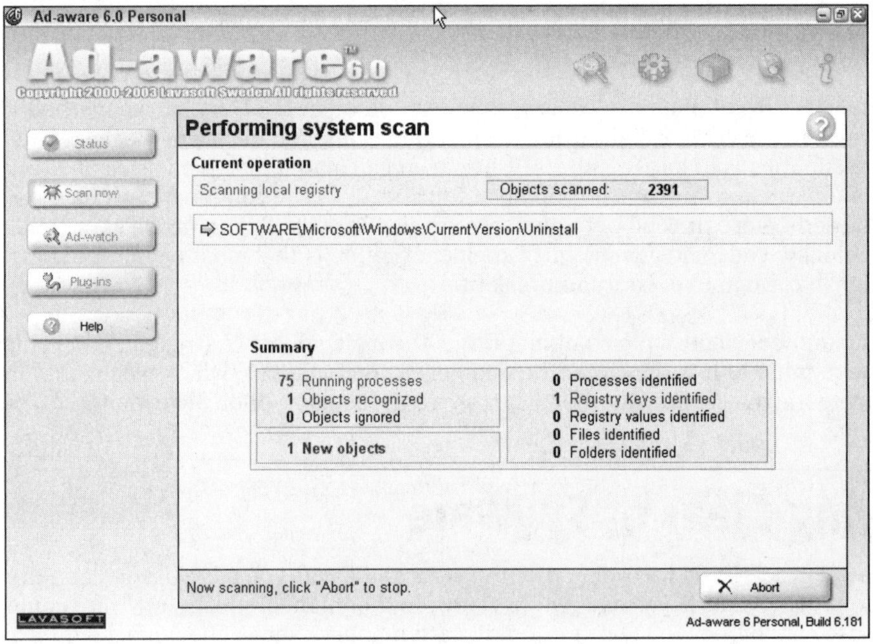

Figure 8-5: Ad-aware is one of the more popular anti-spyware utilities.

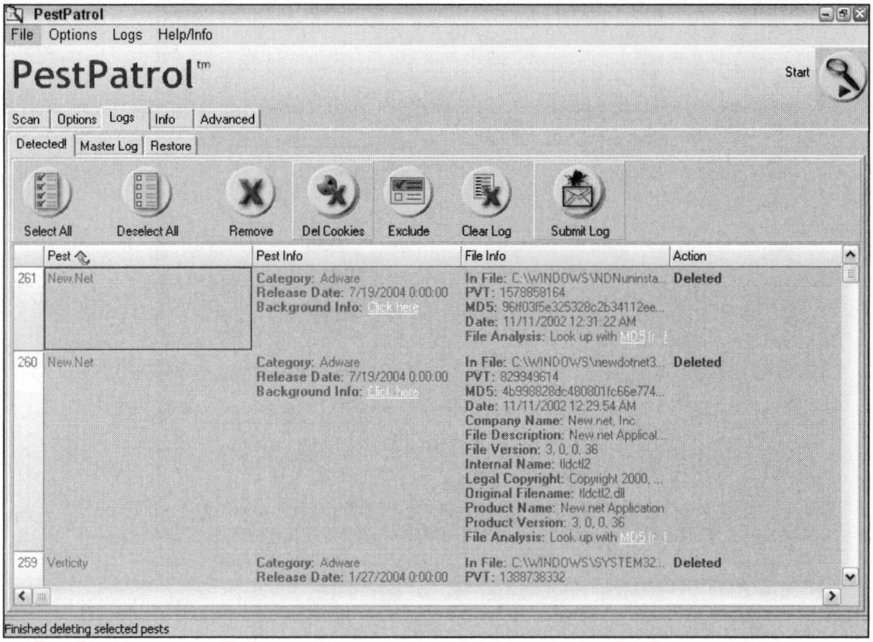

Figure 8-6: PestPatrol's ability to flag and purge nasty spyware is unexcelled.

Cleaning out spyware

PestPatrol is one of the more powerful anti-spyware programs you can run on your PC. It can find and purge all sorts of nasty bits of code — some of which can be used to find out where you surf.

To equip your PC with PestPatrol and then run the program, perform the following steps:

1. **Download and install PestPatrol from** www.pestpatrol.com.

2. **After you install the program, click File and then Start Scan.** PestPatrol immediately starts checking your PC for pesky spyware (see Figure 8-7). During the scanning process, a list of suspected spyware appears in the main window, as shown in Figure 8-8.

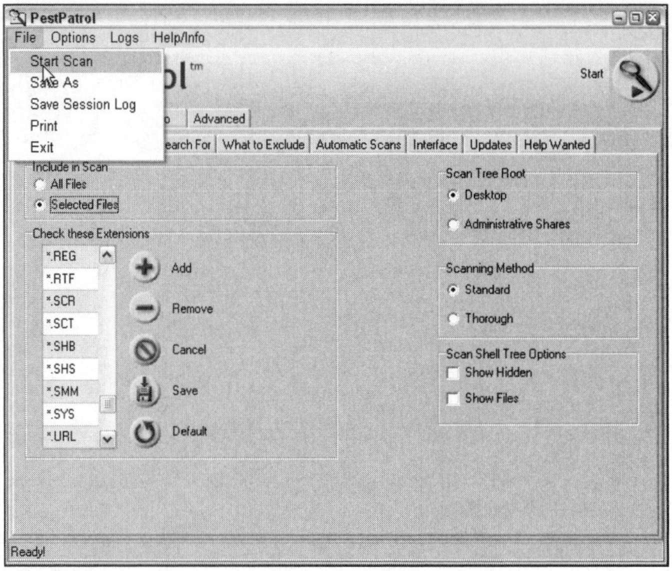

Figure 8-7: PestPatrol checks the PC for spyware.

3. **Either during the scanning process or after the scan completes, click the Select all icon.** Each suspected spyware file is marked for removal from your hard drive (see Figure 8-9).

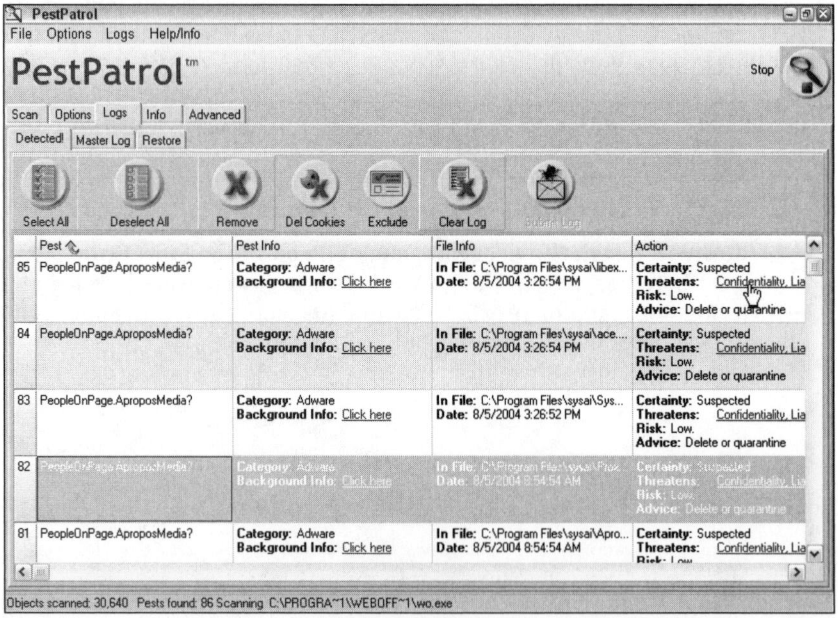

Figure 8-8: PestPatrol lists the spyware it finds.

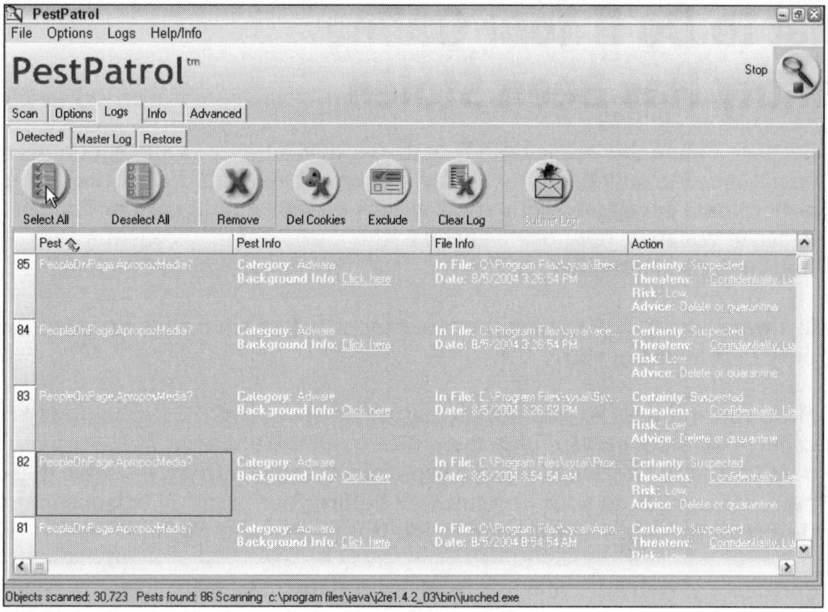

Figure 8-9: Spyware programs marked for removal

4. **Click Remove.** PestPatrol automatically deletes all the marked files from your PC (see Figure 8-10).

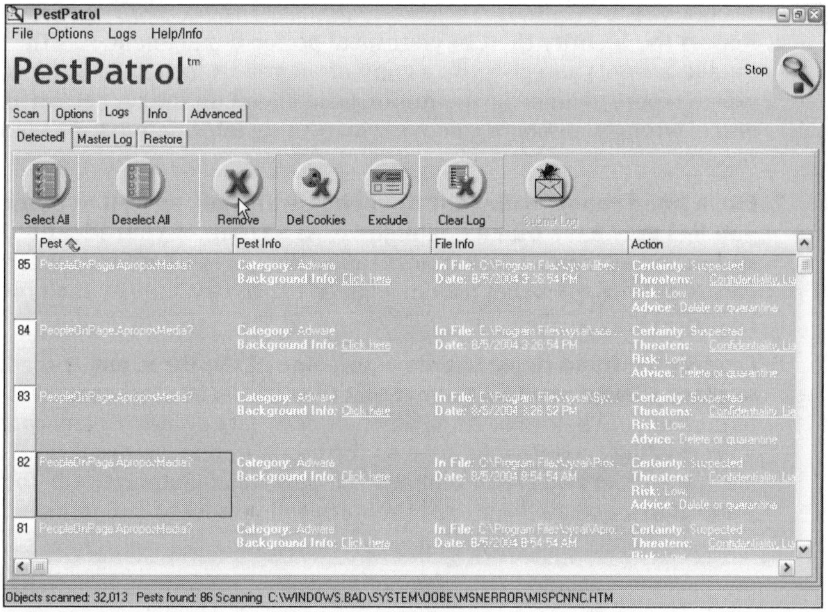

Figure 8-10: Click Remove to delete the files.

What to Do If Your Online Identity Has Been Stolen

Because online thieves seldom broadcast their intentions and accomplishments, sometimes the only time you realize you have been had is after the fact. You may notice some peculiar-looking transactions on your credit card or bank statement. Because you have not physically lost your card, you may consider these weird transactions an anomaly.

In a word, don't. If you think that your identity has been stolen online, you'll have a busy task ahead of you.

First, you will want to find out the nature and scope of the problem. This entails calling customer service or going online to all the financial Web sites you do business with, and checking for any suspicious-looking activity. Because these transactions will appear on your account well before your monthly balance is reported to the credit bureau, you will want to nip this problem in the bud.

Fortunately, Web sites of many retailers and financial institutions have identity theft and fraud-related pages with forms that you can use to file a complaint. Often, this complaint procedure involves filling out a charge-dispute form and then entering the reason why you are contesting the charge. In your case, that just might be identity theft.

If your initial investigation strongly points to the fact that your identity has been stolen, the FTC recommends that you follow at least four steps:

1. **Report the identity theft to your local police department.** Ask the officer to take a report and give you a copy of the report. Sending a copy of your police report to financial institutions can speed up the process of absolving you of wrongful debts or removing inaccurate information from your credit reports.

2. **File a fraud report with your financial institution, as well as other creditors you feel may have billed you unjustly as a result of your identity being stolen.** In fact, some financial institution Web sites offer forms where you can dispute charges that may have been caused by identity theft (see Figure 8-11).

3. **Contact the fraud departments of any one of the three major credit bureaus to place a fraud alert on your credit file.** The fraud alert requests creditors to contact you before opening any new accounts or making any changes to your existing accounts. As soon as the credit bureau confirms your fraud alert, the other two credit bureaus will be notified automatically to place fraud alerts, and all three credit reports will be sent to you free of charge.

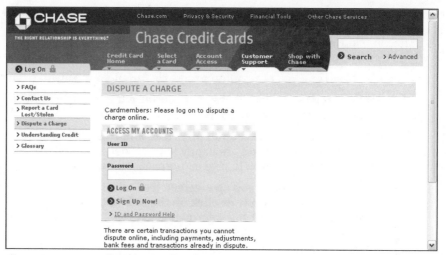

Figure 8-11: An online charge dispute form

Tip The best way to reach the major credit bureaus is by phone. You can reach them at the following numbers:

Equifax: 800-525-6285

Experian: 888-397-3742

TransUnion: 800-888-4213

4. **File a fraud report with the Federal Trade Commission's ID theft center at** `www.consumer.gov/idtheft`. Although the FTC does not resolve specific cases, multiple filings by victims of identity theft can sometimes steer investigators on the trail of the perpetrators.

To sum up, using diligence and common sense can prevent most cases of online identity theft. If it has already happened, don't panic. Just get to work to clear your credit and your name.

Ten Indispensable Techniques for Protecting Your Privacy

1. **Learn about and become familiar with your privacy rights (such as they are) and new laws affecting them.**

2. **Check privacy policies on Web sites you visit and for all companies you deal with.** U.S. laws require companies to state their privacy policies, particularly in relation to sharing your personal data with other companies, and to give you the opportunity to opt out.

3. **Download and use encryption programs for all your sensitive data.**

4. **Perform regular housekeeping to make sure that sensitive information is removed from your hard drive.**

5. **Try to shop at stores that don't offer discounts for providing your personal information.** Many stores are happy to do business and offer good prices without the need for you to give up personal information.

6. **If you get an e-mail or pop-up message that asks for personal or financial information, do not reply or click on the link in the message.** Legitimate companies don't ask for this information via e-mail. If you are concerned about your account, contact the organization in the e-mail using a telephone number you know to be genuine, or open a new Internet browser session and type in the company's correct Web address. In any case, don't cut and paste the link in the message.

7. **Don't e-mail personal or financial information.** E-mail is not a secure method of transmitting personal information. If you initiate a transaction and want to provide your personal or financial information through an organization's Web site, look for indicators that the site is secure, like a lock icon on the browser's status bar or a URL for a Web site that begins "https:" (the "s" stands for "secure"). Unfortunately, no indicator is foolproof; some phishers have forged security icons.

Note   Phishers are e-mailers who fraudulently ask you for your credit card or social security number, in order to steal your personally identifiable information.

8. **Use anti-virus software, and keep it up-to-date.** Some phishing e-mails contain software that can harm your computer or track your activities on the Internet without your knowledge. Anti-virus software and a firewall can protect you from inadvertently accepting such unwanted files. Anti-virus software scans incoming communications for troublesome files. Look for anti-virus software that recognizes current viruses as well as older ones, that can effectively reverse the damage, and that updates automatically.

9. **When shopping online, do business with companies that provide transaction security protection and that have strong privacy and security policies.**

10. **Your operating system may offer free software "patches" to close holes in the system that hackers or phishers could exploit.** For these fixes, check Windows Update at http://windowsupdate.microsoft.com.

Patches for Mac Users

Mac OS X users can set up their computers to receive these patches automatically. Follow these steps:

1. **Click on the Apple icon and choose System Preferences from the menu.**

2. **Click the Software Update icon.** The Software Update dialog box appears.

3. **Click the Update Software tab, and then click the Check for updates check box.** Choose your desired update frequency from the pop-up menu: Daily, Weekly, or Monthly.

4. **Click OK.** Your Mac is now set up to automatically receive Windows Update patches and other fixes.

Summary

In this chapter, you read about issues relating to your privacy and how you can protect it. It is important, as explained, to keep your personal information out of the hands of anyone who doesn't have a need for it and make sure that anyone who does need it only uses it for the intended purpose. I also reviewed safe and secure Web use habits, as well as software that can help you maintain your privacy online. Finally, you learned what to do if, despite every good precaution taken, your personal information is stolen and used for fraudulent activity.

✦   ✦   ✦

Protecting Yourself from Illegal Downloads

✦ ✦ ✦ ✦

In This Chapter

Understanding how copyright law affects you

Applying trademark law to the Internet

Making sure you are legal when distributing copyrighted music

Avoiding copyright violation

✦ ✦ ✦ ✦

Apart from the dangers of file sharing and potentially catching a computer virus, you also are at risk of lawsuits and worse if you download the wrong file or don't have the proper permission to use it. In this chapter, we discuss copyright, trademark, and other intellectual property issues, how the Recording Industry Association of America and other organizations can find you and fine you, and how to ensure that you have the legal authority to use any particular file.

In an age when technology empowers so many activities and capabilities, talking about restraining or limiting the use of the Internet, and of PCs, sounds like retro thinking. That is far from the case, for what we are talking about is the rights of an artist who has labored, bled, cried, or even just gone through the motions to sculpt a song, paint a painting, produce a short film, take that perfect photograph, or write a short story. She may have created a work that can be broken down from the original art into digital sequences of 1s and 0s that form digital data. In doing so, she is certainly entitled to gain something tangible from the fact that her work has touched others to the point that they want to have a copy of that creation for their very own.

You may wonder whether that songwriter or visual artist will miss the $4.99 you have saved by not paying to legally download his work. Perhaps not, but that is not the point. Think how you would feel if you built a model airplane or stitched a quilt, and then your home was broken into, those items were stolen, and they wound up on eBay a few weeks later.

So, downloading is not a right. Legal downloading is a privilege, one in which the creative people of the world and their representatives, have every right to oversee.

Although there are many principles at play that determine whether your downloads are legal, copyright is at the heart of the matter. That being the case, take a look at copyright law — not so much from the statutory standpoint, but why it exists.

Understanding Copyright Law

In a walk-up apartment on the other side of town, a songwriter opens his third beverage of the evening and thinks about a recent love affair that was done too soon. In the corner of his living room, he spots his old guitar, and the words come to him: "Your old boyfriend is back in town, I'm alone and feeling down … gotta stop thinking about what can never be, you're never ever never gonna love me." He titles the song "Gotta, Gotta, Gotta Stop Thinking About You."

A month later, he meets a friend of a friend of a friend, who manages to get him some time in a recording studio. Still heartbroken but salved by his art, he records a CD of his song, which he incorporates into his live act.

Two months later, the song he wrote in pain gets out on the Internet and is available for download through one of the file-sharing services discussed earlier in this book. The songwriter does not even get rent money for the art he created out of sadness.

The framers of the United States Constitution may not have envisioned such a personal aspect to the protection of creative works. In fact, when they wrote the original copyright provisions in the noble document, musical recording technology was nearly a century in the future. Still, the words of the copyright provisions affect how we produce, consume, and exchange creative works:

"To promote the Progress of Science and useful Arts, by securing for limited Times to Authors and Inventors the exclusive Right to their respective Writings and Discoveries" (see Figure 9-1).

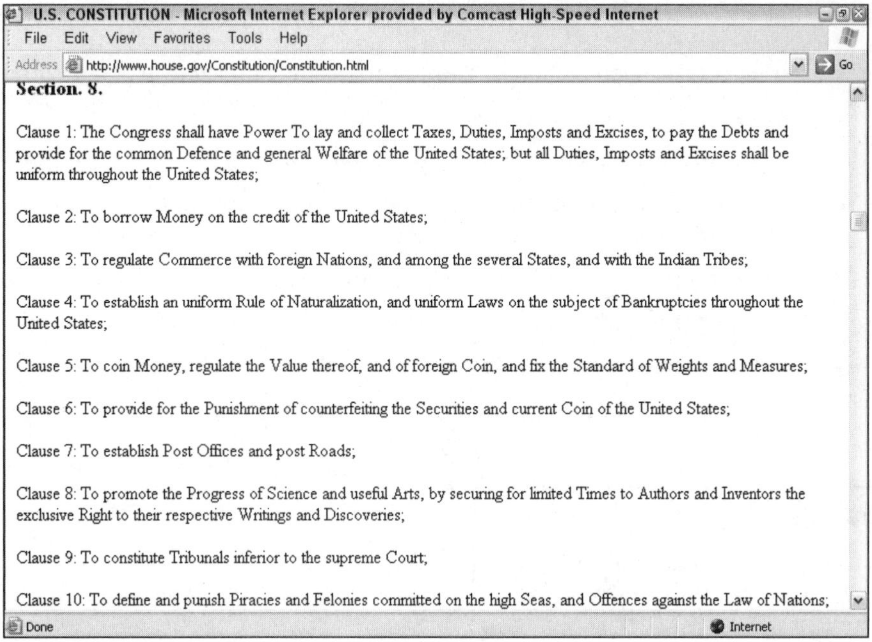

Section. 8.

Clause 1: The Congress shall have Power To lay and collect Taxes, Duties, Imposts and Excises, to pay the Debts and provide for the common Defence and general Welfare of the United States; but all Duties, Imposts and Excises shall be uniform throughout the United States;

Clause 2: To borrow Money on the credit of the United States;

Clause 3: To regulate Commerce with foreign Nations, and among the several States, and with the Indian Tribes;

Clause 4: To establish an uniform Rule of Naturalization, and uniform Laws on the subject of Bankruptcies throughout the United States;

Clause 5: To coin Money, regulate the Value thereof, and of foreign Coin, and fix the Standard of Weights and Measures;

Clause 6: To provide for the Punishment of counterfeiting the Securities and current Coin of the United States;

Clause 7: To establish Post Offices and post Roads;

Clause 8: To promote the Progress of Science and useful Arts, by securing for limited Times to Authors and Inventors the exclusive Right to their respective Writings and Discoveries;

Clause 9: To constitute Tribunals inferior to the supreme Court;

Clause 10: To define and punish Piracies and Felonies committed on the high Seas, and Offences against the Law of Nations;

Figure 9-1: The copyright clause in the U.S. Constitution.

The U.S. Copyright Office administers the copyright law according to the short, but definitive statute you just reviewed. A significant expansion of copyright law in 1976 set the tone for how the copyright statutes exist today. Section 106 of the 1976 Copyright Act gives copyright owners the exclusive right to do, and to authorize others to do, the following:

- ✦ To reproduce the work in copies or phonorecords
- ✦ To prepare derivative works based upon the work
- ✦ To distribute copies or phonorecords of the work to the public by sale or other transfer of ownership, or by rental, lease, or lending
- ✦ To perform the work publicly, in the case of literary, musical, dramatic, and choreographic works, pantomimes, and motion pictures and other audiovisual works
- ✦ To display the copyrighted work publicly, in the case of literary, musical, dramatic, and choreographic works, pantomimes, and pictorial, graphic, or sculptural works, including the individual images of a motion picture or other audiovisual work; and, in the case of sound recordings, to perform the work publicly by means of a digital audio transmission

Works that are protected include the following (see examples in Figures 9-2 and 9-3):

✦ Literary works, such as books, short stories, and magazine articles

✦ Musical compositions, including the lyrics within them

✦ Dramatic works and music, such as an original production in a local theater

✦ Pantomimes and choreographic works, such as a dance performance based on choreographed steps and routines

✦ Pictorial, graphic, and sculptural works, such as a photograph on a Web page

✦ Motion pictures and other audiovisual works

✦ Sound recordings, such as musical CDs

✦ Architectural works, such as unique designs incorporated into a building

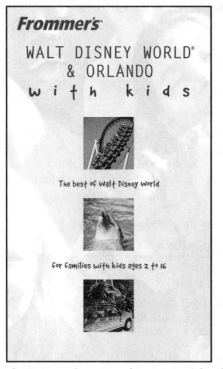

Figure 9-2: Literary works are copyrighted and cannot be duplicated without the publisher's permission.

Figure 9-3: Published photographs are copyrighted.

Copyright law and digital downloading

The concept of digital data ties in with the principle that whether you are talking about online communication, file sharing, or even a photo on a Web site, pretty much everything is translatable to the most basic computer code.

For creators of copyrighted work, as well as those who enjoy it, the PC age has definitely altered the way in which this material is accessed. Rather than grooves in a phonograph record, magnetic tape, or song lyrics existing on sheet music made from dead trees, digital content can be easily manipulated and distributed. Digital distribution does not lack, or have, a conscience.

But you, presumably, have a conscience. That said, the onus is on you to understand the stakes involved. The decisions you make with regard to digitally downloading, purchasing, and trading copyrighted work are affected by these stakes.

Here, then, is how the copyright-protected status of various digital works may affect you, the potential digital downloader:

✦ **Literary works:** Technology exists to scan and then distribute books over the Internet without the author's permission. In fact, a number of sites make this material available.

✦ **Musical works:** This is a separate category from sound recordings, but just as potentially invasive of creative copyright. An example of a highly questionable musical works digital practice would be to cut and paste some song lyrics from a Web page into yours, without the permission of the author.

✦ **Dramatic works:** Sites that offer copyrighted television or movie scripts for download are treading quite thin with this practice.

✦ **Pantomimes and choreographic works:** An example of copyright abuse would be taping a performance of a live dance troupe and then posting a copy of that performance on a video file-trading site.

✦ **Pictorial, graphic, and audiovisual works:** The most obvious copyright violation here would be using a photograph that isn't yours. On the Internet, this would be done by right-clicking on a Web page photo file, saving it to your hard drive, and then reposting it on a Web site without the photographer's permission.

✦ **Sound records:** This is where the predominant abuse of copyright has occurred in the digital age. Typically, this is done by users who use software to "rip" CDs into individual song files. They then make those copyrighted song files available through a file-sharing service such as those discussed earlier in this book (see Figure 9-4). Seldom does the copyright owner ever see any money from this type of distribution.

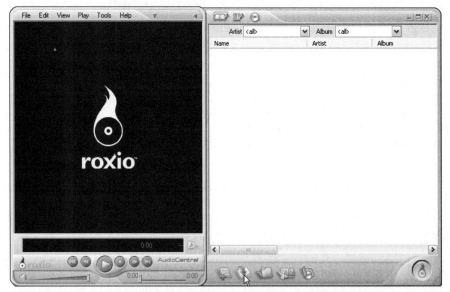

Figure 9-4: CD "ripper" software can slice individual sound files from CDs.

Copyright law exists to protect those who have expended the time, effort, and emotional commitment necessary to produce works that entertain, educate, or enthrall us — sometimes more than one of those.

Changes to copyright law

Even the landmark 1976 changes to copyright law took place before the Internet as we know it today evolved. Back then, computer-to-computer communication was text-based only, and computers occupied whole rooms rather than hutches in dens and laptops toted by traveling businesspeople.

With the substantial potential of the Internet to distribute digital files, several significant changes have been made to copyright law since the 1976 revisions. In this section, we review some of these changes and discuss how they affect digital downloading of music and other copyrighted content.

Updates to copyright law and their effect on digital downloading

In the last 30 years, basic copyright law has changed to further the interest of copyright holders. Several of these changes have had a profound effect on digital downloading. This section details some of these revisions:

U.S. copyright law {Title 17 U.S.C. Section 101 et seq., Title 18 U.S.C. Section 2319} now stipulates that where the infringing activity is for commercial advantage or private financial gain, sound recording infringements can be punishable by up to five years in prison and $250,000 in fines. Repeat offenders can be imprisoned for up to 10 years. Violators can also be held civilly liable for actual damages, lost profits, or statutory damages up to $150,000 per work. This section of the law sets forth the general penalties for "infringing activities," such as downloading music from a file-sharing site and then selling access to it.

Part of copyright law, the Federal Anti-Bootleg Statute {18 USC 2319A} prohibits the unauthorized recording, manufacture, distribution, or trafficking in sound recordings or videos of artists' live musical performances. Violators can be punished with up to five years in prison and $250,000 in fines.

According to the Recording Industry Association of America (which represents most of the major music labels), "two important legal concepts, especially pertaining to the Internet, should be kept in mind — contributory infringement and vicarious liability."

The RIAA interprets the Federal Anti-Bootleg Statute's contributory infringement as occurring "where a person, with knowledge of the infringing activity, induces, causes, or materially contributes to the infringing conduct of another. For example, a link site operator may be liable for contributory infringement by knowingly linking to infringing files." In other words, if you have your own Web site and then link to an illegally obtained music file, it is quite likely you are a "bootlegger."

The RIAA notes on its Web site that "vicarious liability may be imposed where an entity or person has the right and ability to control the activities of the direct infringer and also receives a financial benefit from the infringing activities. Vicarious liability may be imposed even if the entity is unaware of the infringing activities. In the case of a site retransmitting infringing programs, providing direct access to infringing works may show a right and ability to control the activities of the direct infringer, and receiving revenue from banner ads or e-commerce on the site may be evidence of a financial benefit."

In plain, non-legalese English, this means that if your Web page is part of another site, (say, a university or even your workplace) and you link to infringing digital music files on your section of the site, then the site that provides access to your Web page may also be liable for copyright infringement.

Understanding fair use

The Fair Use Doctrine {USC Title 17, Sec 107} of federal law is a complicated area. Basically, it limits the extent of property interest granted to the copyright holder. For example, this might allow citizens to cite a quotation from copyrighted material when the excerpt is used for teaching, research, news reporting, comment, criticism, or parody.

There are some limitations. Whether the court allows you to reproduce, distribute, adapt, display, and/or perform copyrighted works depends upon the nature of the use (commercial purposes, non-profit, educational), the length of the excerpt, how distinctive the original work is, and how the use will impact the market for the original work.

Generally speaking, one is not allowed to take the "value" of a song without permission. Some copyright law experts maintain that such "value" can be as small as a three-second clip—such as that of a famous guitar riff, for example.

In the digital music downloading and distribution world, a violation of "fair use" occurs if your band takes the opening riff of the classic rock hit "Barracuda" by the band Heart, incorporates that riff into your own song, and then distributes the clip over the Internet through a file-sharing service. Even though you have copyrighted your own song and may be okay with digital distribution, there's that offending guitar line that plainly isn't your band's property to copyright and redistribute. You could leave yourself open to copyright infringement.

Understanding the Sonny Bono Copyright Extension Act

The late Sonny Bono (see Figure 9-5) was not only half of the singing, comedically inclined 1960s duo Sonny & Cher, he was also a prolific songwriter, song publisher, and subsequently, a United States Congressman. Bono's career as a copyright holder, and then as a lawmaker, gave him multiple perspectives on how copyright law might be revised to protect copyright owners.

Figure 9-5: A popular entertainer, songwriter, and member of Congress, Sonny Bono was the inspiration for the Sonny Bono Copyright Extension Act.

Passed shortly after Rep. Bono's death in 1998, the law extends U.S. copyright from life of the author plus 50 years, to life of the author plus 70 years. For "works made for hire," the term is extended from 75 to 95 years.

The Bono Act's effect on digital downloading is rather profound. When the copyright law protected musical compositions for up to 50 years after the author's passing, comparatively recent songs passed into the public domain. When music is in the public domain, the legal onus on digital downloading is substantially less.

Now, however, a substantial body of work will take longer to pass into the public domain, making copyright permissions that much more frequent and necessary.

Understanding the Digital Millennium Copyright Act

Of all the copyright protection laws enacted since the dawn of digital technology, the Digital Millennium Copyright Act (DMCA) has proven to be the most contentious.

The DMCA's many powerful supporters — including most of the music business establishment — view the statute as a necessary defensive weapon against millions of digital downloaders who, in the eyes of that establishment, have thievish intentions that must be nipped in the bud.

On the other hand, the DMCA's many opponents look on the act as an effort on the part of the music, movie, and other copyright-intensive industries to keep an inordinate amount of control over how their work is distributed. The sharpest barbs from the DMCA camp criticize the music and movie industries for being both uninformed about, and fearful of, digital file distribution.

Enacted in 1998, the DMCA has many controversial provisions. These include prohibiting the manufacture and distribution of devices designed for the sole purpose of undermining technology used to protect copyrighted works. Some have even argued — with not a great deal of success — that software which "rips" CD sound files into individual tracks runs afoul of the DMCA.

There's more consensus about the DMCA vulnerabilities of hacking software, such as the type that can decode encrypted movie content on a DVD. If you see a movie listed for free download on a peer-to-peer site, it is only one of two things: Either a group of amateur filmmakers has posted it there in a quest for wider recognition, or it is illegal. Is the movie title a familiar one? If so, don't download it.

The DMCA law also spells out the responsibilities of Internet service providers (ISPs) in cases of infringement online. If you are trading unauthorized content over your Internet connection, then your ISP could be responsible as well. If they find out that you are trading files illegally over an Internet connection they provide for you, they could close your account.

Here, the legal situation is not yet crystal clear. Some experts maintain that an ISP is like a phone company. The experts specify a rather exaggerated concept: If a phone line is being used to discuss and plan an illegal act, then no one would say that the phone company providing the line is liable. Others say that because it is easier to track a few transmissions of large digital files rather than just a few random in any of millions of phone conversations, then the ISP is indeed liable.

The DMCA's other major effect is that it provides a simplified licensing procedure for Internet radio stations to stream musical content without having to obtain individual permission from every sound recording copyright owner individually. At the same time, the DMCA assures record companies that they will be fairly compensated for their content played over the Internet. This means that if you listen to a streaming radio station, you will have no legal liability whatsoever.

Understanding the no electronic theft law

This law clarifies criminal penalties for "sound recording infringement." Penalties up to three years in jail and $250,000 fines are now authorized, even where no monetary profit or commercial gain comes from the infringing activity. Plus, the statute of limitations where violations can be prosecuted is extended from three to five years.

There's one provision in the law that should really give you pause. It amended the definition of "commercial advantage or private financial gain" to include the receipt (or expectation of receipt) of anything of value, including receipt of other copyrighted works (as in MP3 trading). Punishment in such instances includes up to five years in prison and/or $250,000 fines. You may also be civilly liable for profits lost to the copyright holder.

The meaning of this for you, the digital downloader, is that if you, for example, download a song illegally, or even legally, and forward it to a friend as an e-mail attachment, you could be facing serious prosecution. Is forwarding that great new Dave Matthews song you downloaded illegally off Kazaa worth the legal risk? "Caution!," indeed.

Understanding Trademark Law

Trademarks and copyright both address protections to the creative process. Other than that general umbrella, though, the parameters of these two types of laws are quite different.

The Far-Reaching Tentacles of Trademark Law

You don't have to be a famous performer or band to be targeted by businesses that believe you have violated their trademark. A few years ago, for example, an Indiana rock band named themselves Neenah Foundry after the name stamped on most manhole covers in their Midwestern town. They subsequently received a "cease and desist letter" from the original Neenah Foundry — an ironworks and casting company headquartered in Neenah, Wisconsin. Although the band felt that they were in the clear, rather than tangle with corporate trademark law, they dropped the "h" and became Neena Foundry. A simple change, but it was apparently enough to keep the Neenah Foundry folks happy.

A trademark indicates the source of a product or service. It can be a familiar advertising slogan, a specific product design (such as the shapes and colors of a pop can), or even a sound strongly associated with a product or service. An example of a trademarked sound is the three-note chime used by the NBC television network for many decades.

When it comes to digital music, the trademark and the copyright work closely together. For example, 1971 saw the release of a trombone-infused, now classic rock hit, "Beginnings" by the group Chicago.

The performance of the song on the album, as well as the lyrics within it, were of course copyrighted. The name of the band, Chicago, is a trademark. In fact, that very generic sounding trademark has its own history. The group was previously known as the Chicago Transit Authority, after the municipal transportation system based in the town where several of the group's founding members were born. The real CTA objected to the use of their trademark. This objection encouraged the group to rename themselves after the city of their origin.

One might think that a band name bearing the title of a large metropolis would not need trademark protection. Oh, but yes, it does. Without trademark safeguards, any other musical group with a similar sound could masquerade as the band Chicago. If the group were lesser known, then the existence of another band with the same name could have impeded the ability of the original trademark rights holder to make money.

What Chicago the band did was to incorporate a unique logo into their trademark. A branding statement as well as trademark protection, Chicago's familiar script style logo is seen everywhere the group is — from concert signage to the band's Web page. The Chicago trademark is followed by an "R", which means that the trademark is registered with the U.S. Patent and Trademark Office.

Trademark Law and the Internet

In the digital world, trademark law does not have as frequent an impact as copyright law does. Still, it is important for you, the digital downloader, to understand how these protections come into play.

Suppose you are thinking of downloading a musical track from a file-sharing service, or even posting the track for distribution through one of these peer-to-peer operations. For consistency, let's go back to the Chicago model. If you distribute or receive one or more of the band's songs through a file-swapping service, without paying for it, that is illegal. If, in the series of music files on your hard drive that you allow the file-swapping service's software access to, you indicate that the group Chicago was the source of those tracks, then it is quite likely that you are violating trademark law.

Distributing Music Legally

If you want to distribute music or even play music within your own multimedia creations legally over the Internet, you should apply for a license to do so.

Internet music licenses come in several forms because of the nature of music copyright itself. Music copyright involves two classifications or entities. The first is what is called the "musical composition." That is the actual lyrics and notes, or what has traditionally been known as sheet music.

The second aspect of music copyright involves the "musical work," which is the actual song. The song is owned either by the songwriter or by his or her music publisher.

In addition to the copyright, you need to obtain another type of permission. The sound recording is the recording of an artist's performance of a particular song. The record company usually owns the performance; less often the recording artist or the CD's producer owns it.

Clarifying the licenses you will need

To explain the type of licenses you will require before you can legally distribute music over the Web, look at this hypothetical example.

With your digital video camera, you shoot some footage of a local off-road race rally. You edit a video clip of the rally for your Web site and would like to include some music. You've picked the perfect song: "What's Too Heavy For You Ain't Even Heavy For Me," by the (again hypothetical) boogie rock trio, the Deacon Little Band.

This band has committed the actual lyrics and notes to sheet music. That's the musical composition. The group's leader, Richard Fowler, composed the song, and in a 50-50 partnership with his music publisher, co-owns the copyright to the piece. You know this because on the Deacon Little Band CD, the publishing and songwriting information, along with the music licensing organization that Fowler and the band's music publisher use (BMI, ASCAP, or SESAC) is printed on the CD's jacket.

Now, suppose the Deacon Little Band records for In Limbo Records out of Atlanta, Georgia. You look on the CD and notice a P (which stands for Protection) in a circle, next to the logo of In Limbo Records. Since the recording is "Protected" by Copyright, you now know enough information to get started seeking a license to use this song on your Web site.

Obtaining a distribution license

To get permission to use a musical composition on the Web, you need to acquire a distribution license. Distribution licenses are obtainable from one of three organizations that have been created to represent songwriters and music publishers:

✦ **ASCAP:** Founded in 1914 and the oldest of the three major publishing rights organizations, the American Society of Composers, Authors, and Publishers represents 190,000 U.S. composers, songwriters, lyricists, and music publishers. The body has worked with songwriters and components ranging from Duke Ellington to Beck, from George Gershwin to Stevie Wonder, from Leonard Bernstein to Madonna, from Garth Brooks to Tito Puente.

✦ **BMI:** Founded in 1939, BMI (which once stood for Broadcast Music International) represents some 300,000 tunesmiths and publishers. Until recent years, BMI was seen as a more contemporary organization than its archrival, ASCAP. In no small measure, this has been due to the richness of BMI's roster, which has included John Lennon, Chuck Berry, Dave Brubeck, David Bowie, Milton Babbitt, Willie Nelson, The Eagles, Thelonious Monk, Carlos Santana, Sir Elton John, The Neville Brothers, The Beach Boys, Aretha Franklin, Waylon Jennings, Charles Ives, The Who, John Kander, Leadbelly, Eric Clapton, John Williams, The Bee Gees, and B.B. King.

✦ **SESAC:** The smallest of the three performance rights bodies, SESAC (once known as the Society of European Stage Authors and Composers) was founded in 1930. Throughout much of its history, SESAC was viewed as a gospel and European music specialist. In recent years, however, SESAC has evolved to be more diverse in the types of works it represents. As a result, it is now more competitive with its larger rivals, BMI and ASCAP.

Obtaining an Internet distribution license from ASCAP

To obtain an Internet distribution license from ASCAP, go to `http://www.ascap.com/weblicense/`.

After you arrive at this page, scroll down until you see the link for Download an "Interactive License" Agreement. Click the link, and a form appears (see Figure 9-6). There are two forms based on license fees: Rate Schedule B and Rate Schedule C. Both forms are in Adobe PDF format and require a copy of Adobe Reader in order to open them.

Rate Schedule B has is based on license fees calculated on revenue. Rate Schedule C is based on usage rights for a projected number of online sessions.

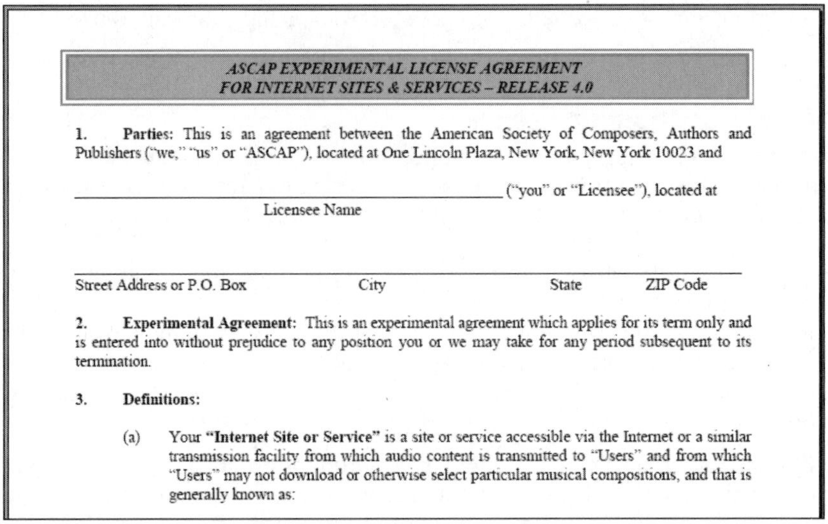

ASCAP EXPERIMENTAL LICENSE AGREEMENT
FOR INTERNET SITES & SERVICES – RELEASE 4.0

1. **Parties:** This is an agreement between the American Society of Composers, Authors and Publishers ("we," "us" or "ASCAP"), located at One Lincoln Plaza, New York, New York 10023 and

_______________________________ ("you" or "Licensee"), located at
Licensee Name

____
Street Address or P.O. Box City State ZIP Code

2. **Experimental Agreement:** This is an experimental agreement which applies for its term only and is entered into without prejudice to any position you or we may take for any period subsequent to its termination.

3. **Definitions:**

(a) Your **"Internet Site or Service"** is a site or service accessible via the Internet or a similar transmission facility from which audio content is transmitted to "Users" and from which "Users" may not download or otherwise select particular musical compositions, and that is generally known as:

Figure 9-6: ASCAP's Internet distribution license application form

If you are planning to make money directly from your Web site content (as opposed to merely using your Web site to make money from selling merchandise), then fill out Schedule B. If you are merely seeking to use music for artistic effect, select Schedule C.

After you complete the form, you can e-mail it to ASCAP as an attached file. ASCAP's e-mail address is `weblicense@ascap.com`.

Obtaining an Internet distribution license from BMI

To obtain a Web distribution license from BMI (or other type of license), point your Web browser to `www.bmi.com/licensing`. Once on the BMI licensing page, click on the link labeled Websites Sign Up Online as shown in Figure 9-7. This takes you to an Account Login screen.

If this is your first visit to the site, you will have to create a login. Click on the KLIK-THRU button to proceed. You are walked through a couple of screens that explain the process you are about to embark on. You end up at the Create an Account page, shown in Figure 9-8, where you create your login account.

Figure 9-7: The link to BMI's Internet distribution license application is on this Web page.

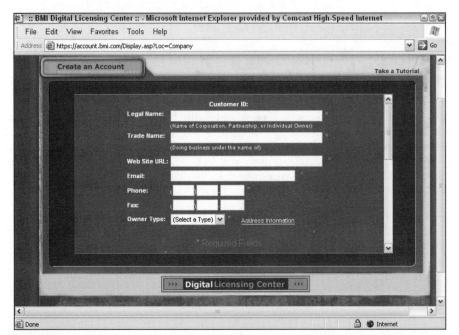

Figure 9-8: The Create an Account page on BMI's Internet distribution license application form.

If you are already a registered user, just enter your login information and proceed. On the first page, you fill in your basic contact information. Click Next, and you reach a page with a Select Business Type pull-down menu, as shown in Figure 9-9. Choose Internet, and Click Next.

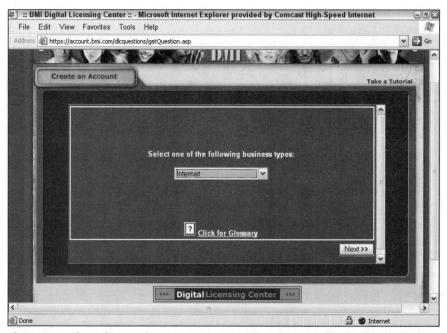

Figure 9-9: The Select Business Type page on BMI's Internet distribution license application form.

You are taken through several screens with radio buttons that ask if your site is U.S.-based and whether it is a for-profit, revenue-generating site. After completing each page and clicking Next, you are asked to complete your account profile. Fill in the rest of the requested data, and then click the Submit Your Name button. Your information is routed to BMI for further processing.

SESAC and Internet music licenses

At the time this book was published, SESAC did not offer an Internet distribution license for its music. Keep checking their Web site at http://www.sesac.com/licensing/internet_licensing1.asp for this feature.

Obtaining a sound recording license

If you intend to obtain a license to broadcast recorded music over the Internet—even as just a music component of a home video you are posting—you need to contact the music company that released the recorded work you wish to extract from.

Because approximately 85 percent of all music sales are transacted by five large music conglomerates, the chances are pretty favorable that the sound recording license you seek will be controlled by of one of these firms.

These are the top five companies and some of the labels under their wings:

✦ Universal Music Group (MCA, Geffen, Mercury, Island)

✦ Warner Music Group (Warner Bros., Atlantic, Elektra)

✦ Sony Music Entertainment Inc. (Columbia, Epic)

✦ BMG Entertainment (BMG, RCA, Arista)

✦ EMI-Capitol Music Group (Capitol, Virgin, Chrysalis)

At the time this book was written, most of the major music companies did not have sound recording license applications posted on their Web sites. Direct contact is the best option. Sound recording license contact information for each of these music companies is provided on the RIAA Web site at www.riaa.com/issues/licensing/howto.asp.

What Can Happen to You

Despite the availability of some great and fully legal digital music and video download Web sites, some Internet users persist in trying to get something for nothing. Whether these people should be prosecuted is a bit beside the point. That's because some of them already have been.

At the time this book was written, the RIAA (Recording Industry Association of America) filed copyright infringement suits against more than 3,000 violators. Additionally, a number of separate infringement complaints have been filed by groups of record companies.

The first word in this book's title is "Caution." At least one dictionary defines the term as "careful forethought to avoid danger or harm" and "close attention or vigilance to minimize risk." As you examine why and how the RIAA was able to locate specific people to sue among millions who have traded music files online, the term caution definitely applies.

Do not misunderstand the term caution in this context. I'm not going to give advice on how not to get caught. Nor will I preach to you not to visit free, file-sharing sites. As long as these sites are available, some—perhaps even you—will be tempted. What I cover in the next section will familiarize you with the arsenal of technical tools the RIAA uses to find those it considers violators.

Hunting for copyright violators

The RIAA starts its search for copyright infringers by using software that scans publicly available directories of peer-to-peer digital download music services and is thus able to identify the Internet service provider of each user. Then the music industry body uses the Digital Millennium Copyright Act to subpoena the ISP for each user's name, address, and other personal information necessary to locate the presumed offender and to sue them.

Based on how this method works, file swappers not intimidated by these RIAA sweeps may take countermeasures to avoid detection. Again, I'm are not recommending these steps, only describing their availability and nature.

The Electronic Frontier Foundation, an online free speech advocacy group opposed to what it considers onerous copyright laws, points out that users of peer-to-peer networks can take the following steps to avoid getting sued:

1. **Make sure there are no potentially infringing files in your P2P shared folder.** This would ordinarily mean that your shared folder contains only files that are in the public domain, for which they have permission to share, or are made available under pro-sharing licenses, such as the Creative Commons license. In addition, all files with potentially misleading filenames that could be confused with an RIAA artist should be removed from your shared folder.

2. **Disable the "sharing" or "uploading" features on your P2P folder that allow other users on the network to get copies of files from any computer on your network.** Disabling this function also prevents other users from scanning any of your online music folders and examining what songs and music files you have stored on your PC.

Caution   On its Web site, the Electronic Frontier Foundation lists Web pages where you can find out how to disable the sharing features on popular peer-to-peer digital downloading services. To reach this resource, go to www.eff.org/IP/P2P/howto-notgetsued.php.

Real-life violations

The RIAA regards itself as a key protector of music companies' legal and business interests. To the chagrin of many who have been served with papers, this organization does not bluff. If they are able to find those digital downloaders believed to be violating copyright law, they will sue for copyright infringement.

Cases in point

A typical RIAA copyright lawsuit involves serving of papers telling the accused that he or she has committed copyright infringement. Sometimes, a dollar amount is specified as redress, and sometimes not. Few of these cases ever come to trial. Most are settled out of court for an average settlement of $2,000 to $3,000, plus a binding promise never to perform an illegal online song swap again.

Occasionally, though, cases are filed that do not fit the mold. The year 2003 seemed to be the year for such complaints. In perhaps the most newsworthy case filed to date, the RIAA sued 12-year-old New York-area resident Brianna Lahara for illegally swapping songs on Kazaa. Brianna's plight made front-page headlines in area newspapers. Press accounts described the girl as being scared and on the verge of tears when she heard she was being sued. Her mother paid $2,000 to settle the case.

Another RIAA legal action in 2003 found the RIAA filing a lawsuit against Jesse Jordan (see Figure 9-10) for converting part of his college computer network "into a marketplace for copyright piracy that is used by others to copy and distribute music illegally."

The complaint went on to say "in addition to operating this piracy marketplace that facilitates direct copyright infringement by others, defendant is committing direct copyright infringement himself by copying and distributing hundreds of sound recordings over his system without the authorization of the copyright owners."

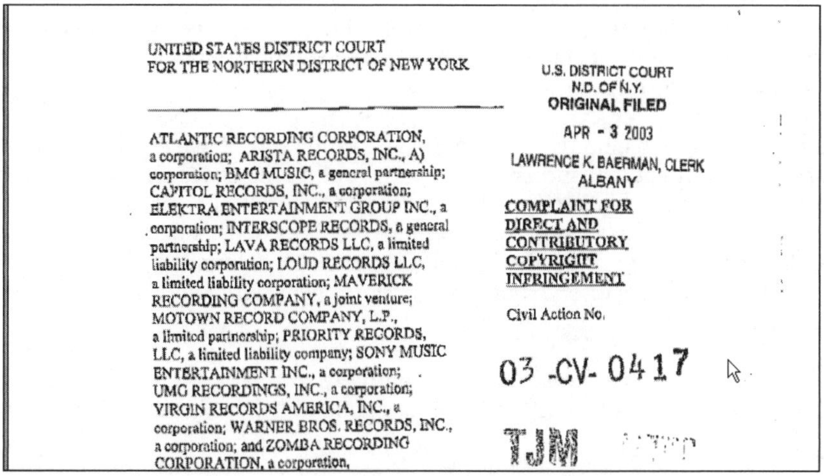

UNITED STATES DISTRICT COURT
FOR THE NORTHERN DISTRICT OF NEW YORK

U.S. DISTRICT COURT
N.D. OF N.Y.
ORIGINAL FILED
APR - 3 2003
LAWRENCE K. BAERMAN, CLERK
ALBANY

ATLANTIC RECORDING CORPORATION, a corporation; ARISTA RECORDS, INC., A) corporation; BMG MUSIC, a general partnership; CAPITOL RECORDS, INC., a corporation; ELEKTRA ENTERTAINMENT GROUP INC., a corporation; INTERSCOPE RECORDS, a general partnership; LAVA RECORDS LLC, a limited liability corporation; LOUD RECORDS LLC, a limited liability corporation; MAVERICK RECORDING COMPANY, a joint venture; MOTOWN RECORD COMPANY, L.P., a limited partnership; PRIORITY RECORDS, LLC, a limited liability company; SONY MUSIC ENTERTAINMENT INC., a corporation; UMG RECORDINGS, INC., a corporation; VIRGIN RECORDS AMERICA, INC., a corporation; WARNER BROS. RECORDS, INC., a corporation; and ZOMBA RECORDING CORPORATION, a corporation,

COMPLAINT FOR DIRECT AND CONTRIBUTORY COPYRIGHT INFRINGEMENT

Civil Action No.

03 -CV- 0417

TJM

Figure 9-10: The copyright infringement lawsuit filed by the RIAA against Jesse Jordan.

The RIAA summarized the circumstances by stating the "defendant's (Jordan's) conduct has caused and continues to cause Plaintiffs grave and irreparable harm." Artists named that suffered from harm as a result of Jordan's actions include Santana, Usher, the Smashing Pumpkins, Pink, and the Dave Matthews Band.

The suit was settled when Jordan paid the RIAA $12,000.

Yet another high-profile action against file sharers occurred in August 2004, when the Federal Bureau of Investigation served warrants at a home in the Houston area, as well as at the offices of small Internet Service Providers in Texas, New York, and Wisconsin. The warrants sought evidence about the operators of five "hubs" of the Underground Network, an organization of 7,000 users who, Federal prosecutors charged, repeatedly have violated federal copyright laws by facilitating the unauthorized file-swapping of copyrighted movies and music.

Such violations carry a maximum $250,000 fine and five years imprisonment. The case had not yet been brought to trial when this book was published.

Caution   From time to time, newspaper articles note a new round of RIAA lawsuits. These accounts can strike terror into online swappers' hearts. Because news of these suits often comes weeks before the defendants are actually served, part of the terror is uncertainty. But have you been sued? Go to `http://www.eff.org/IP/P2P/riaasubpoenas/`. This page has a form where you may enter a user name or search for your IP address in a legal database to determine whether a subpoena has been issued.

What to do if you have been sued

No matter how authoritative and comprehensive the advice, no Web site can take the place of personal legal counsel. If the RIAA sues you, then you should immediately contact an attorney.

That said, some groups unfavorable to RIAA lawsuits offer legal advice and input to those sued by the music industry body. The Subpoena Defense Alliance, a project of the Electronic Frontier Foundation, maintains a list of attorneys at `www.subpoenadefense.org/legal.htm`. Many of the links on this page are to Web sites of law firms that provide legal assistance to RIAA defendants. Additionally, some of these Web sites offer articles about your legal rights and alternatives open to you.

Most people who receive RIAA lawsuits eventually settle for a relatively small portion of what was demanded in the initial complaint. Case law is still evolving.

Ten Vital Ways to Protect Yourself Legally when You Download or Distribute Music and Video

1. **Understand the justification for copyright law.** It is meant to protect the rights of artists and others who create visual, literary and other works.

2. **Understand what types of digital content are protected under copyright law.** Typically, these include music, sound recordings, recordings of public performances, books, movies, and even choreographed dance routines and pantomimes.

3. **Learn how to recognize copyrighted material.** In most cases, such works will carry the insignia ©.

4. **Understand the principle of Fair Use — and the limited provisions it offers you to draw from copyrighted music or other creative works.** You may be able to take a few seconds from a song for your own purposes, but not too much.

5. **Understand how the provisions of the Digital Millennium Copyright Act affect you.** Copyright violations are now punishable by a $250,000 fine per unauthorized use of copyrighted work, plus a five-year jail sentence.

6. **Understand how trademark law works in relation to brand names, slogans and other protected material sometimes distributed by file sharers.** Generally, even if the material you distribute through a file-sharing service is not copyrighted, you cannot legally distribute it if the musical act, or even name of the song, belongs to, or disparages, a known brand, company or trademarked advertising slogan.

7. **Learn how to obtain a distribution license for posting copyrighted music on the Internet.** The two main music publishing licensing services, BMI and ASCAP, offer this feature on their Web sites.

8. **Learn how to obtain a Sound Recording license for posting copyrighted music on your Web site, or on your own digital files.** BMI and ASCAP's Web sites offer these resources.

9. **Keep current with the latest lawsuits and other legal action against file sharers accused of Internet-based copyright violations.** Thousands of file swappers have already been sued by the Recording Industry Association of America, and there is no indication the suits are going to stop.

10. **Learn what to do if you have been sued by the RIAA, or other organization representing the rights of copyright holders.** Call a lawyer, and be prepared to dig in to your pocket. Most of these suits have been settled out of court for amounts ranging from $2,000 to $3,000.

Summary

In this chapter, you learned the basics of copyright law and why this law exists to protect songwriters, musicians, and other artists who create, record, and perform their work. You also learned that trademark law can work with copyright law to protect artists' rights.

If you intend to distribute copyrighted music over the Internet, this chapter explained how to comply with copyright law, by seeking the appropriate licenses to do so. Finally, you learned what's at stake for you in the legal arena if you do not exercise the proper caution and become either an illegal or careless digital music downloader.

✦   ✦   ✦

Legal and Safe Fun with Downloaded Media

In This Part

Chapter 10
Safely Downloading
Music to Portable
Devices

Chapter 11
Creative and Legal
Music and Video
Projects

Safely Downloading Media to Portable Devices

✦ ✦ ✦ ✦

In This Chapter

Transferring tracks
from PCs to portable
devices

Introducing portable
music players

Using portable music
player software on
your PC

Downloading and
watching movies
on your notebook
computer

Downloading musical
ring tones to your
cell phone

✦ ✦ ✦ ✦

Sometime this weekend, take a jaunt to your favorite
city or county park. You will see picnickers, couples,
people with their dogs, and in this mix of humanity, you may
also notice plenty of folks carrying around portable devices.
Through earphones, they are listening to music while power
walking, running, or cycling.

Although some of these mobile music listeners have taken
along their own CDs, an increasing number are walking, running, or biking to the rhythms of MP3 song files downloaded
from the Internet and transferred to these portable devices.

This is a different type of music consumption than the standard
walkman model, where CDs (or in earlier versions, cassettes)
are used. Still a popular method, listening to music tracks on a
walkman most often involves purchasing a CD at a music store,
inserting the CD into the portable player, and then hitting the
street or running track.

MP3 or similarly enabled portable music players work on
another model. You purchase and download music from the
Internet, store it in a music library on your hard drive, and
then, at a time and place of your choosing, transfer your digital music files from PC to your portable player.

In this chapter, you learn about how to safely and efficiently purchase, download, and transfer MP3s and other audio and video files from the Web to your portable music or video player. I introduce you to some of the leading portable music players available, tell you how to configure them, and then lead you through the song purchase and download process.

Also in this chapter, you learn about safe media downloads for portable DVD players, personal digital assistants, and even cell phones. I conclude with some tips to guard your privacy when downloading to and using these mobile entertainment devices.

Using iPod and iTunes

iPod is Apple Computer's hugely popular portable music player. There are several versions, the largest of which holds 10,000 songs. Although iPod can work with almost any MP3 music directory, it is directly configured for easy interchange with iTunes, the online music store from Apple.

For the most part, iTunes' selections are programmed in the AAC (Advanced Audio Coding) format. Apple, which played a big part in formulating this music technology standard, claims with some justification that AAC compresses (condenses) audio much more efficiently than MP3. Apple also correctly notes that AAC compression produces music tracks that are almost up to CD standards.

Downloading and installing iTunes on your computer

Before you can buy digital music from iTunes to transfer to your iPod, you need to download and install the iTunes software on your PC. This procedure varies from some other music stores, where the transactions take place on a Web site. To download and install the iTunes software on your PC, perform the following steps:

1. **Point your Web browser to the Apple iTunes site at** www.apple.com/itunes/download/.

2. **Scroll down the page and, depending on your computer's operating system, click either the "Windows 2000 or XP" or the "Mac OS X" radio button (see Figure 10-1).**

3. **Click Download iTunes.** This kicks off the download process. A file download dialog box opens. This box contains an "executable" installation file that you need to save to your PC.

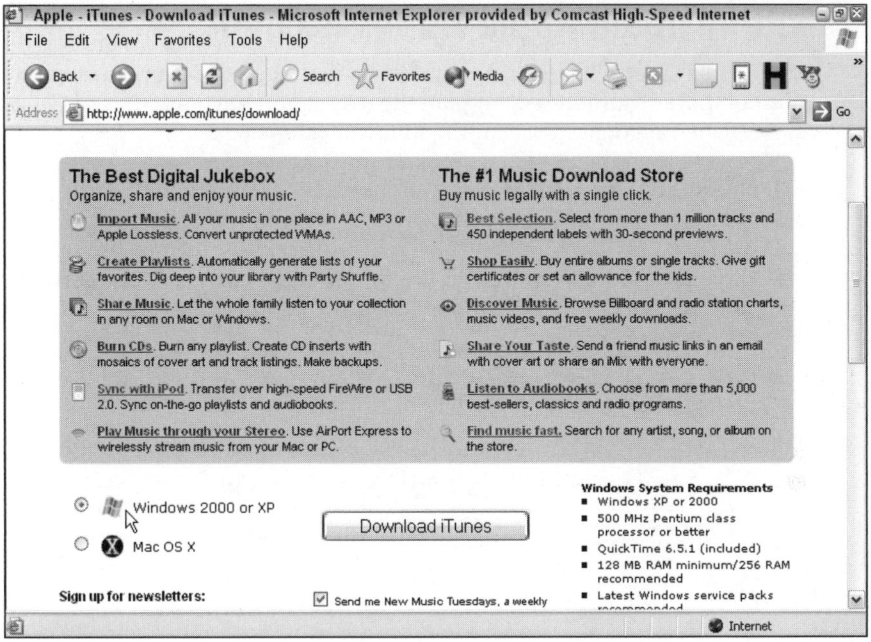

Figure 10-1: Before downloading iTunes, click your operating system's radio button.

4. **Click Save.** The installation file downloads to a default directory on your hard drive.

5. **After the file downloads, go to Windows, click Start ⇨ Run, choose the name of the directory, and then choose the name of this installation file.** This begins the actual iTunes download.

6. **When the download completes, follow the onscreen instructions for installing iTunes on your PC.**

iTunes has one of the most substantial music libraries on the Internet. At the time this book was written, iTunes offered more than 1 million tracks from all five major labels and more than 600 leading independent labels, giving it the status of the largest fully legal downloadable music catalog.

The most efficient way to add music to your iPod is by going online using your PC, purchasing songs from the iTunes Music Store (`www.itunes.com`), and then transferring your selections from your PC to your portable iPod. When you click Buy, the music is downloaded to your hard drive and imported into your iTunes library.

Setting up an Apple iTunes account

Before you can purchase music on iTunes, you need to set up an account and have your computer "authorized" to play the music you have purchased. To set up an Apple iTunes account, perform the following steps:

1. **Open the iTunes software.**

2. **Click Music Store in the Source list.**

3. **Click the Account button in the upper-right corner of the store.** If no other user is signed in to the iTunes Music Store on your computer, the Account button says Sign In.

4. **Click Create New Account.** Fill out the contact and other information requested (see Figure 10-2).

Figure 10-2: To open an iTunes account, click Create New Account.

Before you can listen to your music purchases, you need to authorize your computer to play the music you bought. A maximum of three computers can be authorized to play given tracks at one time. Although authorization may sound rather controlling and intimidating, it is Apple's way of protecting the copyrights on the music that it sells. The three-computer limit thwarts any strategy of making numerous copies of digital music files by distributing them to a large number of computers. Fortunately, though, you do not have to go through too much trouble to authorize your PC or Mac. Your computer becomes authorized the first time you use that computer to set up your account or when you play a song that you purchased (and enter your Apple ID and password).

To authorize a computer, simply play a song you have purchased from iTunes on your computer. The first time you authorize your computer, you'll need to enter your Apple ID and password. iTunes tracks are encoded with information that, once the songs are distributed to more than five computers, prevents those songs from being played on any more computers. This is a built-in digital safeguard against file sharing.

Finding music on iTunes

As mentioned, iTunes encodes songs in a digital file format called AAC or Advanced Audio Coding. These are MPEG-4 type files. Apple, as well as most consumer electronics reviewers, agrees that MPEG-4 AAC rivals CD quality.

To find music on iTunes that you can play on your PC or transfer to your iPod, perform the following steps:

1. **Open the iTunes software and log into your account.**

2. **Click Music Store.** The main Music Store page opens, with a display and list of highlighted music available for purchase from iTunes.

3. **In the Main Music store page, fill in the name of a recording artist, album, song, artist, or composer in the Search box and click Search Music Store.** A list of tracks available for purchase appears (see Figure 10-3).

Figure 10-3: A list of tracks that match what you've searched for appears.

4. **Highlight and then click the titles of the track or tracks you want to purchase.** On most tracks, a 30-second sample of the song will play on your computer (see Figure 10-4).

Figure 10-4: Highlighting iTunes tracks to sample and purchase

Purchasing music on iTunes

iTunes has a branded *1-Click* technology that makes it easy to purchase the music you have found in your search and have listened to. The process involves just a few easy steps.

In the previous set of steps, I searched for tracks from Sheryl Crow and selected "A Change Would Do You Good." To use the 1-Click option to buy a track you have selected from iTunes, perform the following steps:

1. **Move the iTunes slidebar to the right until the Buy Song icon appears (see Figure 10-5).**

2. **Click the Buy Song icon.** The Apple Account box opens.

3. **In the Apple Account box, type your username and password (see Figure 10-6) and click Buy.** Your music purchases are charged to the credit card number you supplied when you opened your Apple Account.

Figure 10-5: The iTunes Buy Song icon

Figure 10-6: Filling out the Apple Account box

4. **After your credit card is approved, your new track or tracks are added to your iTunes Library.** To see a list of tracks in your iTunes Library, go to the Source bar and Click Library. A list of songs you have downloaded appears in iTunes' main window (see Figure 10-7).

Caution

On iTunes, all sales are final. Each time you click a Buy button, your music purchases are charged to the credit card on your Apple Account. You cannot cancel a purchase or receive a refund for a purchase. Because it prevents people from buying large numbers of songs that they do not intend to pay for, this is largely a copyright-protection strategy on Apple's part.

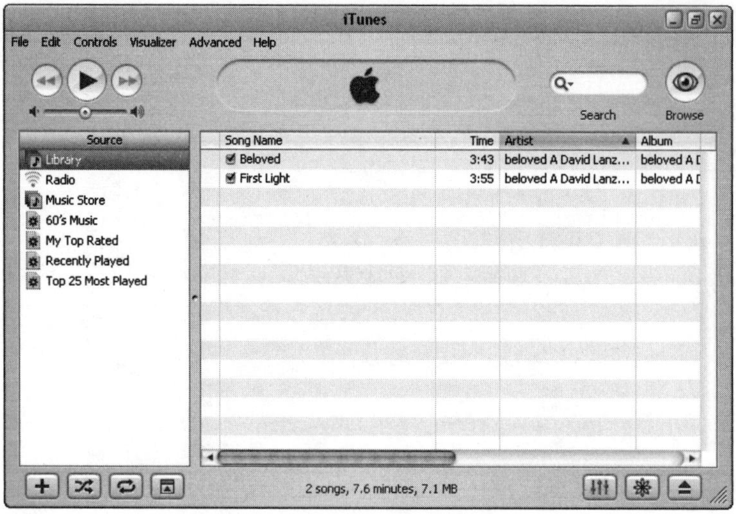

Figure 10-7: Viewing a list of downloaded songs

Transferring music from iTunes to your iPod

In order to move your newly purchased digital music files from your PC to your iPod, you need to perform two separate procedures: Connect your iPod to your computer, and then transfer the digital song files from your computer to your iPod.

Connecting your iPod to your computer

The exact way in which you perform this procedure has much to do with the type of operating system your computer runs on. If you have a Mac, you will want to connect your iPod using the special FireWire cable that came with your iPod. With Mac OS X 10.3.4 or later and an iPod (with Dock Connector) or iPod mini you can also use your USB port.

To connect iPod to your computer, you can do one of two things:

✦ Plug the cable into a FireWire or high-powered SB 2.0 port on your computer, and then connect the other end to iPod.

✦ If you have a Dock or synching cradle, connect the cable to a FireWire or high-powered USB port on your computer and connect the other end to the Dock. Put iPod in the Dock.

Transferring songs from iTunes to iPod

Part of the process of transferring songs from iTunes to an iPod is automated. When you connect your iPod to your computer and your computer is on, it automatically calls up the iTunes software and looks for newly purchased and added tracks. iTunes transfers new songs you've added.

If you prefer, you can also transfer tracks manually between your iTunes software and your iPod. To do this manually, follow these steps:

1. **Connect iPod to your computer.** How you connect the iPod depends on your computer type.

2. **Open iTunes.** The iTunes Source list opens.

3. **Click iPod in the iTunes Source list.** The Source list appears in the main iPod left frame, containing a list of the portable devices that are compatible with iTunes and that you have installed software for. If you have installed iPod software, iPod will appear on the Source list.

4. **After clicking iPod in the iTunes Source list, click the Options button.** A series of choices appears in the Source list frame.

5. **Click Manually manage songs and playlists, and then click OK.**

6. **In the Source list, click Library.** A list of the tracks in your iTunes Library appears in the main window.

7. **In the list of tracks in your iTunes Library click to select a track to transfer to your iPod.** If you want to transfer more than one track, hold your Control key down and then click to highlight each track you want to move to your iPod.

8. **Drag the song to the iPod icon in the Source list.** The songs will begin transferring automatically from iTunes to your iPod.

Introducing Other Portable Media Players

When it comes to media players you can carry around with you, a number of choices are available. Although there are some differences in style, size, weight, battery life, and the controls you use to operate the device, most of these players are far more similar than different.

The similarities involve how you, the user, download digital files from your PC to these players and how these products store, list, and retrieve the files you have downloaded to them.

Later in this chapter you learn how to securely and efficiently transfer files from your PC to some of these leading products. This is a different process from the tightly integrated iPod-iTunes transfer process, which involves a specific series of actions between purchasing music on iTunes and then moving those selections along to your iPod. The digital download and transfer process in other devices is somewhat more open-ended, with several music and media software products configured to work on multiple brands.

Before I describe the transfer process, though, it stands to reason that you want to select a portable music player. Because no one music player has an inarguable quality edge over another, this decision is far from a slam-dunk. Like purchasing an automobile, your choice in portable digital music hardware should be an aesthetic decision as well as one based on quality.

To help you in your decision, the next sections offer an overview of some of the more popular digital music players available today. With an eye on your budget, I've included a sample of music players at various price ranges and digital music file storage capacities.

RCA/Thomson Lyra

The Lyra is one of the more well-established MP3 players and has been around since 2000. Several models are available, including the economically priced RD1080 (see Figure 10-8). On its 128MB built-in flash memory multimedia card, the RD1080 stores more than two hours of digital audio. The device has a flash card slot for an additional several hours of storage.

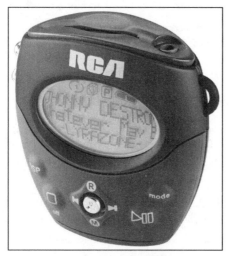

Figure 10-8: The Lyra RD1080

The RD1080 weighs just two ounces and is 2.3"x2.4" inches in size. It runs on two AAA batteries and comes with stereo headphones, a carry case with a belt clip, a USB connection cable, and a CD-ROM with music transfer software.

At the time this book was written, the RD1080 had a suggested retail price of $119.99, but was available on the RCA site (www.rca.com) for only $99.99.

Rio Cali

Listening to music while running is one of the more popular things people do with their portable digital players.

The very act of running, of course, produces (hopefully productive) strain—not only on the body doing the actual physical exercise, but also on any devices that are attached to the body. That's why runners who want their digital music on the go should consider a sturdy model that can attach with an armband and comes with headphones that won't slip off when you pound the pavement or track.

The $179.99 Rio Cali 256MB Sport (see Figure 10-9) is one such model. It can hold up to eight hours of Windows Media Audio (a format for playing music tracks in Windows Media Player on PCs or compatible portable devices) or four hours of MP3 music. That equates to more than 120 WMA or 60 MP3 tracks. It weights 1.8 ounces measures 2.5"x2.6". For you fitness freaks, it comes with earphones, an armband, and an integrated stopwatch/timer.

Figure 10-9: The Rio Cali

Creative Rhomba

The Creative Rhomba portable music players have some of the largest digital music storage capacities of any portable model. The Creative Rhomba Jukebox 20GB (see Figure 10-10), for instance, can house up to 340 hours of digital music and supports both the MP3 and WMA formats. Unlike most other non-Apple devices, it is fully compatible with iTunes, Apple's online digital music purchase and downloading service.

The Creative Rhomba Jukebox 20GB weighs 14 ounces, is 5.5"x5.5", and is available for less than $250 at several online retailers.

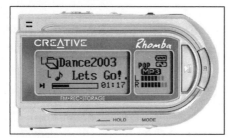

Figure 10-10: The Creative Rhomba Jukebox 20GB

Samsung YP55V

Samsung, the Asian electronics giant, offers several MP3 players. Of these, the YP55V is one of the most popular models and regularly gets high marks from consumer electronics product reviewers for its surround sound style audio playback capabilities.

It has 256MB of digital file storage space, which, in this model, equates to up to 15 hours of playback time. It can handle both MP3 and WMA files. The device runs on one AAA battery, is 8"x8" in size, and has FM receiver and voice recording functions. The YP55V has a suggested list price of $249.99.

ARCHOS Gimini 220

One of the more advanced digital music players, the $349.95 ARCHOS Gimini 220 (see Figure 10-11) has a 20GB, 5,000-song capacity. More than just an MP3 player, the Gimini also has photo-display, audiotape recording, and an optional FM radio, from which you can record broadcasts and save them as MP3 files.

The ARCHOS Gimini comes with the Musicmatch Jukebox software. It also includes the built-in ARCHOS Double Browser, an in-player application that lets you manage your digital music files, as well as any other digital files — such as photo and voice files — currently stored on your Gimini.

Cross-Reference   For more information on Musicmatch Jukebox, see Chapter 1.

Figure 10-11: The ARCHOS Gimini 220

Transferring files to portable music players

In this section, you explore ways to move your files between PC-based music management software and your portable digital music devices.

Depending on the software and portable players you use, digital music file transfer can take one of two forms:

✦ **Using digital music library software configured to work on numerous devices.** Depending on the software, you probably need to download a module or other component into the music library software so it can communicate with your portable player.

✦ **Using proprietary digital music library software configured to work with specific devices.** iTunes is one such package. Rio Music Manager, which works with Rio Forge and other Rio digital music players, is another example.

The next sections describe software-to-player digital music transfer from non-brand-specific music library software, and then from specific, branded digital file management software. Because the file transfer process is similar among music library software of all types, I use two examples: RealPlayer for non-brand specific transfers and Rio Music Manager for Rio Forge.

Equipping RealPlayer to work with your portable device

RealPlayer, a leading digital media utility, supports digital music file transfer between PCs and numerous portable digital music players.

First, you need to ensure that RealPlayer supports your device. If it does, you must instruct your copy of RealPlayer to install some computer code to ensure that your RealPlayer can work with your device.

To equip RealPlayer to work with your portable digital music player and then transfer files, follow the next two sets of steps:

1. **Download and install RealPlayer from the RealNetworks site at** `www.real.com.` You will need to turn your computer off, and then on again before you can use RealPlayer.

2. **Open RealPlayer, and click Burn/Transfer.** The main Burn/Transfer screen opens, as shown in Figure 10-12.

3. **In the main Burn/Transfer window, click Add A New Device.** The Add A New Device screen opens, as shown in Figure 10-13.

4. **Scroll down the Add A New Device list until you see the name of the digital music player with which you want to equip RealPlayer to work and click on the name of that device**. An information screen opens on the right with a description of the device, as shown in Figure 10-14.

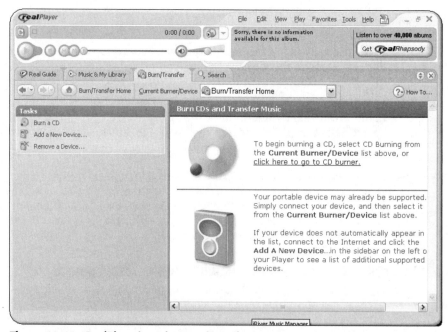

Figure 10-12: RealPlayer's main Burn/Transfer screen

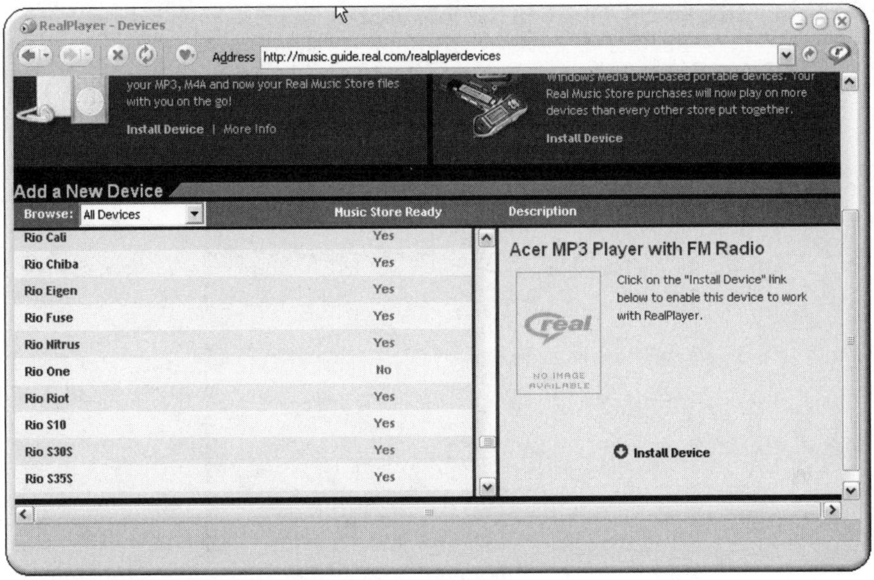

Figure 10-13: RealPlayer's Add A New Device menu

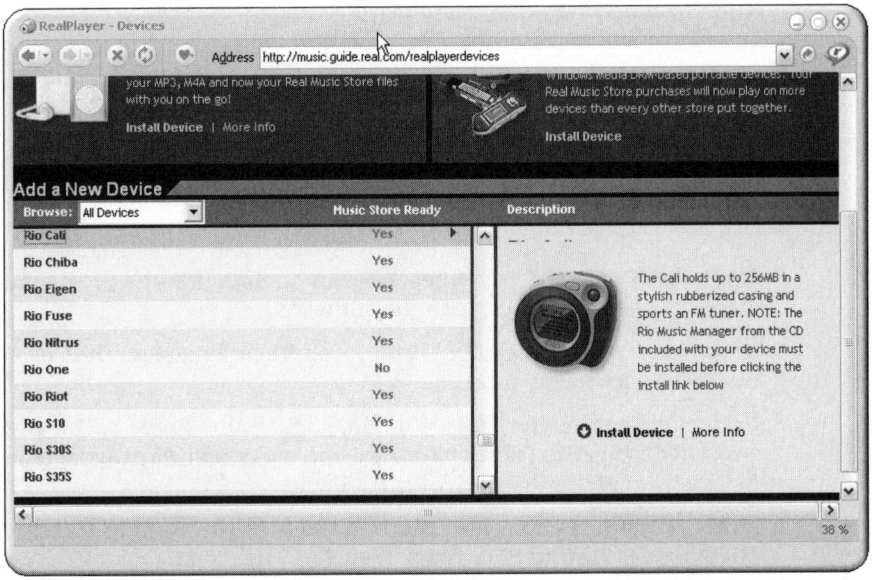

Figure 10-14: Choosing your specific device yields a description of the device to be installed as a file transfer option.

5. **Click install device in the information screen.** Your copy of RealPlayer contacts the RealNetworks (maker of RealPlayer) Web site and downloads the code for your new device into RealPlayer. You see an AutoUpdate dialog box while this is working (see Figure 10-15).

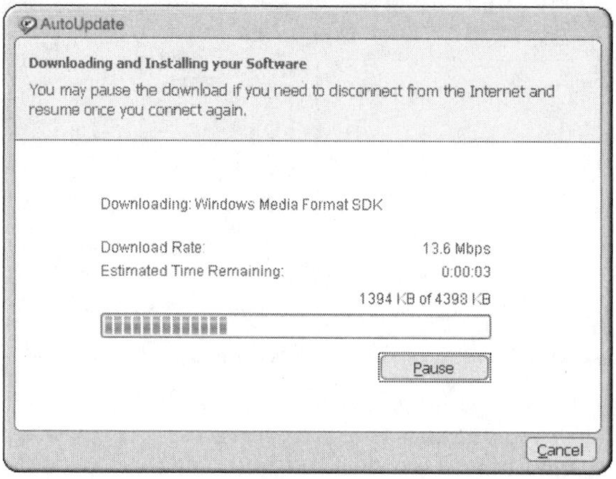

Figure 10-15: Code for the newly installed portable device installs into RealPlayer.

6. **Restart your computer after the download completes.** You will be prompted to restart. RealPlayer is now configured to work with your portable device.

Once you've made sure your portable device will support RealPlayer, you need to get some files on to your portable digital music player! To transfer files, follow these steps:

1. **Open RealPlayer.** After you restart your computer in the previous set of steps, you will need to reopen the software.

2. **In the View menu, click My Library and Burn/Transfer.** The Current Burner/Device menu appears.

3. **In the Current Burner/Device menu, click on the name of the device you want RealPlayer to transfer files to.** You must have already installed the device you choose in order for this to work.

4. **In My Library, click on the names of the files you want to transfer to your portable device and click Start Transfer.** The digital music files you have selected are transferred to your digital music player.

Equipping Rio Music Manager for file transfer

Application-specific digital music utilities such as Rio Music Manager are configured to work with specific portable digital players — in this case, several MP3 players offered by D&M Holdings U.S., Inc., manufacturer of the popular Rio line of portable music players.

Before you can use Rio Manager with your Rio Cali or other player, you need to install it on your PC. Here's how:

1. **Locate the installation CD that came with your Rio device, and place it into your PC's CD-ROM drive.** The installation software launches automatically.

2. **Click the Rio Music Manager INSTALL NOW prompt, and follow the onscreen instructions for saving Rio Music Manager to a directory on your PC.**

3. **When the installation is complete, reboot your computer.** When you reboot, your Rio Music Manager software is installed on your PC.

4. **After reboot, click My Music.** Rio Music Manager scans your PC and builds a list of your digital music files. After the process is complete, these files are added to your music library.

Copying digital music files from your PC to your Rio

Now that you have installed Rio Music Manager on your PC, you are ready to start transferring digital music files to your Rio. Here's how:

1. **Make sure that your Rio Cali or other model is connected to your PC either by cable or docking station.**

2. **Choose Start ➪ Programs ➪ Rio Music Manager.** The Rio Music Manager utility opens.

3. **In the Device List, click the Media Library icon.** Your Media Library opens, as shown in Figure 10-16.

4. **In the Media Library click to highlight the name of one or more tracks.** If you want to highlight multiple tracks, press and hold down the Control key and then click on the name of each track you want to transfer (see Figure 10-17).

5. **Click the CD icon next to the name of each track you have selected.** These tracks are copied to your Rio.

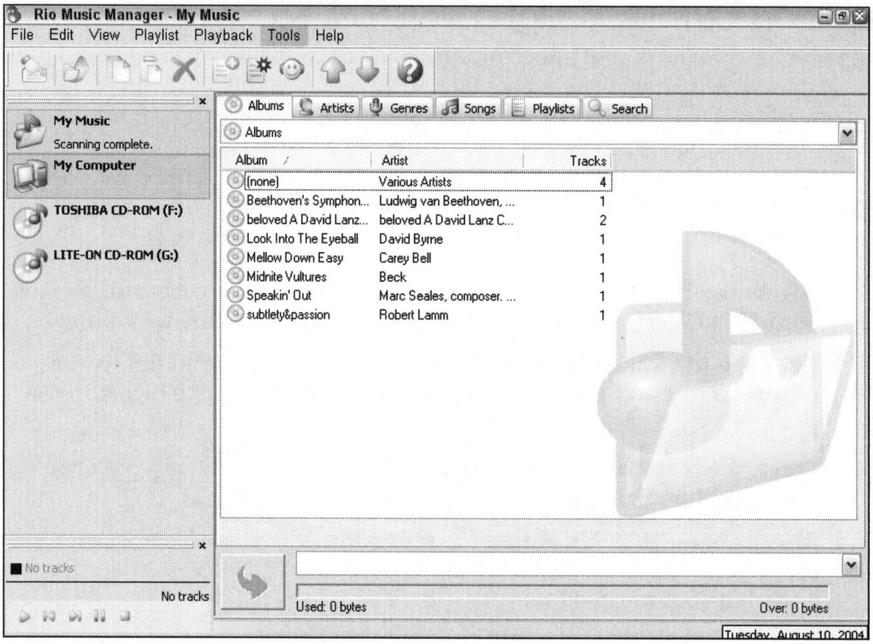

Figure 10-16: Rio Music Manager's Media Library

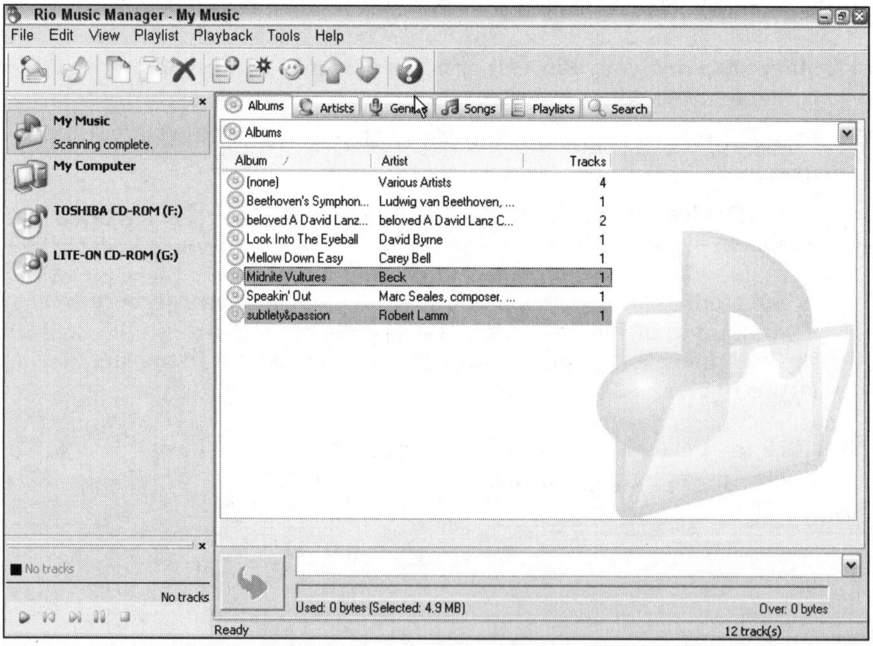

Figure 10-17: Selecting multiple tracks to copy from the Rio Music Manager to the Rio Cali

Enjoying Downloaded Digital Media on Other Portable Devices

The limits of current technology combine with copyright concerns to place some barriers to unimpeded enjoyment of digital audio and video content on portable devices. It would be nice to be able to legally download a DVD movie, transfer it to your portable DVD player, PDA, or cell phone, and watch it there. It should just be a matter of time until this is both technically feasible and legal.

That said, there are still ways to turn your laptop, PDA, or cell phone into an entertainment center of sorts. In this section, I explore two of these safe and legal options: downloading a movie to your laptop computer and downloading an MP3 music file to your cell phone.

Downloading a movie to your laptop

Sites such as MovieLink (`www.movielink.com`) and Cinema Now (`www.cinemanow.com`) make it possible to view movies for specific lengths of time or download them to keep.

Because of the potential for unlicensed duplication, copyright restrictions now in effect generally limit viewing of movies you have downloaded to the device you downloaded it on. In other words, you technically (and legally) cannot burn a CD or DVD of your video file, nor can you copy a downloaded movie file from your PC to your laptop.

A Cineplex On Your Laptop? Yes, Eventually

With the average full-length motion picture costing many tens of millions of dollars to produce, the movie industry is understandably very, very afraid of unauthorized duplication of crown jewel titles. Still, elements of an eventual marriage between full-length movies and portable devices are starting to appear. Much of this early momentum is due to the DivX format, a proprietary type of digital compression used to condense movies so they can fit on a CD. Movies compressed in this manner, however, are still encoded in DivX. With the exception of Windows Media Player 9 and two DivX-only offerings (BSPlayer v1.00 and Global DivX Player v1.0), it is a format not readily understandable by today's generation of media player software or playable on portable devices.

That may be changing. In Summer 2004, a Hong Kong-based company called Shinco announced a DivX-compatible portable media player with a 9"-view screen. The company intends for its product to work with DivX movies — many of which are already available for purchase on the DivX movies site at `www.divxmovies.com/search/index.php`. Yet, until more portable DivX players come out and the file transfer technology matures to ease movement of DivX movies between PCs and portable devices, you are cautioned to wait for all pieces of this promising delivery technology to come together.

That said, there's nothing to prevent you from firing up your portable notebook computer, going to a site such as MovieLink or Cinema Now, and buying access to or a copy of a movie. Then you can play the movie anywhere you go with your laptop—a park, an airplane, or wherever you choose.

Downloading a movie to your laptop is as simple a process of going online with your notebook computer and accessing MovieLink, Cinema Now, or another movie rental site. After you rent or purchase and download the movie, it is available for viewing using one of several media player software programs, including RealPlayer and Windows Media Player.

Caution   Movie files are huge. A 90-minute feature can take up about 550MB on your hard drive. Before you download your movie, make sure that you have at least double that available space. In your Windows notebook PC, click Start ⇨ My Computer and then check the free space on your local disk (usually Drive C:).

In this example, you learn how to select and legally download a digital movie file from MovieLink to your notebook PC. To do this, perform the following steps:

1. **Point your Web browser to the MovieLink Web site at** www.movielink.com **(see Figure 10-18).**

Figure 10-18: The MovieLink Web site

2. **In the menu on the left click on the category of the type of movie that interests you.** A list of movie titles fitting that classification appears.

3. **Click on the title of the movie you want to download.** A separate page opens for your selection (see Figure 10-19).

4. **Click the radio button next to the media player you want to use to view your clip in your notebook computer.**

5. **Click Rent.** Your selected movie begins downloading to your notebook PC. When the download is complete, you receive a notification of the directory in which your film is stored.

6. **When the download is complete, open your media player, click the File menu, and then go to the folder and filename for your movie.** The digital movie file starts playing automatically.

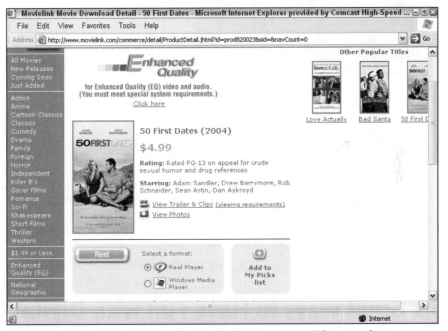

Figure 10-19: Each MovieLink selection has its own page with a Rent button.

Downloading ring tones

If you have a digital cell phone, you may be able to obtain digital music files for your device. Commonly called ring tones, these files are actually MP3-encoded song snippets.

The best way to obtain ring tones is through your cellular phone device. A number of newer phones have color-coded feature icons and menus. If your phone has a menu called "tones" or "ring tones," click it to open a list of tonal choices.

Some carriers, such as Sprint PCS, list tones by artist and style (see Figure 10-20).

Using your phone keypad, browse through the list and choose one to your liking. Hit the "Select" button or one similarly named. Your choice downloads to your phone and plays the next time you receive an incoming call. But choose wisely ... a bodacious ring tone in a crowded place will turn heads — the wrong way!!

Figure 10-20: Many cell phone service providers make MP3 ring tones available for download.

Six Great Ways to Have Fun with Digital Media on Portable Devices

1. **Learn how to find tracks on iTunes and other legal music services.** Most offer searchable databases of songs, tracks, and artists.

2. **Become knowledgeable about portable music players.** Several brands are available, and are described in this chapter, including iPod, RCA Thomson/Lyra, and Rio Cali.

3. **Learn how to install and use proprietary software that most portable music players come with.** This software is either downloadable from the Web sites of these portable music player manufacturers, or it comes on a CD you get when you buy the product. This software helps you transfer your files from your PC to your portable device.

4. **Understand how to use RealPlayer to transfer digital music files from your PC to your portable device.** RealPlayer supports most portable music players.

5. **Learn how to download a full-length feature movie from a legal Web site to your laptop, and then watch it wherever you take your computer.** Movies take up a lot of storage, but the convenience of being able to watch a movie on your notebook computer while you are on a flight is pretty cool.

6. **Understand how to purchase, download, and install ring tones to your cell phone.** Often, ring tones are MP3 files of familiar songs.

Summary

Want to watch your own movie on your next airplane trip? How about listening to your favorite rock, jazz, country, or classical tunes when you are out jogging — without paying for a whole CD of songs you don't know or want? In this chapter, you've explored how to safely and legally obtain music and video you can listen to and view while on the go. You've also reviewed some leading portable players and discussed how to transfer downloaded digital entertainment files to these devices.

✦   ✦   ✦

Creative and Legal Music and Video Projects

◆ ◆ ◆ ◆

CHAPTER 11

In This Chapter

Using audio and
video together

Finding music
to accompany
your video

Using video and
audio editing
software

Using multimedia
scrapbooks

Learning what
content you can
legally add to your
presentation

◆ ◆ ◆ ◆

Music and moving images can form a scintillating combination. This has been true since the early days of cinema, when the villain's dirty deeds were accompanied by minor-key piano music that served to accentuate the mysterious deeds he was about to commit. Or what about any of hundreds of romantic dramas, where sweeping strings played to a couple's embrace?

Okay, so you are not a professional filmmaker, but you could be one of the more than 10 million people worldwide who own a digital video camera. With this equipment, you can make your own movies. Your subject could be as simple as your baby's first steps (not simple to your baby, though!), scenes from a family vacation, or bird watching on a Saturday morning.

After you record your video, you can transfer it from your digital video camera to your PC. With the movie file on your PC, you can edit and select parts of it, and then use any of several software programs to add your legally downloaded music, thus combining video and audio elements to create your own production!

Working with Digital Video Editing Software

With digital video editing utilities, you will transfer files from your digital video camera to your PC and then edit your video files on your desktop. Most editing software allows you to include music with your videos as you edit them or add your favorite songs later on.

I won't spend a great deal of time on video editing intricacies, but take a look at some of the more popular video editing tools. Although dozens of excellent video editing utilities are available, several are very familiar to a wide range of users. These include Pinnacle Studio (`www.pinnaclesys.com`), Adobe Premiere (`www.adobe.com`), Final Cut Pro (`www.apple.com/finalcutpro/`), and uLead Video Studio (`www.ulead.com`) shown in Figure 11-1. These programs can be downloaded from the vendors' respective Web sites, purchased in a box version, or bought in a store.

Transferring video files from camera to PC

Although this is not a book about digital video cameras and production techniques, it is still useful for you to familiarize yourself with the process of how to transfer the videos you have taken and then how to edit them. Why? Because you can have the greatest music in the world, but if your videos are not up to snuff, few people will want to watch them.

Figure 11-1: uLead Video Studio is one of the more popular video editing software programs.

That being the case, let me review how to move your video files from your digital video camera to your PC. In this scenario, I attach a video camera to a PC by means of a cable called a FireWire.

Note   FireWire cables are also referred to as "IEEE 1394," after a technical standard adapted by the Institute of Electrical and Electronics Engineers.

To transfer a video from your digital video camera to your computer, perform the following steps:

1. **Load the software you will use to edit your video.**

2. **Attach one end of your Firewire cable to the DV port in your camera.**

3. **Attach the other end of your Firewire cable to the Firewire port in your PC.**

4. **In your editing software, click the Capture (or similarly named) icon.** The Start Capture icon appears.

5. **Click Start Capture.** Your digital video should begin transferring (see Figure 11-2). After the transfer process completes, you should see an acknowledgement that the transfer has been successful.

Once you have transferred your video from your digital camcorder to your desktop, you are ready to edit it. In some programs, you can reach the Edit command by means of a pull-down menu or wizard interface.

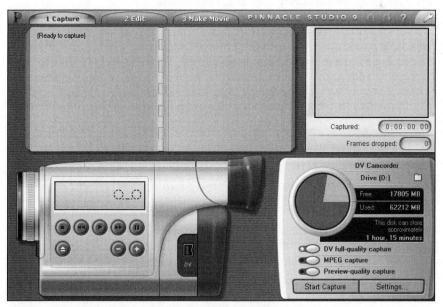

Figure 11-2: Using the Capture feature in Pinnacle Studio 9

In this example, I use Pinnacle Studio to depict video editing and how to add music to your videos along the way.

Finding free and legal music for your Web site

There are numerous places to find free and legal music for your Web site, or even for your own multimedia projects that you want to burn on CD and distribute to friends.

That being said, some music resources are of questionable legality.

If you are looking for "free" and "legal" music, consider that phrase. Many of the excellent music download Web sites we have explored throughout this book charge small fees for most of their selections. On the other hand, free sites may not own the rights to legally offer distribution of these music files. The challenge, then, is to find other resources where you can obtain free music.

Caution   Just because a music file is legally downloadable, or even freely downloadable, that does not mean it is legal for you to post it. If you are looking to post music on your own site, you can try to contact the copyright owner. A better bet, though, is to try and work with some of the free, licensed music included with numerous Web site authoring and multimedia editing programs.

Finding legal music files included in video editing programs

A number of sound and video editing programs, including uLead Video Studio, Adobe Premiere, and Pinnacle Studio, offer pre-included music tracks you can use to include with the video clips you want to prepare for your Web site or for download.

Most often, these are not recognizable hits by well-known artists, but are one of the following:

✦ Original compositions by music artists working for the video editing software developer or one of their business partners

✦ Versions of classical music works, most of which have expired copyrights due to their age

Although these categories sound quite limiting, a wealth of resources is available through each of these two sources. You examine them in the next section.

Working with music in video editing software libraries

In most cases, music in video editing software can be accessed from either the Album or Toolbar menu. This section examines how to use Pinnacle Studio to place legal music in a video file on your PC for eventual posting to a Web site.

To include legal music in a video clip edited with Pinnacle Studio, you need to perform the following steps:

1. **Capture the video.** Typically, hooking up your digital video camera to your PC starts this process.

2. **Click Capture.** The video is transferred from your digital video camera to your PC. When the transfer is complete, the digital video files appear as a series of images in the Pinnacle Studio preview pane.

3. **Click the Edit tab, then drag the images you want to include from the Preview pane into the editing windows.**

4. **Click Toolbox.** A pull-down Toolbox menu with series of options appears that lets you add sound, text, and other elements to the video that you are editing.

5. **In the Toolbox menu, click Generate Background Music.** A list of legal music you can incorporate into your video clip appears (see Figure 11-3).

6. **Highlight a selection appropriate to your video clip.** Choose music that is appropriate for the video you are showing.

7. **Click Add to Movie.** The music you have chosen is now included in your clip.

8. **Click the Make Movie tab.** Pinnacle Studio saves your new production as an .avi file, with your music included.

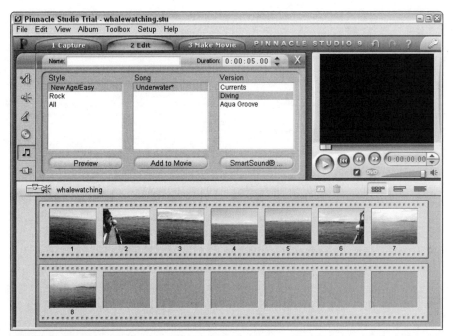

Figure 11-3: Pinnacle Studio offers a library of free music clips you can incorporate into your video production.

Including legal music from CDs in your video clips

Several companies offer compilation CDs with dozens of music tracks that you may choose from to include in your videos or place on your Web page. Although the CD on which these legal music tracks are included is usually quite economically priced, the CD is not free. What's free is the music on the CD.

One of the best resources for such compilations is published by the Elettro Network and can be purchased at any large computer or office supply store or ordered from the Elettro Web site at www.elettro.com (see Figure 11-4).

Adding music from your complilation CD

In this project, I use Pinnacle Studio to add music to a video. My source for the music is Elettro's 100 Top Downloads Compilation CD. This CD contains works representative of several musical styles.

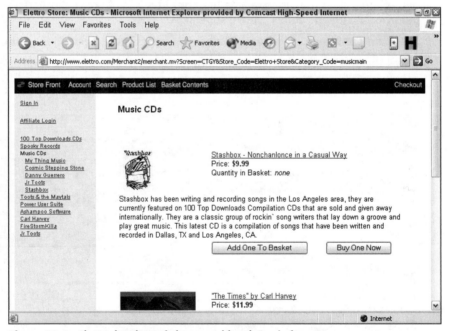

Figure 11-4: Elettro has lots of cheap and legal music for you.

To add music to a video clip you intend to post on your Web site, perform the following steps:

1. **With the video production that you are editing open in Pinnacle Studio, click Toolbox.**

2. **Insert your music CD into your computer's CD-ROM or DVD drive.**

3. **Choose Toolbox ⇨ Add CD Music (see Figure 11-5).**

4. **Click in the Track field to choose a song from the CD.** Scroll through the list and click to highlight the song from the CD you want to add to your video.

5. **Click the Add To Movie tab, to the right of the Toolbox menu** The music track you selected is added to your video. It's that simple!

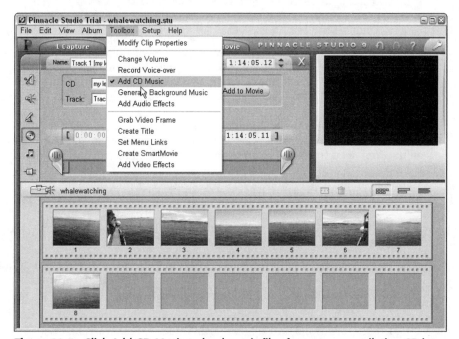

Figure 11-5: Click Add CD Music to load music files from your compilation CD into Pinnacle Studio.

Creating and Sharing Multimedia Scrapbooks

Multimedia scrapbooks allow you to integrate legally downloadable music with your photographs, and then incorporate that information into a slideshow.

You can then configure your slideshow with cool background colors, and you can specify how often you want the images in your slideshow to change from one to the next. A typical rotation time is around five seconds.

After you save your slideshow, you have several options. You can e-mail it to friends, burn it to a CD, or even post it on your Web site.

Producing a music slideshow with PHOTOJAM 4

Several multimedia slideshow software products are available. These include Photo 2VCD Studio (available for download from several Web sites), as well as the slideshow capabilities bundled into Microsoft PowerPoint and Adobe Photoshop Elements. One of the most popular, if not *the* most popular, slideshow products is PHOTOJAM 4 from AtomShockwave. A trial version is downloadable from the AtomShockwave Web site at www.shockwave.com/sw/content/photojam.

Once you've downloaded and installed PHOTOJAM 4 onto your hard drive, you are ready to begin. For this example, I want to organize some photos into a photo album. You need to configure your photo album before you can add music to it.

To prepare a music slideshow of a selection of your photographs, you need to open PHOTOJAM 4 and perform the following steps:

1. **With PHOTOJAM open, click the Create button.** A Browse for Folders box opens.

2. **In the Browse for Folders box, click the folder that contains the photos you want to use and then click the names of the photos you want to add to your slideshow.** The photos load and appear as a series of thumbnails in PHOTOJAM (see Figure 11-6).

3. **Click Transitions and select a Transitions effect.** You can choose from effects such as Dissolve (where one picture dissolves into the next) or Fade (where one picture fades out until the next image appears).

4. **Select a style(s).** This choice determines how your photos will appear and whether they have any tint or special effects coloring.

5. **Select music.** A menu of available music appears, listed by genre (Pop, Rock, Alternative, Jazz, Classical, etc.) and title of track (see Figure 11-7). If you prefer, you can add to this list by clicking the Get All Music button. This loads a list of all tracks currently in the PHOTOJAM library.

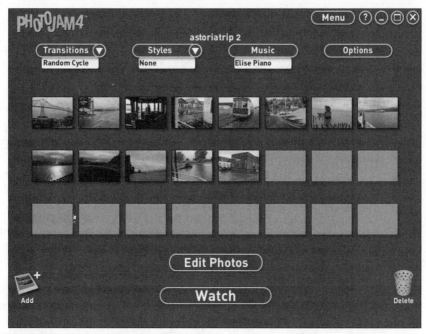

Figure 11-6: In PHOTOJAM, photos to be added to a slideshow first appear as thumbnails.

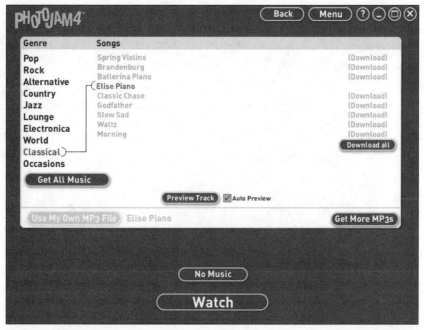

Figure 11-7: PHOTOJAM has a substantial library of legal music for your slideshow.

6. **Click Preview Track. The track plays in PhotoJam.**

7. **Click Watch.** This plays your new photo slideshow with the musical track you selected.

8. **To close the preview, Click on the slide show.** A white strip appears, with Edit, Share, and Menu buttons.

9. **Click Share.** A "How would you like to share your PhotoJam:" dialog box appears.

10. **Choose your option from the list in the dialog box (see Figure 11-8).** You can either e-mail your new music and photo slideshow as a link, save it as an HTML page for posting on your own Web site, prepare it to burn to a CD, create it as an "Executable" file that will automatically open when you click on the filename, turn it into a screen saver, or even prepare your new PHOTOJAM file so you can watch it on your television set. Click the radio button next to your choice, and then click Share. Depending on your choice, PhotoJam will start the process you have selected for sharing your slideshow.

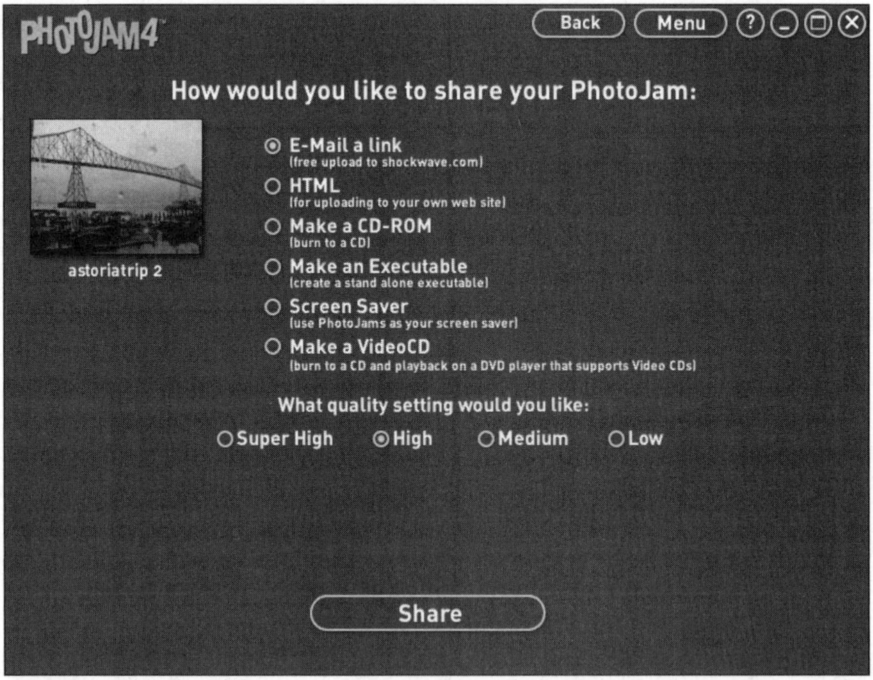

Figure 11-8: PHOTOJAM users have many ways to distribute their musical slideshow to friends and family.

Legal Restrictions

I cannot emphasize this point strongly enough. Just because you have paid for music online does not mean that you automatically have the right to include it in a slideshow or other fun multimedia product.

The best way for me to help you understand the extent of your potential legal vulnerabilities here is by going over the choices available to you as you design your project, and then include some frank commentary about where you stand legally, should you take that route.

What will get you into trouble

If, for whatever reason, you have illegally obtained MP3s or other music files already stored on your hard drive, you may be tempted to incorporate one of those songs into a project with other elements — such as your photographs or videos.

I admit that I have been tempted. As a pretty enthusiastic amateur photographer, I have taken many shots of mountains and seascapes. To me, those images evoke new-age music. I have numerous new-age MP3 tracks on my hard drive. A few were obtained at no charge, before the music industry complained and started to seek legal redress against this practice.

As most of us learn in our lives, temptation is not always a good thing. Unless you have obtained these tracks legally (through a service such as Real Rhapsody or Apple's iTunes), you have no business incorporating such tracks into your slideshow. If you just want to make a slideshow for friends, well, don't anticipate being served with a civil suit by the copyright holder or their trade association. If you want to post the slideshow on your Web site, or even send it out by e-mail, that's when the ground underneath your feet will start to turn slippery.

You also want to refrain from taping performances of uncopyrighted works. This is especially true with classical music, where the copyright (if it existed at all) is likely to be long gone. Yet if you are thinking about extracting your music from a classical CD, well, there are performance rights that must be dealt with. In other words, although Beethoven's music is not copyrighted, that recorded symphonic performance is.

What might get you into trouble

In many cases, copyright and usage is a gray area. In the digital age, that keeps the lawyers and judges quite busy.

Typical iffy practices include assuming that you have the right to use the music in your project because you have paid for it, such as via an iPod download or your purchase of a CD. That is quite likely not the case. Your vulnerability depends on whether the copyright holder has licensed the track or tracks for unlimited distribution. If you are unsure, stay away.

What won't get you into trouble

As we discussed earlier in this chapter, you can obtain legal, paid-for music in many places. How is this done? On compilation CDs, or in slideshow software, the company issuing the product has, more than likely, contracted with songwriters for unlimited distribution. Yet reading the fine print is never a bad idea. In some cases, your only vulnerability will be if you make your own CD with musical background from legal sources, and then sell it.

Six Clever Ways to Have Fun with Downloaded and Legal Digital Media

1. **Learn how to transfer files from your digital video camera to your PC.** This is an easy process, usually done by connecting your camera to your computer with a cable, and then using the Capture setting on a digital video-editing program to receive your files.

2. **Learn how to use video editing software to view, select, and edit your video files.** Although video editing is beyond the scope of this book, most video editing software makes the process easy.

3. **Learn how to incorporate your legal music downloads into the video you are producing.** Many video editing software utilities also come pre-bundled with music you are able to use. Additionally, several Web sites and free music compilation CDs are available for this purpose.

4. **Discover how to add legal music to a slideshow of your digital photographs.** After you get the images from your digital camera, seek out any one of several easy-to-use utilities, such as AtomShockwave's PhotoJam 4. Most of them come with tracks you can use.

5. **Use cool digital effects.** Once you have selected music for your digital photo slideshow, choose interesting digital effects to make your production even more compelling to watch.

6. **Know what is legal to use and what isn't.** Understand how to use digital music safely and legally, while avoiding risks if you do not do so. And, know how to check legality of use if you aren't sure.

Summary

If you own and use a digital camera, digital video camcorder, or both, you can create multimedia slide shows and video clips. This chapter reviews how to transfer your videos and photos from your camera to your PC, edit your files, and then combine the photographs and video you have taken and edited with free and legal music.

The chapter also explains how to find these free and legal music files on the Internet, on special CDs, and even within some popular photo and video editing programs. You have also learned that just because you have legally purchased a music track you are not automatically entitled to put it in a slide show. With that concern in mind, I've included some usage guidelines that will help you decide whether you can legally include the songs you wish on the music or video project you are creating.

✦　　✦　　✦

Appendixes

P A R T

IV

♦ ♦ ♦ ♦

In This Part

Appendix A
Music and Video
Services

Appendix B
Useful Information

Appendix C
Chronicle of a Typical
Digital Download

Glossary

♦ ♦ ♦ ♦

Music and Video Services

There are numerous ways to find, download, and share music and video files online. In this appendix, I list some of the best direct-download and file-sharing sites. Those that have already been covered in the chapters are not listed here (see Chapters 2 and 3 for those sites). Note that these are not recommendations; the software, terms and conditions, privacy policies, pricing, and other attributes of these sites may change or disappear at any time.

Getting Files through Direct Downloads

Direct-download sites usually sell music files, by the track, by the album, or both. Often you'll need to download proprietary player software to use the music files, but because the files are for sale, it's less likely that you'll be infected by a virus or get low-quality recordings.

Music

Why go to a music store and pay $14.99 for a CD with only a couple of songs you are interested in? Why drive to the store at all, when you can download the tracks you want inexpensively and legally? In addition to the legal music download sites I have already covered in this book, here are some others worthy of checking out.

BuyMusic (www.buy.com)

This site requires at least Windows Media Player 9 and features a library of more than 500,000+ songs, priced around $0.79 per track.

Sony Connect (www.connect.com)

This site requires Windows 98 SE, ME, 2000 Professional, or XP, Internet Explorer 5.5 or better with 128-bit encryption, and a download of SonicStage 2.0. The tracks are around $0.99, and the albums are around $9.99. Sony Connect boasts 500,000+ songs.

eMusic (www.emusic.com)

eMusic uses Download Manager 2.0; versions for Windows, Mac, are Linux are available. This site is subscription-based with prices for its more than 500,000 songs ranging from $9.99 to $19.99 for 40 to 90 songs downloaded. The site also offers unlimited free CD burning privileges, a feature not universally available on other digital music sites.

MusicNow (musicnow.fullaudio.com)

MusicNow requires Windows 98 SE, 2000, ME, or XP, and uses Windows Media Player. Its library contains 100,000+ songs with tracks priced around $0.99.

MusicRebellion (www.musicrebellion.com)

MusicRebellion uses a flexible and often-changing pricing model for some tracks. It requires a non-subscription account and recommends Windows Media Player. WMA and MP3 files are provided.

Streamwaves (www.streamwaves.com)

Streamwaves has more than 450,000 songs and is subscription-based for around $7.95 to $14.99 per month. It streams music for you to listen to, but doesn't allow saving tracks. The site does allow 30-second samples for non-subscribers, but full song access for subscribers.

Wal-Mart (musicdownloads.walmart.com)

Wal-Mart's site requires Windows and at least Windows Media Player 9. It offers a large selection of music with tracks priced at less than $1.

Video

Most of you have gotten into your car, fought traffic, looked for a parking spot, and gone into your local video store to buy or rent a DVD. And, when you rent a DVD, you have to put up with the inconvenience of going back to the store to return it. Now, sites are available from where you can download movies to your PC and depending on the site, watch them on your PC as often as you want or within a given period of time. And there are no traffic jams or crowded parking lots to put up with.

MovieLink (www.movielink.com)

This site requires Windows 98 SE, ME, 2000, or XP; and, RealPlayer 8 or newer or Windows Media Player 9 or newer. Internet Explorer with 128-bit encryption is also necessary. It offers hundreds of movies and allows rental of movies only for around $2.99 to $4.99. Movies may be stored for up to 30 days, but can be played only within a 24-hour window as long as it falls within the 30-day storage limit.

MovieFlix (www.movieflix.com)

MovieFlix requires Windows and Windows Media Player, RealOne or RealPlayer 10. The site offers thousands of movies priced around $6.95 for unlimited use.

Using File-Sharing Services

File-sharing services provide file-sharing software that connects to the popular file-sharing networks (groups of people using one or another of the file-sharing protocols). Generally, you can share or download any files you find, so they are not grouped into music and video.

eMule (www.emule-project.net)

One of the biggest peer-to-peer file-sharing clients, eMule connects to the eDonkey2000 network, a peer-to-peer platform for sharing music and video files. Unlike so many other file-sharing services, eMule is free of adware and spyware. You can also preview your songs and videos before they are fully downloaded to your computer.

Piolet (www.piolet.com)

This is a proprietary file-sharing P2P protocol network. It has a built-in playlist manager for organizing your downloaded files, as well as text and voice chat to communicate with other users.

Blubster (www.blubster.com)

This is another proprietary file-sharing P2P protocol network. Once your Blubster program connects with another Blubster-enabled PV, you can search and download MP3 files from all PCs hooked up to the network. After you download these files, you can play them on Blubster's integrated media player and chat about these files with other logged-on Blubster users. Blubster claims downloads at greater speeds than most other P2P networks.

MLDonkey (www.nongnu.org/mldonkey)

MLDonkey connects to multiple P2P networks, and it's Linux-based. Not Windows-compliant, its most frequent use is on computers running Linux or the Mac OS X operating system. This utility has sophisticated controls for configuring the transfer speeds of digital files to your available bandwidth.

Gnucleus (gnucleus.sourceforge.net)

This is a Windows-based application that connects to Gnutella (G1 and G2) networks. Released in 2000, it was the first Windows-based Gnutella peer-to-peer application.

Direct Connect (www.neo-modus.com)

This provides direct, P2P connections with other users, and it's for Windows and Mac OSX. Users have the technological ability to share any type of media or data file, with no restrictions — except for copyright, of course.

✦   ✦   ✦

♦ ♦ ♦ ♦

Useful Information

Numerous anti-virus software solutions, anti-spyware products, file-sharing network protocols, and file types are available. In this appendix, I've listed some relevant information on each of these topics.

Knowing the Anti-virus Software Makers

Anti-virus software can catch nasty computer viruses you have unintentionally loaded on to your PC. This list of anti-virus software makers and products is not an endorsement, but is here as a guide to some of the more popular such utilities.

AVG (www.grisoft.com/us)

Grisoft, founded in the Czech Republic and incorporated in Delaware in 1998, makes and distributes both free and purchased versions of its AVG anti-virus software. The software detects viruses of many types and can heal some infections. The free version has no technical support, but works fine. After it's installed, you'll be prompted to install regular updates of virus signatures.

eTrust EZ Antivirus (www.mye-trust.com)

This popular, $29.99 program from information management software company Computer Associates provides complete protection, detection and elimination of thousands of computer viruses, worms, and Trojan Horse programs.

McAfee (www.mcafee.com)

McAfee offers Internet Security Suite for $49.99 after a $20 mail-in rebate. It includes anti-virus, Personal Firewall Plus, SpamKiller, and Privacy Service services.

Symantec (www.symantec.com)

Symantec currently offers Norton AntiVirus for $49.95 and Norton Internet Security for $69.95. Norton AntiVirus detects problems, removes viruses, blocks worms and scripts, and provides for automatic updates. Internet Security includes Norton AntiVirus, Personal Firewall, and AntiSpam.

Panda Software (www.pandasoftware.com)

Panda software offers Titanium, Platinum, and Platinum Internet Security starting at $19.95 with six months service included. It includes the latest updates and provides daily updates.

Using Anti-Spyware Programs

Anti-spyware programs can root out nasty computer code placed on your PC by certain e-mails and through some Web pages you visit. Spyware can track your Web movements and then report back to the company or company client. Too often, this results in you receiving an incessant barrage of pop-ups as well as large bunches of unwanted e-mail.

Ad-Aware (www.lavasoft.com)

Ad-Aware is a fast, easy to use, downloadable utility that can spot, quarantine, or completely remove pesky spyware from your PC. Free and inexpensive versions are available for download from Lavasoft, the Sweden-based developer of this popular product.

PestPatrol (www.pestpatrol.com/Products/PestPatrolHE/)

PestPatrol is a powerful tool that detects and removes Trojan horses, spyware, adware, and tools used by hackers to discover your credit card numbers and other personally identifiable information. It's available via download for $39.95 from the PestPatrol site.

Using File-Sharing Networks

You can find file-sharing applications on many Web sites, but the networks they connect to are common to many of the applications. In fact, some applications boast that they can connect to multiple file-sharing networks, while others boast of proprietary protocols and networks that only they can connect to. One of the primary differences in file-sharing networks is whether they use a central server (centralized) or not (decentralized or distributed).

Gnutella and G2 (www.gnutella.com)

These are peer-to-peer networks used by several file-swapping software products that allow all desktop and laptop computers in the network to act as servers and share their files with all other users on the network. G2 is a scaled-down version of the original Gnutella, but one that is reputed to work faster.

Freenet (www.freenet.sourceforge.net)

As with Gnutella, Freenet is a peer-to-peer network architecture that allows all desktop and laptop computers in the network to act as servers and share their files with all other users on the network. Freenet comes equipped with encryption (file-scrambling, security capability).

Understanding File Types

Most music, video, text, and spreadsheet applications have file types. These file type designations ensure that the relevant software utility or utilities will be able to recognize these files for what they are, and then open them up for you to use. These file types are usually indicated by extensions at the end of the file name.

For example, if a music clip entitled "Are You Trying To Tell Me Goodbye?" is also an MP3 file, the last extension at the end of the file name (areyoutryingtotellme-goodbye.mp3) indicates the file type. Then if the media software program you are using recognizes the file type as one it is equipped to play, it will open and play the file.

Table B-1 lists many common media and related file type extensions as well as their names.

<table>
<tr><td colspan="2">Table B-1
Common Media Files Types</td></tr>
<tr><td>*Extension*</td><td>*Description*</td></tr>
<tr><td>.$$$</td><td>Temporary file</td></tr>
<tr><td>.aif</td><td>Audio Interchange File Format or AIFF</td></tr>
<tr><td>.au</td><td>Sound file</td></tr>
<tr><td>.avi</td><td>AVI movie format</td></tr>
<tr><td>.bak</td><td>Backup copy</td></tr>
</table>

Continued

Table B-1 *(continued)*

Extension	Description
.brx	Browse Index found on multimedia CD-ROMs
.cda	CD Audio track
.cgi	Common Gateway Interface
.cmf	SoundBlaster file
.dll	Dynamic link library
.doc	Document file
.jpeg	JPEG image file
.jpg	JPEG image file
.mff	MIDI File Format
.mov	QuickTime Movie
.mp2	MPEG Layer II compressed audio
.mp3	MPEG Layer III compressed audio
.mpe	MPEG
.mpeg	MPEG movie file
.mpg	MPEG movie file
.ra	RealAudio
.ram	Real Audio
.rm	Real Media
.tif	TIFF graphics file
.tiff	TIFF graphics file
.txt	Text file
.voc	Sound Blaster
.wav	Sound file
.wma	Windows Media Audio
.zip	File compressed using WinZip or PKZIP

✦   ✦   ✦

Chronicle of a Typical Digital Download

A major purpose of this book is to show you how to safely use music software and Web sites to find, download, and play your favorite songs on your PC or on portable devices. I have suggested several easy-to-use services where you can choose from hundreds of thousands of inexpensive tracks to find those that you want to listen to over and over.

Although I have covered a wide gamut of sites with music available for download, I have repeatedly stressed the virtues of obtaining your songs from inexpensive, legitimate music download sites rather than those that make it possible for you to obtain something for nothing. Downloading copyrighted material for free from some peer-to-peer sites is inviting, even tempting, but this comes at a potential price to your computer's security—and because the music industry is fed up with this practice, perhaps your own personal liberty. And don't forget the artist and songwriter who labored hard to come up with the notes and words that have moved you to the point where you want their work as part of your music collection. Denying them their legal (and moral) share of a few cents a track just isn't right.

That fact established, you might be eager to try out one of these convenient and easy-to-use legitimate music download sites. Most sites work more or less identically: You sign up for an account, you search or browse for work by certain artists or in certain genres, and you see a list of songs or CDs that match what you are looking for. Then, you order the track or tracks, and you download them to your PC. After they're downloaded, you can play them on your PC or, as I explain in Chapter 11, transfer them to your portable music player.

To show you how quick and easy this process can go for you, I performed just such a transaction on Musicmatch Jukebox. I signed up, looked for tracks by one of my favorite recording artists (Canadian singer-songwriter Alanis Morrisette), bought the track for only 99 cents, and then played the song on my PC. So read along as I describe this legal, inexpensive, and simple process.

Signing up for a Musicmatch Jukebox Account

To sign up for a Musicmatch Jukebox account, you need to enter a credit card number, along with accompanying personal information. After you have filled out all the required information and made your choices, click Submit (see Figure C-1).

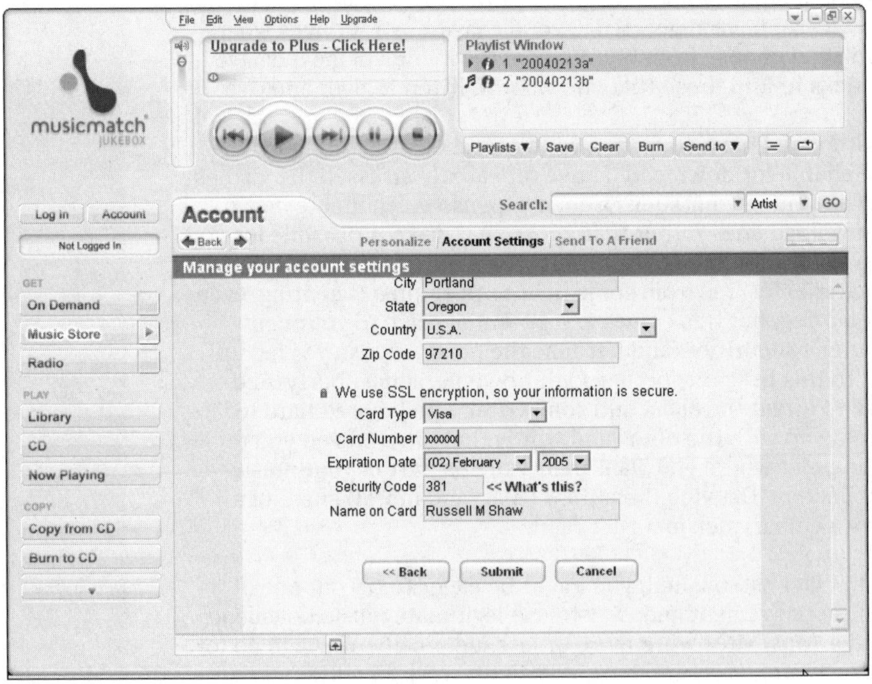

Figure C-1: Signing up for a Musicmatch Jukebox account

Cross-Reference In Chapter 1, I introduced Musicmatch Jukebox as one of the most popular, legal music download services.

Understanding Your Account Settings

The Musicmatch Jukebox account is now set up, and the Manage your account settings screen appears. This screen, shown in Figure C-2, summarizes Musicmatch's rules for secure downloading and CD-burning.

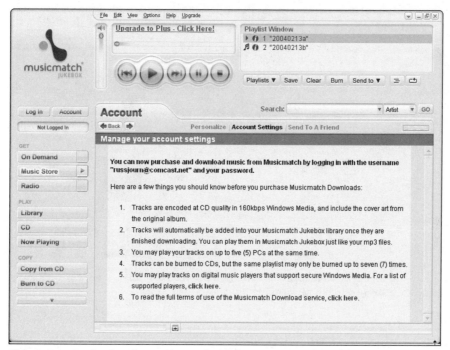

Figure C-2: Reviewing the Musicmatch Jukebox account options and rules

Accessing the Music Store

Your Musicmatch Jukebox account is set up, and you are ready to access the Music Store to browse and search for tracks. Click Music Store to reach this utility in Musicmatch Jukebox, shown in Figure C-3.

Figure C-3: Accessing the Musicmatch Jukebox Music Store

Searching for music by artist

After you're in Music Store, suppose that Alanis Morrisette is one of your favorite artists, and you want to search for Alanis Morrisette tracks available for purchase in the Music Store. You type Alanis Morrisette in the search field (see Figure C-4). To begin your search, click GO.

Figure C-4: Searching for tracks by artist

Finding music tracks by artist

The Musicmatch Jukebox Music Store's search engine has found a total of 74 tracks by Alanis Morrisette. To see the search results, go to the Search Results main window, shown in Figure C-5, and click on the name of the artist you have been searching for tracks by—in this case, of course, Alanis Morrisette.

Choosing a track to download

To see a list of tracks (rather than a list of albums), click the Tracks tab. A list of all tracks by the artist whose music you have been searching for appears.

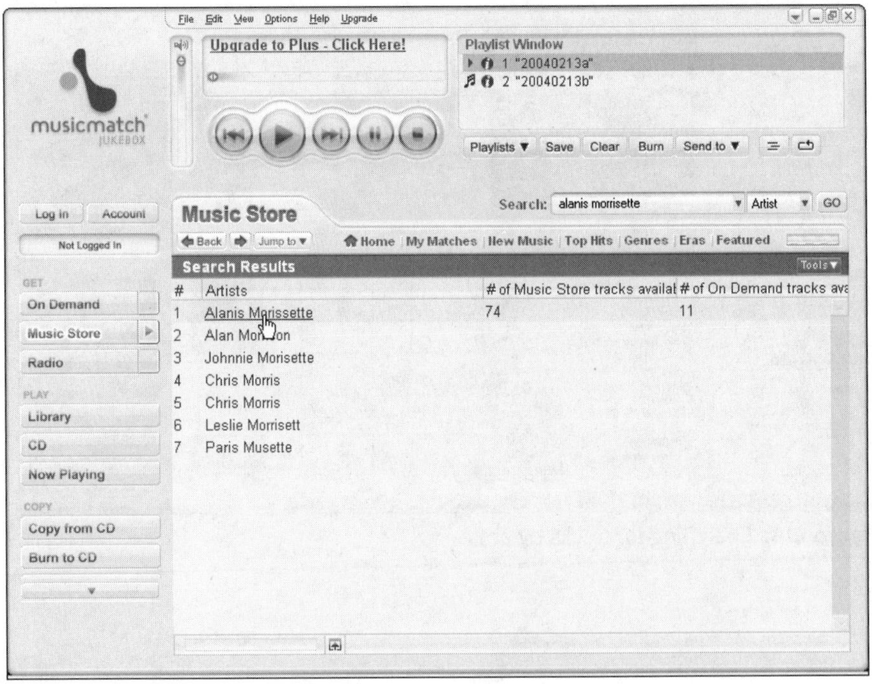

Figure C-5: The Search Results page

Locating the Buy Track icon

After perusing the list of Alanis Morrisette tracks available for purchase, you have decided on the song, "You Learn," from her "Jagged Little Pill" album. To start the purchase process, click the Buy Track icon, as shown in Figure C-6.

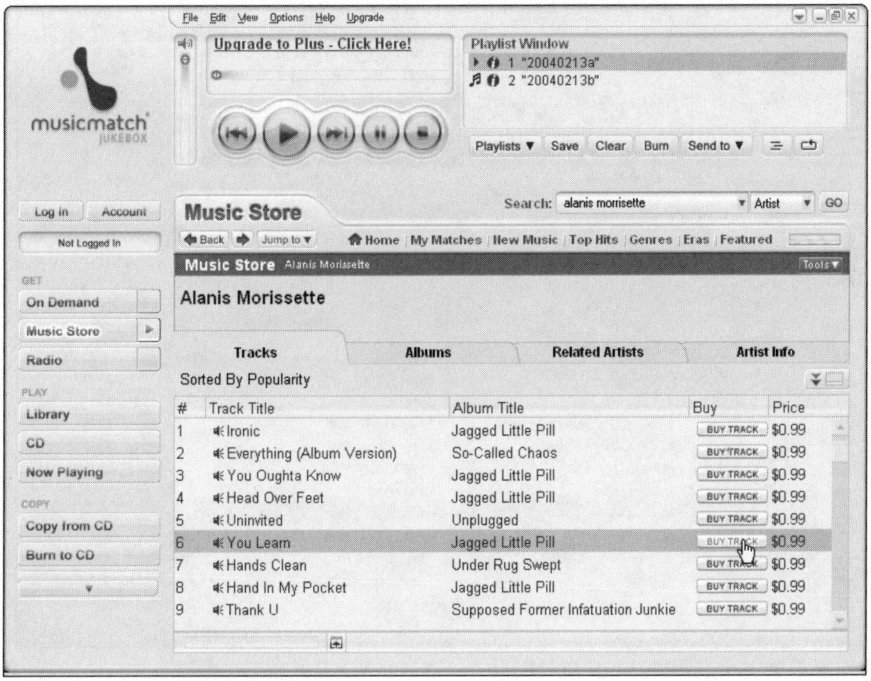

Figure C-6: The Buy Track icon

Confirming your purchase

Before your purchase is processed, a Confirm/Cancel box pops up. If you want to go ahead with your legal music purchase, click Confirm (see Figure C-7).

Figure C-7: Confirming your purchase

Logging on to purchase your track

At this point, Musicmatch Jukebox asks you to log in. Because you have already created your account, just go to the Log In section on this page. Enter your user name and password, and then click the Log In icon, as shown in Figure C-8.

Once you click the icon, the song you purchased downloads to your PC. On a fast broadband connection, the process takes less than one minute.

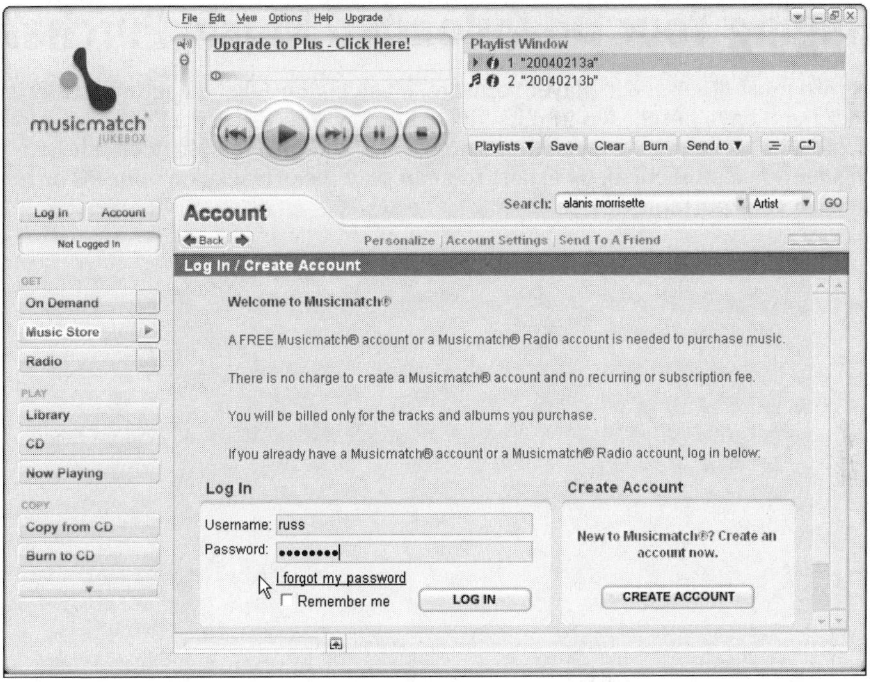

Figure C-8: Log in to Musicmatch Jukebox to proceed with your download.

Listening to Your Downloaded Track

Your download of Alanis Morrisette's song "You Learn" is now complete. Immediately after the download finalizes, Musicmatch Jukebox automatically plays the song you purchased (see Figure C-9).

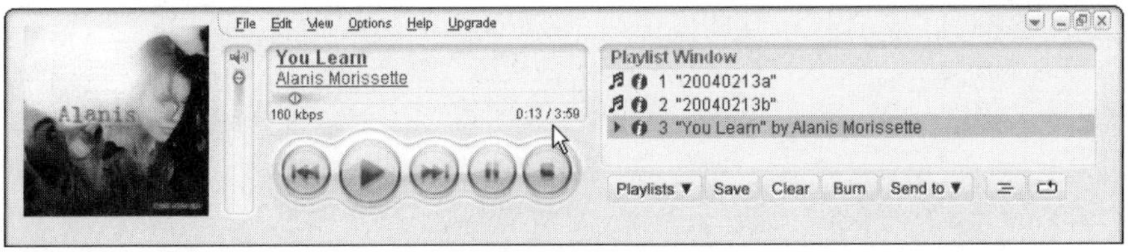

Figure C-9: The track you purchased has downloaded and is now playing in Musicmatch Jukebox.

Managing Your Downloaded Music Purchases

As with most other music player software, Musicmatch Jukebox automatically inserts tracks you have purchased into its Music Library. You will see a list of downloaded music files on your PC—even those not purchased through Musicmatch Jukebox. This view is alphabetical, by artist. You can play these tracks on your PC or transfer them to your portable device.

✦   ✦   ✦

Glossary

ActiveX. A set of interdependent Microsoft technologies for dynamic applications. Active X technology implemented on Web pages, and enabled on Web browsers, makes it possible for Web sites to become animated using multimedia effects.

Affiliate. A music company affiliated with a digital music Web site.

AGP. Accelerated Graphics Port, is a high-speed video card standard ideal for PCs that display multimedia applications.

Applet. Small program application.

Application. A software program that generally runs on top of the operating system.

ASP. Standing for Active Server Page, it is Microsoft technology for dynamic Web pages that enable code that shows moving action, such as an animated advertisement for a downloadable music file from a guitarist shown playing his instrument.

Authentication. The act of verifying the identity of a person or process attempting to use a computer resource.

Authorization. Allowing access to a Web site, such as a digital-download site that requires authorization of a password and of credit card information to process orders.

Autoresponder. A piece of software at a business e-mail address that automatically generates an e-mail reply. An example is a "thank you for your question, we will get back to you shortly" autoresponder sent out by a digital download music site in response to a question from a user.

Bandwidth. Name for available data carrying capacity, commonly used in reference to the speed/size of your Internet connection. This is usually defined in terms of megabytes (MB) or kilobytes (KB) per second, such as 56Kbps for Internet dialup and 1.5 MB for some DSL connections.

Beta Software. Unreleased software in late stages of development; typically ready for public download, but is usually not supported by the vendor. Many music player software programs release beta versions as upgrades to "official" versions.

Binary. Number system consisting only of zeros and ones; the number system computer calculations are actually performed in.

BIOS. Basic Input/Output System, runs under the operating system, contains basic settings for date/time, hard drive, boot disk, and so forth.

Bit. Single data item, either on or off, represents the 1 or 0 for binary calculations.

Blog. A Web log, often where individuals post their observations and thoughts in chronological, online diary form. There are tens of thousands of Blogs about music and movies. You can search for them on the Blog index Technorati, at www.technorati.com.

Bluetooth. Wireless communications technology for short range communication between devices (usually this is up to 33 feet).

Bookmark. Also called a Favorites list; saves URL or location in browser. If you want to place a music download site in your Internet Explorer's Favorites list, open the page, click Favorites, and then click Add To Favorites.

Bot. Robot, refers to robot software automatically running across the Internet

bps. Bits per second.

Broadband. Internet connections running faster than 56Kbps, usually refers to a cable modem, DSL, or wireless broadband connection. Now also used for wireless broadband connections.

Browser. Software application such as Internet Explorer, which is designed to access Web sites, capable also of downloading files and performing e-mail functions.

Buffer. Temporary storage place for data; often used to hold data while burning a CD to coordinate the process of sending and burning data without losses.

Burn. Recording data on CD or DVD, refers to use of laser to "burn" spots onto CD or DVD.

Cable modem. Specialized modem offered by cable television providers, which hook up the modem to your computer. In turn, these modems are connected to cable television lines maintained by these systems, often have nothing directly to do with the TV.

Cache. Storage spot for data while processing, speeds up processing by storing some data in a Web browser's memory. This makes it possible for browsers, and even some media players, to hold content in their cache for quicker retrieval.

Chipset. Group of chips designed to work together on a motherboard (the main board of a computer, usually containing the circuitry for the central processing unit, keyboard, and monitor).

Client. An application that runs on a PC. Your Web browser and e-mail program are examples of clients.

Codec. Stands for compressor/decompressor. It's hardware or software that encodes/compresses and decodes/decompresses audio and video data streams. The purpose of a codec is to reduce the size of digital audio samples and video frames in order to speed up transmission and save storage space.

Configuration. Process of setting options, generally refers to software, including operating systems, utilities, and desktop applications.

Cookie. Small string of data that is placed on your hard drive when you browse to some Web sites, generally harmless, although sometimes used to track browsing for advertising purposes.

CPU. The central processing unit is the main data processing chip on your computer.

CRM. Content Rights Management; refers to your rights to use data such as music and video files. Also refers to systems designed to restrict your ability to copy or share files.

DDR. Double Data Rate; type of RAM (Random Access Memory) that is faster than other types of computer memory. This is done via a memory chip that increases performance.

Defragment. Process of organizing files so your computer can access them more quickly.

DHCP. Dynamic Host Configuration Protocol; used to dynamically assign IP addresses for Internet access. Your ISP probably uses it to assign you a new IP address each time you log on.

DLL. Dynamic Link Library; file type used in conjunction with many desktop applications on Windows, such as most music and video player software utilities.

DNS. Domain Name Server; translates domain names to IP address of Web server.

Domain name. Easy-to-read and remember name for IP address of a Web site. Example: www.itunes.com.

Download. To receive a file or files into your computer.

Driver. Software utility for making printers and other devices (including software devices) run.

DSL. Digital Subscriber Line; broadband Internet connection over phone connections.

DVD. Digital Video Disc; high-capacity disk generally used to hold full-length movies, also capable of storing ordinary data (such as music files) in large amounts.

Encryption. Process of coding data so it is unintelligible unless user has appropriate "key" to de-encrypt.

Ethernet. Very common technical standard for how networks that tie computers together operate.

FAT32. File Allocation Table. For example, a 32-bit FAT table computer organizes a hard disk and tells what sectors are used for which software programs and files.

Firewall. Methods for restricting traffic to and from your computer using software, hardware, or both; packet-based, firewalls read packets (short portions of data coming into your computer) and decides which data packets to let through.

Firewire. Standard for transmitting data from a peripheral device, such as a digital video camcorder, to a PC.

Flash. Non-HTML file type (.swf) that provides rich media to Web pages; most browsers can display this file type. Flash also stands for Flash memory, where files, such as songs are video clips are held on small cards that fit into portable music and video players. Most portable MP3 players use some form of Flash memory.

Freeware. Software without cost or obligation, may still be licensed. Sometimes, the freeware creator asks for a small donation or fee to subsidize their expenses.

FTP. File Transfer Protocol; standard for transmitting files across the Internet. Differs from downloading or e-mail in the fact that when you transfer a file using FTP, you are directly accessing the computer system of your recipient.

GIF. Graphics Interchange Format; image file type. It is one of the two most common image file types displayable in most browsers. (The other is JPEG.)

Gigabyte. One billion bytes, which equates to 1000 megabytes or 1 million kilobytes.

GIGO. Garbage In Garbage Out; bad input to a program will likely result in bad output.

GUI. Graphical User Interface; Windows-style interface most programs now use.

Hit. Commonly refers to HTTP request to Web server for single file of a Web page. For example, if you type in **www.musicmatch.com** in your Internet Explorer Web browser, and your browser takes you to that page, that's one hit. If you navigate to other pages on the site, that's one more hit for each page.

Host. Server computer from which files may be requested (also other services).

HTML. HyperText Markup Language; basic language code of Web pages.

HTTP. HyperText Transfer Protocol, basic protocol used for communications between Web server and a client, such as your Internet-connected PC.

Hypertext. Computer text displayed with ability to take users from one Web page to another when they are connected to the Internet and click on the link.

Icon. Small graphic symbol, such as a Download Here icon on a music Web site.

IM. Instant Messaging. It is now possible to transfer music files via IM.

ISP. Internet Service Provider; such as the company you use to access the Internet.

Java. Programming language for creating animations over the Internet. For example, a cartoon of a guitar player using his instrument is most likely a Java application

JavaScript. Script for running small Java applications via your Web browser.

JPEG. Image file standard, often used for photos. Stands for Joint Photographic Experts Group, the organization that wrote the standard.

Kbps. One thousand bits per second. With the growth of broadband connections of more than one million bits, most Internet connections expressed as Kbps (such as 56 Kbps for dialup) are usually considered slow.

LAN. Local Area Network, where two or more computers are tied in together. This can be done by cables, or wirelessly.

Latency. Refers to communications time across networks (generally); often used to note excess communications time when noticeable by humans or delays cause processing problems. Latency sometimes happens when you try to play online computer games over slow, dial-up Internet connections.

LCD. Liquid Crystal Display. A display technology that uses rod-shaped molecules (liquid crystals) that flow like liquid and bend light. LCDs are used in many MP3-enabled PDAs, as well as other portable devices.

Linux. High-powered operating system based on supercomputer operating systems, but ported to PC-clones. It is free in principle, but available in several desktop software utilities that charge for their product offerings.

Megabyte. One million bytes.

Megahertz. One million hertz, or cycles per second.

Mirror. Site or host containing duplicate files, used to provide multiple, separate download sites for common files. For example, if you are downloading RealPlayer from the Real.com site, you may be given a choice of downloading from one of several mirror sites in different states and countries.

Modem. Modulator-demodulator; communications device for dial-up and cable Internet access, translates between a computer and communications networks.

Motherboard. Main circuit board in your computer.

MP3. Format for audio files. The MP is the first two letters of Motion Picture Experts Group, a group of technologists who drafted several multimedia file transmission standards in use today.

MPEG. Motion Picture Experts Group; format for movie files. The latest is MPEG-4, which is designed to transmit video and images over a narrower and can mix video with text, graphics, and animation.

Multimedia. Files containing multiple media types, such as music and video clips.

NIC. Network Interface Card; device connecting your computer to the network cable.

NNTP. Network News Transfer Protocol; the protocol for Newsgroups.

OCR. Optical Character Recognition; used to recognize text characters in image files. This is a common feature of scanners.

Packet. Name for small sets of data packaged for transmission across network or Internet.

Parse. "Read" a file and separate its contents into relevant portions. For example, to parse an HTML document means for a program to read the document and separate its contents into HTML tags and their content.

Partition. Portion of a hard drive formatted as a separate drive. More than one partition is allowed per drive, and each partition may be formatted with a different file system if desired.

PDA. Persoanl Digital Assistant. Some newer PDAs can play MP3 and video files.

PDF. Portable Document Format. A file format for PDF files created with Adobe Acrobat software. PDF's main advantage is that it can be used to display documents similar to the form they would show if they were in print, such as in a book or magazine. An example is a user's manual posted for download from the customer support section of a Web site offered by a portable music player manufacturer.

Pixel. Individual color dot in an image. For example, if your music player software's main screen shows a promotion for a music group, the images accompanying that promotion are pixels, or color dots.

Plug-in. Software that attaches to your browser for playing back specialized file types.

Pop-up. A Web page that, often without your consent, appears on your monitor when you click on another page or link. Often, pop-ups are advertisements. For example, when you click on a music Web site, you may see an ad for a CD.

Protocol. Communications format for how computers and networks communicate with each other, both internally and over the Internet.

QuickTime. Apple media player application program that can play multimedia video and audio files encoded in the QuickTime (.mov or .qt) format.

RAM. Random Access Memory, a type of computer memory that can be accessed randomly; that is, any byte of memory can be accessed without touching the preceding bytes. The most important thing for you to remember is that some multimedia software programs require a specific amount of RAM (such as 256KB of RAM) to work on your PC.

Resolution. Sampling rate or amount of data collected for media files; the higher the resolution the better the quality and larger the file size. This standard is applied for video or photos seen in Web sites or viewed on portable media players.

ROM. Read Only Memory. This is a type of computer memory on which data has been prerecorded. Once data has been written onto a ROM chip, it cannot be removed and can only be read.

Root. Main folder (all other folders are subfolders of this) in a hard drive partition, or highest privileged user on a computer system.

Router. Device routing Internet or network traffic across network of computers.

Server. Software that serves other software (clients). Web server and e-mail server software are common examples.

Shareware. Software freely shared, but licensed and sometimes with fees to help pay the cost of development.

Skin. Data that creates a customized, often "cool" look for software applications. An example is a skin for media player software that runs on a PC.

Spam. Any unsolicited or obnoxious, generally commercial message sent via e-mail or newsgroups, also includes pop-ups and misuse of HTML for getting unwarranted search engine rankings (search engine spam).

Spyware. A small software program that inserts itself in your PCs Web browser, follows which Web sites and pages you visit, and then reports that information to the spyware distributor or third party.

Streaming. Process of sending data for playback, in which data is continuous instead of sent as complete files.

TCP/IP. Transmission Control Protocol/Internet Protocol; combination of protocols used for almost all Internet communications.

TIFF. Tagged Image File Format; image file format in full or minimally condensed resolution. An example would be a high-resolution product photo of a portable music player, with the photo downloadable from the Web site of the company that made the product.

TTL. Time To Live; parameter set for packets to be dropped after attempted delivery on Internet fails or times out.

Upload. To send a file from your computer to a Web site, a Web server, or to one or more e-mail recipients.

URL. Uniform Resource Locator. This is another term for a Web site address, such as www.musicmatch.com.

USB. Universal Serial Bus, which is able to connect a PC to peripheral devices, such as mice, modems, scanners, and keyboards.

VGA. Video Graphics Array; format for video signals from your video card to your monitor.

Virus. Software that reproduces itself on your computer, attempts to spread itself, and may cause damage or spy on your activities (also worm and spyware).

WHOIS. System for looking up domain name registration.

Worm. A program that once it is transmitted to a PC, replicates itself to other PCs on the Internet or over a network — usually with harmful or annoying results. For example, some worms can cause your e-mail programs to send out bogus notes to everyone in your e-mail programs' address book.

Zip. Very common compression format. You'll often find files in .zip format for download or upload. You need a zip utility such as PKUNZIP or WinZIP to unzip the file.

Index

Symbols

.$$$ file type (temporary file), 235

A

ActiveX, 129, 247
Ad-Aware anti-spyware software, 156, 234
affiliates, definition, 247
AGP (Accelerated Graphics Port), 247
.aif file type (Audio Interchange File), 235
anti-spam software, 121–127
anti-virus software manufacturers, 233–234
Apple
    iTunes (*See* iTunes)
    .mov files, 25
applets, 247
applications
    definition, 247
    desktop software applications, 7
ASCAP distribution license, 177–178
ASP (Active Server Pages), 247
associating files, 91–92
.au files (sound files), 235
audio, streaming, 4
audio books, iTunes, 17
audio cards, overview, 79–80
audio video interleave files (Microsoft). *See* .avi files
audiovisual works, copyright law and, 170
authentication, 247
authorization, 247
autoresponder, 247
AVG Anti-virus software, 105
AVG anti-virus software, 233
.avi files (AVI movie format), 25, 235

B

backups, listening to music and, 39
.bak files (Backup copy), 235
bandwidth, 247
BBBOnline, 152–154
BearShare
    installation, 58–60
    introduction, 56
    overview, 57
    system requirements, 58
    third-party software, 56–57
beta software, 248
binary, definition, 248

BIOS (basic input/output system), 84, 248
bits, 88, 248
BitTorrent file-sharing network, 47
blogs, 248
Blubster file-sharing service, 231
Bluetooth technology, 248
BMI distribution license, 177, 178–180
bookmarks, 248
boot disk, operating systems, 85
bots, 248
bps (bits per second), 248
broadband connections
    definition, 248
    streaming music and, 40
browsers, description, 248
.brx files (Browse index on multimedia CDs), 236
buffers, 248
burning CDs. *See* ripping CDs
BuyMusic direct download site, 229
bytes, overview, 88

C

cable modem, 248
cache, 249
cases, 78
CD/DVD drive, overview, 80
.cda files (CD Audio track), 236
CDs, burning from iTunes downloads, 31
.cgi files (Common Gateway Interface), 236
Children's Seal Program, TRUSTe and, 151–152
chipsets, 249
clients, 249
.cmf files (SoundBlaster), 236
codec, 249
configuration
    definition, 249
    firewalls, 63
connections
    file-sharing applications and, 71
    physical Internet connections, 134–135
cookies
    definition, 249
    threat potential, 112
copyright law
    consequences of violations, 181–184
    digital downloading and, 169–171
    DMCA (Digital Millennium Copyright Act), 173–174

Continued

copyright law (continued)
   electronic theft law, 174
   Fair Use Doctrine, 172
   ISPs and, 174
   music download use, 223–224
   overview, 166–169
   protected works, 168
   Sonny Bono Copyright Extension Act, 172–173
   updates pertaining to digital downloads, 171–172
   violator detection, 182
cost, direct-download sites, 23
CPU
   definition, 249
   overview, 79
crackers, overview, 113
cracking passwords, network security and, 139
Creative Rhomba portable media player, 199–200
CRM (Content Rights Management), 249
cryptography (encryption), 155

D

DDR (Double Data Rate), 249
defragmenting disk drive, 87, 249
desktop software application, definition, 7
DHCP (Dynamic Host Configuration Protocol), 249
digital video editing, software, 213–219
Direct Connect file-sharing service, 232
direct downloading
   background of sites, 17
   domain name registration for site, 18
   ease of use of site, 23
   file downloads, 16–17
   file sharing comparison, 4–5
   iTunes, 16
   legal issues, 4
   library of site, 23
   music sites, 229–230
   Musicmatch, 6–7
   Napster and, 15–16
   price for downloads, 23
   privacy policies, 26–27
   quality issues, 4, 12
   security issues, 4, 10–11
   site use, 15–23
   sites, searching for, 17–22
   software license agreements, 25–26
   system issues, 4, 12–13
   Terms and Conditions, 26
   tips for consideration, 13
   user interface familiarity, 40
   video sites, 230–231
disk drives. See hard drive

disks, downloads, 8
distributing music, licensing, 176–180
DLL (Dynamic Link Library), 249
.dll files (dynamic link library), 236
DMCA (Digital Millennium Copyright Act), 173–174
DNS (Domain Name Server), 249
.doc files (document), 236
domain names, 18, 250
downloading. See also direct downloading; illegal
       downloads
   considerations before, 39–40
   copyright law and, 169–171
   from direct-download sites, 16–17
   from disk, 8
   from e-mail, 8
   fake sites, 40
   FTP sites, 8–10
   illegal sites, 40
   iTunes, 190–191
   music files, 3–4
   RealRhapsody, 33–34
   ring tones, 209–210
   video files, 3–4
dramatic works, copyright law and, 170
drivers, 250
drives
   BIOS (basic input/output system), 84
   POST (power-on self test), 84
DSL (digital subscriber line), 250
DVDs
   burning from iTunes downloads, 31
   description, 250

E

e-mail
   downloading from, 8
   personal privacy and, 148
   security, 120
   threat potential, 111–112
   threat protection tips, 130
eDonkey, 60–61
electronic theft, copyright law and, 174
eMule file-sharing service, 231
eMusic direct download site, 230
encrypted Web sites, security and, 141
encryption, 154–155, 250
Ethernet, 250
eTrust EZ Antivirus software, 233

F

Fair Use Doctrine, copyright law and, 172
FAT-16 file system properties, 96

FAT-32 file system properties, 96
FAT (file allocation table) file systems, 85, 250
file extensions
    music, 24–25
    viewing in XP, 89
file management
    file properties, 95–96
    folders, 95
    introduction, 93–95
file sharing
    applications, selection tips, 71–72
    direct downloading comparison, 4–5
    Kazaa, 5–6
    legal issues, 11–12
    Napster and, 44
    overview, 43–45
    quality issues, 12
    security issues, 10–11
    security risks, 136–138
    system issues, 12–13
    tips for consideration, 13
file-sharing networks
    BitTorrent, 47
    Freenet, 46
    Gnutella, 46
    iMesh, 47
    Overnet, 47
    overview, 45
    P2P connections, 46
    Web sites, 234–235
file-sharing services
    BearShare, 56–60
    eDonkey, 60–61
    Kazaa, 67–70
    LimeWire, 62–64
    Overnet, 60–61
    overview, 47
    Shareaza, 48–55
    Web sites, 231–232
file systems
    downloads and, 93
    FAT (file allocation table), 85
    fragmented files, 86–87
    groups, 98
    permissions, 97–98
    users, 98
file types
    associations, 91–92
    media files, 235–236
    viewing in XP, 89
filenames, music, 24–25

files
    bits, 88
    bytes, 88
    properties, 95–96
    track sizes, 5
    types, 24–25
firewalls
    configuration, 63
    definition, 250
    network security and, 141–144
firewire, 250
Flash, 25, 250
floppy drive, overview, 80
folders, description, 95
fragmented files, disk drives, 86–87
Freenet file-sharing network, 46, 235
freeware, definition, 250
FTP (File Transfer Protocol)
    description, 135, 250
    sites, search engines and, 8–10

G

GB (gigabytes), 88, 251
GIF (Graphics Interchange Format) file format, 251
GIGO (Garbage In Garbage Out), 251
Gimini 22 (ARCHOS) portable media player, 200–201
Gnucleus file-sharing service, 232
Gnutella file-sharing network, 46, 235
graphic works, copyright law and, 170
groups, file systems, 98

H

hackers, overview, 113
hard drive
    defragmenting, 87
    fragmented files, 86–87
    labeling, 85
    overview, 80
    space for downloads, 40
hardware
    audio cards, 79–80
    cases, 78
    CD/DVD drive, 80
    CPU, 79
    disk drives, 85–87
    floppy drive, 80
    hard drive, 80
    laptops, 78
    modems, 80
    motherboard, 79
    network cards, 80

Continued

hardware *(continued)*
    notebooks, 78
    partitions, 85–87
    RAM, 79
    speakers, 80
    video cards, 79–80
hits, 251
host, 251
HTML (Hypertext Markup Language), 251
HTTP (Hypertext Transfer Protocol), 135, 251
hypertext, 251

I

icons, 251
identity theft, 115–116, 160–161
illegal downloads
    consequences of violations, 181–184
    copyright law and, 166–174
    introduction, 165–166
IM (Instant Messaging), 251
iMesh file-sharing network, 47
installation
    BearShare, 58–60
    considerations before beginning, 39–40
    iTunes, 190–191
    iTunes software, 31
    Kazaa, 69–70
    LimeWire, 64
    Morpheus, 66–67
    Musicmatch software, 33
    Napster software, 29
    RealRhapsody, 33–34
    Shareaza, 49–52
inter-networks, 134
interfaces, direct-download sites, 40
Internet
    FTP, 135
    functioning of, 134–136
    HTTP, 135
    as network, 135–136
    network threats, 136–140
    physical connections, 134–135
    protocols, 135–136
    SMTP, 135
    TCP/IP, 135
    trademark law and, 176
iPod, 196–197
ISPs (Internet service providers)
    copyright law and, 174
    definition, 251

J

Java, 251
JavaScript, 251
.jpeg files (JPEG images), 236, 251
.jpg files (JPEG images), 236

K

Kazaa
    file sharing on, 5–6
    installation, 69–70
    overview, 67–70
    privacy policy, 68
    services, 6
    Supernodes, 5–6
    system requirements, 68–69
    Terms and conditions, 68
    third-party software, 68
KB (kilobytes), description, 88
Kbps, 251

L

LAN (Local Area Network), 251
laptop computers
    hardware, 78
    movie downloads, 207–209
latency, 251
LCD (Liquid Crystal Display), 252
legal issues. *See also* copyright law; trademark law
    CD ripping, 12
    direct downloading, 4, 11–12
    file sharing, 11–12
    music download use, 223–224
libraries
    direct-download sites, 23
    Shareaza, 53
license agreements
    considerations before software installation, 39
    distribution licenses, 177–180
    software, direct-download sites and, 25–26
    sound recording license, 181
LimeWire
    installation, 64
    overview, 62–63
Linux
    description, 252
    file system properties, 96
listening to music, backups and, 39
literary works, copyright law and, 170
Lyra (RCA/Thomsom) portable media player, 198

M

Macromedia, file extensions, 25
MailWasher Pro anti-spam software, 122
malfunctioning software, threats and, 103–105
MB (megabytes), 88, 252
McAfee antivirus software, 233
media file types, 235–236
Media Player, Shareaza, 54
media players
    Creative Rhomba, 199–200
    Gimini 220 (ARCHOS), 200–201
    Lyra (RCA/Thomson), 198
    music transfer, 201–206
    RealPlayer and, 201–204
    Rio Cali, 199
    Rio Music Manager and, 205–206
    YP55V (Samsung), 200
Megahertz, 252
Messenger, popups and, 109–110
.mff (MIDI file format), 236
.mg2 files, specifications, 25
Microsoft
    audio video interleave files, 25
    waveform files, 25
mirror sites, 252
MLDonkey file-sharing service, 232
modems
    description, 252
    overview, 80
monitors, specifications, 79
Morpheus
    installation, 66–67
    privacy policy, 65
    system requirements, 66
    Terms and conditions, 64
motherboard, 79, 252
Motion Picture Experts Group files, extensions, 25
.mov files, specifications, 25
.mov files (QuickTime movie), 236
MovieFlix direct download site, 231
MovieLink direct download site, 231
.mp4 files, specifications, 25
.mp2 files (MPEG Layer II compress audio), 25, 236
.mp3 files (MPEG Layer III compress audio), 25, 236, 252
MP3 sites, registration, 8
.mpe files (MPEG), 236
MPEG (.mp3) files, 25, 252
.mpeg (MPEG movie file), 236
.mpg files (MPEG movie file), 236
MSN Music
    overview, 36–38
    privacy policy, 38

    system requirements, 38
    Terms and Conditions, 38
multimedia, definition, 252
multimedia scrapbooks, PHOTOJAM 4 music slideshow, 220–222
music
    direct-download sites, 15–23, 229–230
    distribution, licensing, 176–180
    downloading, 3–4
    file extensions, 24
    file types, 24–25
    filenames, 24
    iTunes, 16
    legal restrictions on downloads, 223–224
    slideshows, PHOTOJAM4 and, 220–222
    video clips and, 218–219
    video editing software libraries, 216–217
musical works, copyright law and, 170
Musicmatch
    direct downloads, 6–7
    origins, 32
    privacy policies, 32
    software installation, 33
    system requirements, 32
    Terms and conditions, 32
MusicNow direct download site, 230
MusicRebellion direct download site, 230

N

Napster
    as direct-download site, 15–16
    file sharing and, 44
    privacy policies, 28
    software installation, 29
    system requirements, 28
    Terms and conditions, 28
network cards, overview, 80
network security
    encrypted Web sites, 141
    firewalls, 141–144
    Internet as network, 135–136
    Internet functioning and, 134–136
    password cracking, 139
    passwords, default, 138–139
    physical connections, 134–135
    physical security, 141–144
    protection tips, 144–145
    securing network, 140–144
    server exploits, 138–140
    spoofing and, 139–140
    threats, 136–140
Network Solutions, whois searches, 18–19

networks
    file-sharing. *See* file-sharing networks
    Internet as, 135–136
NIC (Network Interface Card), 252
Nigerian bank account scam, 114
NNTP (Network News Transfer Protocol), 252
notebook computers, hardware, 78
NTFS file system, 96–98

O

OCR (Optical Character Recognition), 252
open-source software, file-sharing applications
        and, 71
operating systems
    boot disk, 85
    overview, 82–83
Overnet file-sharing network, 47, 60–61

P

packets, 252
Panda Software anti-virus, 234
pantomimes and choreographic works, copyright law
        and, 170
parsing, 252
partitions, 85–86, 253
passwords
    cracking, 139
    default, security and, 138–139
PDAs (personal digital assisstant), 253
PDF (Portable Document Format) files, 253
peer-to-peer. *See* P2P (peer-to-peer)
permissions, NTFS file permissions, 97–98
personal privacy
    BBBOnline, 152
    encryption and, 154–155
    identity theft, 160–161
    introduction, 147–148
    PGP (Pretty Good Privacy) and, 154–155
    privacy services, 150–154
    spyware and, 155–159
    TRUSTe and, 150–152
PestPatrol anti-spyware software, 156–159, 234
PGP (Pretty Good Privacy), personal privacy and,
        154–155
PHOTOJAM 4 music slideshow, 220–222
physical security of networks, 141–144
pictorial works, copyright law and, 170
Piolet file-sharing service, 231
pixels, 253
players, default, 40
plug-ins, 253

popup ads
    file-sharing applications and, 71
    Messenger and, 109–110
    threat potential, 108–111
popups, definition, 253
portable media players
    overview, 189–190
    transfers to, 197–206
POST (power-on self test), 84
P2P (peer-to-peer)
    file-sharing networks, 47
    Kazaa and, 5
    Napster and, 27
privacy policies. *See also* personal privacy
    BearShare, 58
    considerations before software installation, 39
    direct-download sites, 26–27
    iTunes, 31
    Kazaa, 68
    Morpheus, 65
    MSN Music, 38
    Musicmatch, 32
    Napster, 28
    RealRhapsody, 33
    Sony Connect, 36
properties, files, 95–96
protocols, 43–44, 253
public key cryptography (encryption), 155

Q

quality issues
    direct downloading, 4, 12
    file sharing, 12
QuickTime, 25, 253

R

.ra files (RealAudio), 25, 236
.ram files (RealAudio), 25, 236
RAM (Random Access Memory), 79, 253
real audio files, extension, 25
Real Networks files, extension, 25
RealMedia, file extensions, 25
RealPlayer
    portable devices and, 201–204
    RealRhapsody and, 34
RealRhapsody (Real Network)
    downloading, 33–34
    installation, 33–34
    privacy policy, 33
    RealPlayer and, 34
    system requirements, 33
    Terms and conditions, 33

recording, sound recording license, 181
remote access threats
    cookies, 112
    e-mail, 111–112
    malfunctioning software, 103–105
    overview, 102–103
    popups, 108–111
    spyware, 108
    Trojan horses, 112
    viruses, 105–107
    worms, 107–108
resolution, 253
RIAA (Recording Industry Association of America),
        copyright violations and, 181–184
ring tone downloads, 209–210
Rio Cali portable media player, 199
Rio Music Manager, portable devices and, 205–206
ripping CDs
    description, 248
    legal issues, 12
.rm files (RealMedia), 25, 236
ROM (Read Only Memory), 253
root folder, 253
routers, 254
.rv files, specifications, 25

S

scam artists, threat potential, 114–115
scripting, Web-browsing security and, 129
search engines, FTP sites and, 8–10
searches
    legal downloads, Web site music, 216
    Shareaza, 54
security. *See also* personal privacy; threats to PC
    anti-spam software, 121–127
    direct downloading, 4, 10–11
    e-mail, 120
    file sharing, 10–11
    file-sharing risks, 136–138
    identity theft, 160–161
    introduction, 119–120
    networks (*See* network security)
    networks, threats to, 138–140
    networks, tips for, 144–145
    password cracking, 139
    passwords, default, 138–139
    spam and, 120–121
    spoofing and, 139–140
    Web-browsing security, 127–130
servers, 138–140, 254
SESAC distribution license, 177, 180

Shareaza file-sharing service
    application download, 49
    installation, 49–52
    Library tab, 53
    Media Player, 54
    overview, 48
    Search tab, 54
    system requirements, 49
    third-party software, 48
    user interface, 53
shareware, 254
sharing files. *See* file sharing
SMTP (Simple Mail Transfer Protocol), description, 136
software
    anti-spyware software, 234
    anti-virus manufacturers, 233–234
    beta software, 248
    default player, 40
    desktop software application, 7
    digital video editing, 213–219
    installation, considerations before, 39–40
    iTunes installation, 31
    license agreements, direct-download sites and,
        25–26
    malfunctioning as threat, 103–105
    Musicmatch installation, 33
    Napster, installation, 29
    proprietary, direct-download sites, 23
    spam, anit-spam software, 121–127
Sonny Bono Copyright Extension Act, 172–173
Sony Connect
    overview, 34
    privacy policy, 36
    system requirements, 35
    Terms and conditions, 35
Sony Connect music direct download site, 230
sound recording license, 181
sound records, copyright law and, 170
space for downloads, installation considerations, 40
spam
    anti-spam software, 121–127
    definition, 254
    security from, 120–121
speakers, specifications, 80
spoofing, network security and, 139–140
spyware
    Ad-aware and, 156
    anti-spyware software, 234
    definition, 254
    description, 20

Continued

spyware (continued)
    file-sharing applications and, 71
    Kinko's case, 155
    PestPatrol and, 156–159
    threat potential, 108
    threat protection tips, 130
streaming, definition, 254
streaming audio, 4, 40
streaming video, 4
Streamwaves direct download site, 230
Supernodes, Kazaa, 5–6
.swf files, specifications, 25
Symantec anti-virus software, 234
system issues
    direct downloading, 4, 12–13
    file sharing, 12–13
system requirements
    BearShare, 58
    eDonkey, 61
    iTunes, 31
    Kazaa, 68–69
    Morpheus, 66
    MSN Music, 38
    Musicmatch, 32
    Napster, 28
    RealRhapsody, 33
    Shareaza, 49
    Sony Connect, 35

T
TCP/IP (Transmission Control Protocol/Internet
        Protocol), 135, 254
Terms and conditions
    BearShare, 58
    considerations before software installation, 39
    direct-download sites and, 26
    iTunes, 30–31
    Kazaa, 68
    Morpheus, 64
    MSN Music, 38
    Musicmatch, 32
    Napster, 28
    RealRhapsody, 33
    Sony Connect, 35
threats to networks, file-sharing security risks,
        136–138
threats to PC. See also security
    crackers, 113
    hackers, 113
    identity thieves, 115–116
    Nigerian bank account scam, 114
    overview, 101–102

remote access, 102–113
scam artists, 114–115
tips of overcoming, 116–117
.tif files (TIFF graphics files), 236
.tiff files (TIFF graphics files), 236, 254
track sizes, download sites, 5
trademark law, 174–175
Trojan horses, threat potential, 112
TRUSTe
    complaints about violations, 153–154
    personal privacy and, 150–152
TTL (Time To Live), 254
Tunes
    account setup, 192–196
    audio books, 17
    burning CDs/DVDs, 31
    downloading to computer, 190–191
    installing to computer, 190–191
    iPod and, 190–197
    iPod and, transferring music to, 196–197
    locating music, 193–194
    offerings, 30
    origins, 16, 29
    privacy policies, 31
    purchasing music, 194–196
    software installation, 31
    system requirements, 31
    Terms and Conditions, 30–31
.txt files (text), 236

U
uploading, 4, 254
URLs (Uniform Resource Locator), 254
USB (Universal Serial Bus), 254
user interface
    direct-download sites, 40
    file-sharing applications and, 71
    Shareaza, 53
users, file systems, 98

V
VGA (Video Graphics Array), 254
video
    cards, overview, 79–80
    digital video editing software, 213–219
    direct-download sites, 15–23, 230–231
    downloading, 3–4
    editing, legal music files, 216–219
    file transfer from camera to PC, 214–216
    file types, 24–25
    laptops, downloading to, 207–209
    streaming, 4

violations of copyright law and download restrictions, 182–184
viruses
    anti-virus software manufacturers, 233–234
    definition, 255
    threat potential, 105
.voc files (Sound Blaster), 236

W

Wal-Mart direct download site, 230
.wav files (sound file), 25, 236
waveform (Microsoft) files, extension, 25
Web-browsing security, 127–130

Web sites
    encrypted, security and, 141
    information collected, notification, 148–150
    legal music for, 216
whois searches, 18–19, 255
.wma files (Windows Media Audio), 236
worms, 107–108, 255

X–Y–Z

YP55V (Samsung) portable media player, 200

.zip files (file compressed using WinZip or PKZIP), 236, 255